QUANTUM CRISIS 3

Best Selling Author of
Quantum Crisis-II and Quantum Crisis-III

RAJ D. RAJPAL
B.Sc.(Honors), D.A.P.R., D.M., D.C.S., D.M., M.B.A. (Ohio)

QUANTUM CRISIS-I

Financial crises have afflicted mankind from times immemorial. This publication is the first of a three-book commentary on the financial and credit problems facing the world today. In order to better understand this entire problem. It is critical to start from the origin of such world financial crises.

This book looks in detail at the most infamous and difficult financial crises in the past four hundred years. In this journey, the story weaves through diverse countries from Japan in the East to Scandinavia and the United Kingdom in Europe to the United States.

It has been found that a very common pattern exists in world financial crises, both past and present. Human greed and fear are the two essential components of all financial crises. Human greed accompanied with massive market speculation resulted in a run up in asset prices, creating an "asset bubble". This run up was then followed by a period of aggressive and uncontrolled selling of assets leading to a market meltdown. In the process, several investors and ordinary citizens got burnt — the winners at the other end of the table were the very privileged investors, who due to special insider information or connections with royalty and wealth got away with fraudulently earning an unprecedented amount of money.

The lessons to be learnt from this book are three fold. Firstly, there is a dire need for more transparent investor education. Secondly, there is an immediate and urgent need for financial authorities to both develop comprehensive market regulation and to monitor risk management systems. Thirdly, there must be serious consideration of a way of Financial Life, which leads to a fundamental re-evaluation of human relationships. It is possible to be rich, yet honest and the book is dedicated to protecting the achievement of uncommon success in common circumstance.

QUANTUM CRISIS-I
Origin of Global Financial Crises

ISBN : 978-0-9783550-3-6

Best Selling Author of
Quantum Crisis-II and Quantum Crisis-III

Best Selling Author of
Quantum Crisis-I and Quantum Crisis-III

RAJ D. RAJPAL
B.Sc.(Honors), D.A.P.R., D.M., D.C.S., D.M., M.B.A. (Ohio)

QUANTUM CRISIS-II

The global financial and credit crisis of 2007-2009 is like no other in the history of Mankind. This crisis has been sudden and unprecedented in the scale of its appearance and impact on humans all across this planet. It has fundamentally changed the nature of all financial relationships. A crisis of this magnitude and impact calls for a special and wide understanding of its causes, results and future implications. Development of this understanding constitutes the primary objective of this publication.

Slowly but surely the US real estate mortgage crisis escalated into a US banking crisis, which then metamorphosed into a more dangerous international banking and credit crisis. The crisis spread its wings universally. This worldwide financial impact reinforces the fact that the world financial network is truly interconnected in every way. When America sneezes, Europe catches a cold while Asia inherits a transmitted flu.

The main culprits behind this crisis were the large investment and commercial banks in the US, who spread risk across the world through sale of specialized, synthetic financial products. Using a process called "financial securitization" — risk of different qualities got wrapped up and sold as investment products globally. When Americans started defaulting on their mortgages, these toxic investment assets lost value and brought the entire money, credit and banking system to its knees.

This book attempts to navigate through some very complex financial territory and provides a 360 degree view of the crisis — attempting to propose some novel and radical ways of solving the problems inherent in this unfolding crisis. It is a must read for all individuals wanting an honest and unbiased analysis of this crisis.

The author prays that the new found understanding acquired through this book results in the reader saving, protecting and growing his nest egg more vigorously.

QUANTUM CRISIS-II
The Great Financial & Credit Crisis
2007 - 2009

ISBN : 978-0-9783550-4-3

Best Selling Author of
Quantum Crisis-I and Quantum Crisis-III

Best Selling Author of
Quantum Crisis-I and Quantum Crisis-II

RAJ D. RAJPAL
B.Sc.(Honors), D.A.P.R., D.M., D.C.S., D.M., M.B.A. (Ohio)

QUANTUM CRISIS-III

This book represents the final installment of the "Quantum Crisis" 3-book series. While "Quantum Crisis-I" deals with the origin of the financial crisis, "Quantum Crisis-II" expounded the 2007-2009 global financial credit crisis. This book is a natural progression and attempts to provide solid time-tested savings, investment and risk management strategies to assist an investor accumulate his wealth better in a post-crisis world.

In terms of financial planning processes, several good ideas are propounded in terms of retirement strategies, college education funding options, home investment and credit card reduction strategies. In addition, investment and insurance strategies as well as small business wealth creation processes are discussed. The purpose of all these separate and diverse strategies is to integrate the reader's financial portfolio with a view to to performing effectively and efficiently.

Since life is one big "ball of wax" comprised of a multitude of activities and relationships, the author urges the reader to step aside from his daily routine and look at the wider value of his Financial Existence. Personal health and wellbeing strategies, personal development processes and good mental, emotional and spiritual balance are all stressed as important components of a good overall financial Life. Is there any value to money if you are unhappy and imbalanced in the process?

The author prays that an understanding and application of the numerous financial strategies help the reader better control costs, avoid future financial losses while aiding in the orderly and systematic growth of his hard earned wealth.

QUANTUM CRISIS-III
Winning Investment Strategies
To Prosper Through
The Global Financial and Credit Crisis

ISBN : 978-0-9783550-5-0

Best Selling Author of
Quantum Crisis-I and Quantum Crisis-II

AUTHOR SUGGESTS YOU READ ALL THREE BOOKS
SEQUENTIALLY FOR FULL UNDERSTANDING OF
GLOBAL FINANCIAL & CREDIT CRISIS

1

THIS PAGE IS LEFT BLANK INTENTIONALLY

QUANTUM CRISIS II-
THE GREAT FINANCIAL AND CREDIT CRISIS 2007-2009

By

RAJ D.RAJPAL

B.Sc. (Honors). G.C.E. (Cambridge), D.A.P.R., D.M., D.C.S., D.P.S.,
M.B.A. (Ohio)

FROM THE BEST-SELLING AUTHOR OF:

QUANTUM CRISIS 1:
THE ORIGINS OF GLOBAL FINANCIAL CRISES
&
QUANTUM CRISIS III
WINNING INVESTMENT STRATEGIES TO PROSPER THROUGH THE
GLOBAL FINANCIAL AND CREDIT CRISIS

PIONEER COMMUNICATION PUBLISHERS

BOOKS BOUTIQUE

FINANCE SERIES
QUANTUM CRISIS 1: ORIGINS OF FINANCIAL CRISES
QUANTUM CRISIS 2: THE GREAT FINANCIAL & CREDIT CRISIS
QUANTUM CRISIS 3: WINNING INVESTMENT STRATEGIES
OFFSHORE INVESTMENTS: THE MILLIONAIRE VISION
OFFSHORE HAVENS: THE FOUR BEST-KEPT SECRETS OF
MILLIONAIRES

SALES AND MARKETING SERIES
QUANTUM SELLING
QUANTUM SALES MANAGEMENT
QUANTUM MARKETING

MANAGEMENT SERIES
QUANTUM ETHICS

SELF-IMPROVEMENT SERIES
QUANTUM PUBLIC SPEAKING
YOU HAVE IT ALL NOW: YOUR LIFE IS TRULY YOURS TO
DISCOVER & ENJOY

OTHER FORTHCOMING BOOKS
UNCONDITIONAL LOVE
UNCONDITIONAL YOGA
UNCONDITIONAL HEALTH
UNCONDITIONAL WEALTH
UNCONDITIONAL HEALING
UNCONDITIONAL SPIRITUALITY
UNCONDITIONAL WEIGHT LOSS

QUANTUM CRISIS II-
THE GREAT FINANCIAL AND CREDIT CRISIS OF 2007-09

By

RAJ D.RAJPAL

B.Sc. (Honors), D.A.P.R., D.M., D.C.S. (U.S.), D.P.S., M.B.A. (Ohio)

National Quality Award Winner
Sales Coach and Public Speaker
Trainer, Bob Proctor Basic Program, Canada
Sales Trainer, Counselor Selling Program, U.S.A.
Trophy Winner, Public Speaking, Indo-American Society.
Provisional Applicant, Million Dollar Round Table, U.S.A.
Diploma, Graduate Advertising & Public Relations Program.
Trainer, Bob Proctor Advanced Motivation Series Program, Canada.
Uni-Lever Gold Medal Recipient-Graduate Marketing Management.

PIONEER COMMUNICATION

PUBLISHER:
PIONEER COMMUNICATION, CANADA
Orders for additional books can be placed directly at:
rdrajpal@yahoo.com
National Library of Canada
Rajpal Raj D., 1951–
Quantum Crisis/Raj D. Rajpal
Includes Index
ISBN: 978-0-9783550-4-3

This book is dedicated to the understanding of the serious challenges facing us--- as we set out to conquer this great global financial and credit crisis.

Awareness, understanding and meaningful investor actions are required in addition to total integration of personal, financial and spiritual priorities. This will help protect both one's inner peace and external wealth while guaranteeing a more sane and profitable future for our children.

TABLE OF CONTENTS

PART 2 – THE REAL FINANCIAL & CREDIT CRISIS 2007–2009

CHAPTER 5
BACKGROUND OF PAST GLOBAL FINANCIAL CRISES
TYPES OF FINANCIAL CRISES
BANKING CRISES
SPECULATIVE BUBBLES AND CRASHES
INTERNATIONAL FINANCIAL CRISES
WIDER ECONOMIC CRISES
CAUSES AND CONSEQUENCES OF FINANCIAL CRISES
LEVERAGE
ASSET-LIABILITY MISMATCH
UNCERTAINTY AND HERD BEHAVIOR
REGULATORY FAILURES
FRAUD
CONTAGION
RECESSIONARY EFFECTS
THEORIES OF FINANCIAL CRISES
WORLD SYSTEMS THEORY
MINSKY'S THEORY
CO-ORDINATION GAMES
HERDING MODELS AND LEARNING MODELS

CHAPTER 6
TIMELINE OF GLOBAL FINANCIAL CRISIS OF 2007–2009
PRE-PANIC PHASE
PRELUDE TO PANIC PHASE
START OF THE FINANCIAL CRISIS

PREFACE

2007 was a particularly challenging year for most investors. What started as a faint Headwind developed into a massive hurricane of unbelievable strength. The speed and impact of this financial hurricane was unprecedented in modern history.

October 2007 marked the beginnings of this financial hurricane. The impact of this unbelievably vital and destructive headwind was felt all over the world. The first manifestation of this devastation was felt intimately in the country, which represented the epicenter of this crisis---- the United States of America. The US stock market price values reflected the early symptoms of this larger financial malaise. In October 2007 it swung up and down ---- but the general trend was downwards. Stock prices depreciated expeditiously-----and this deep downward price decline spread to bond and commodity contracts too. Commodities, which were always thought to be a great hedge against future inflation, also saw precipitous drops in value. Nothing seemed safe anymore. All markets simultaneously tanked----- it was an unbelievable sell off. And, to add misery to madness, the Federal Reserve continued its path to lower interest rates, simultaneously decimating investors' interest savings and retirement returns for the older segment of the population.

All of a sudden nothing was safe anymore. All the financial advisors and their advice were not worth a dime. In the backdrop of this vast destruction of investor and public wealth, was a notion in my mind that this was a subject worth investigating. I visualized myself being in a position to practically and positively assist a common investor in understanding and resolving these current and future financial risks. Looking at my over two decades of experience in risk management, I took upon myself the challenge to write a book which would, for the first time explain to the public the history, causes and effects of this financial tsunami. But to be valuable book, I would then have a continuing obligation and responsibility to present valid risk management initiatives to the personal investor with an end view of developing strategies to protect such investor's nest egg----- irrespective of whether this nest egg was a modest sum of money in a bank account or a multimillion dollar estate.

With these thoughts and feelings, I started this project of writing this monumental thesis. This book is more than sixty chapters long (counting present and future editions to this book).

The author humbly submits that an understanding of the causes and effects and practical action steps by an investor to mitigate such astronomic risks will go a long way to protect and enhance your life savings and life values.

May this book assist you in accomplishing such objectives.

INTRODUCTION

This book's history starts in the United States. Where it ends is anyone's guess. But to be absolutely candid and forthright, the entire blame for this crisis rests in the hands of the most powerful country in the world--- the United States of America. Since this country marks the very epicenter of this financial earthquake, it is important to start the story in Part 2 with the goings on financially in this part of the Western World. This book therefore focuses greatly on this epicenter. How quickly we resolve this global financial and credit problem will rest on how well the financial repair is conducted in the United States.

The great financial and credit crisis of 2007-2009 amplified itself when greedy banks, insurance companies and other financial intermediaries/institutions (within the massive financial system) decided to systematically exploit the opportunities available to them. This was done with a view to maximize their profits with no consideration of what impact such profits would have on the global financial system.

At this time of our financial histories in the US, interest rates were very low----- this encouraged risk-taking by ordinary investors and speculators alike. With a negative real rate of borrowing, financial institutions lent billions of dollars out. This money landed up in everyone's hands. Such money was being invested in the ever-expanding real estate market as investors purchased homes and commercial properties with little or no money down (with very few credit restrictions).

This upward demand for real estate resulted in real estate prices hitting the roof nationally. Along with this investment behavior was the accompanying actions of investors to speculate in the stock and commodity markets. This resulted in ever increasing prices of everything from homes to office buildings to stock prices. The unlimited amount of capital available in the marketplace was largely due to a financial innovation called SECURITIZATION. Securitization was the magic financial engineering concept and technique, which assisted such financial institutions in creating and transporting these massive amounts of risk to third parties. By employment of the securitization process, banks, as one example, transferred their credit risks of lending money to third parties. In this process, banks were ably assisted by their evil counterparts in the investment banking system. The investment banks packaged and repackaged such bank loans into securities and sold them to different banks and investors all over the world. This is how an American problem became an international financial problem with "toxic assets" infecting all countries in the world and decimating global bank balance sheets. Let us try to understand the securitization process a bit better since this can be traced to the real roots of this financial and credit crisis. Securitization is a process where ordinary banks would resell their loans to investment banks, which then packaged them into loans of different tranches/qualities. Tranche 1, for example, could be loans made to individuals with good credit.

Tranche 2 were loans to individuals with average credit while Tranche 3 were loans made to questionable credit risks, like sub-prime borrowers.

Using this financial process banks were able to offload their loans to third parties. The third party would make an investment based on its risk-return requirement. If it wanted to earn a higher return it would invest in Tranche 2 as compared to Tranche 1.

As loan growth exploded in the US, more and more people were being allowed to borrow money to buy houses, which they could never afford (to pay back) by fraudulent banks and mortgage brokers. But this process of upward moving house prices could not go on forever. When the subprime borrowers started defaulting on their loan obligations, this started the process of collapse of the credit markets. There was so much money floating around and no investor really knew what any lenders portfolio was worth. This created confusion and finally panic in the marketplace. Where was one to invest? How would one know if one would get their money back after investing in say, a bank or other financial institution? Frankly, no one knew, because the toxic assets were neatly distributed in different parts of the financial system. Also no financial institution was willing to come clean on their real exposure to toxic assets. We got into an environment where everything was suspect. This resulted in the extreme stand by banks, which stopped trusting each other. Even for one bank to lend to another overnight became a problem. This started the credit crisis.

Since banks stopped or restricted lending, businesses could not get loans to continue their activities--- this resulted in them laying off workers, who now stopped spending money since they had less of it. The crisis had run a full circle. Easy lending, lots of money around, speculation and growth of asset markets followed with distrust, lack of confidence and a credit crisis. This resulted in job layoffs, lower consumer spending and a general lack of investor confidence. And the bottom line was that this crisis was impacting what hurts most, which is an average individual's ability to earn (as a result of a lost job) and his accompanying inability to spend. When you looked at the effect of this crisis on a macro-level, it invariably lead to economic disruption and downturn accompanied with a higher national unemployment rate, lack of consumer confidence and lower production of Gross National Product.

Many factors lead to this crisis. Inefficient and ineffective bank supervision, too lax an interest rate policy by the Federal Reserve and the massive securitization of loans by investment banks and regular banks all hand a hand in this crisis.

This book will slowly but surely take you through all the historical and actual steps in this evolving crisis. In the process, it will give you a bird's eye view of the problem and a 360-degree understanding of the crisis. It will then move forward to discuss policy prescriptions and most importantly look at what you can as a private investor do to protect and grow your nest egg.

This introduction serves to preview what is going to follow in his book. Read on--- the book is interesting and lively. May this presentation assist you in living a better financial and personal life and protect your hard earned assets.

CHAPTER 1

MISSION STATEMENT

The purpose of this book is unique in the sense that it tries to understand the whole picture reflecting the universal financial and credit crisis. This particular crisis is like no other since the Great Depression and therefore needs patient and clear understanding. The problems surrounding this crisis are very complex---- causes of this crisis which appear like simple concepts presented by the media and other vested interests do not reflect the fundamental reasons triggering this problem. There are numerous causes, some which appear on the surface and others more subliminal. In fact, it is the dangerous combination of a variety of lethal causes all acting at the same time, which has precipitated this crisis.

The book revolves around three different time curtains representing the past (Quantum Crisis 1), the present (Quantum Crisis II) and the future (Quantum Crisis II & Quantum Crisis III). The first part outlined in Quantum Crisis 1, talks about what money represents and how and where it derives its power and influence from. This part continues as a historical journey into how money was created and what shape and form it appears in the present. The second part outlined in Quantum Crisis II, goes into the past history of bubbles, depressions and public mania.

This history is critical in understanding what has happened in the past and how the string of past, present and future events are interlinked.

In this process, the reader understands that "financial crises" existed through many past centuries in almost every country in the world. Causes of the prominent crises are then elucidated with a moral or policy prescription at the end of each historical crises point. It is surprising that wise economists, financial institutions and representative governments have still not learnt to spot these irrational exuberances in advance----- nor have they learnt to set up effective risk management and risk mitigation systems to control such negative wealth destruction occurrences.

Part 3 outlined in the second half of Quantum Crisis II, explains what went wrong with the current global financial and credit crisis and what we can do to solve this problem immediately with the least amount of pain.

Part 4 outlined in Quantum Crisis III then goes to the most important part of this publication---- which is, what you, as an ordinary investor can do to protect and build your nest egg. It is not enough to know and understand this crisis. What is critical at this stage is to apply this newfound knowledge to grow your wealth and guarantee your lifestyle for generations to come.

In short the mission statement is part history, part an understanding of current problems with the second half discussing causes and policy prescriptions to solve this problem in addition to preventing such financial catastrophes in the future.

And the last part talks about the most important person in the world--- which is, of course YOU with all the financial challenges you must now face as you struggle to protect and grow your wealth.

In closing, the mission statement is to educate, enlighten and grow your understanding of the financial world in a straight, plain and factual manner. May this mission statement serve to protect you in every shape and form conceivable.

CHAPTER 2

PHILOSOPHY BEHIND A CRISIS

Times have indeed changed today. The global crisis in front of us has fundamentally changed the nature of our relationships with each other. In times of plenty and prosperity when no thought was given to money, people lived in nice homes and had secure jobs. The family looked forward to two vacations, one in the summer and one around Christmas. When money was not immediately available there was the reliable credit card, which could stave off any scarcities. While all of this was happening, inflation was generally controllable and there was always enough to spend in spite of the daily increases in the cost of living. And our marvelous home, the ultimate bastion of free enterprise would quietly go up in value every year. Everything was fine and dandy. This was until the global financial crisis hit home. And hit home it did and the effect was a very severe jolt into reality.

The first manifestations of the crisis were the plunging values of homes in most neighborhoods. In early 2005 the deceleration had started in the United States--- first with slight drops till suddenly home prices started decreasing exponentially. The final housing shock arrived sometime in 2008 when the mortgage on the home was greater than its market value ------this provided a homeowner with his first glimpse with scarcity and poverty. Still things were going along fine till the stock market tanked in 2008.

And October 2008 was like no other month or year. At around this time the US Government refused to bailout the investment banking firm, Bear Stearns, and everything went downhill subsequent to that. 2009 was a time of increased change as national consumer confidence plummeted and the US started losing jobs in the first two months of the year at a rate in excess of 500,000 jobs per month. Now, you had zero or inappreciable equity in your home, your stock market portfolio had tanked by over 50% and you either had or were in danger of losing your job. Suddenly there was a real crisis---- it was a personal crisis of unbelievable portions and the only story out there was one of personal survival.

This crisis changed in many ways the relationship between people. Everyone was so self-consumed in his or her financial and life issues that there was very little time for retrospection of the wider issues, which had created this problem. One of such issues was the relationship between the people and the global financial system. Did the controllers/primary players in the financial system have the right to decimate individual wealth? And how much greed (on their part) was enough? And now that the destruction was complete who would save us? America, which had always believed in the free enterprise system where the markets would sort out what is right and return to equilibrium suddenly realized that this business model, was ineffective and inefficient in solving the massive new financial problems.

Suddenly the Government had to sort out the mess to redistribute resources so that the problem could be solved and resources could be properly allocated among the different players in the financial system. And what about the financial architecture surrounding the financial system? Something was seriously wrong here too in a way where a few powerful constituents like global banks, investment banks, insurance companies and mortgage related entities proved that in the name of greed they had the power to destroy the otherwise worthwhile financial architecture?

The philosophy behind this crisis starts with a self-examination on the part of all components of this global financial system to understand their individual roles and effects and to design proper systems to insure stability and prosperity to everyone. As the financial crisis developed, it showed how few powerful constituents could destroy the lifestyle of billions of people worldwide.

The philosophy behind the crisis needed to deal with human values---- the basic values of self-respect, concern about other individual's rights and a desire to work cooperatively and peacefully knowing there was enough for everyone. The current crisis brought to the fore several ethical issues that expressed them in the total callousness and indifference of some financial players to the detriment and ruin of hundreds of small and medium sized players. And this abuse of ethics involved primarily the large financial organizations like the commercial and super powerful investment banks along with their brethren in insurance and mortgage companies.

Such large corporations in the United States (predominantly) violated the rights of everyone else to survive and prosper and given the interrelatedness of the global financial system such unconscionable and criminal behavior resulted in people suffering all over the world. All of a sudden there were 20 million people out of work (in early 2009) in China due to reduced global demand for their products in addition to millions of people displaced in Asia, Europe and Australia people who due to no fault of their own had become indirect negative beneficiaries of the global financial scam perpetrated by a few super large financial institutions in the United States.

Looking at this massive and catastrophic effect on individual's lives---- this destruction and suffering point to a time which has now come for the world to become one. By this I mean, there is a great and extreme need for humans to work co-operatively and peacefully in every field of endeavor. Globalization has become the first step, which has brought people and cultures in intimate contact with each other---- this has all started with a need to serve the needs of international business. However this movement is only the beginning.

The philosophy of good business ethics is intimately connected with this need for companies and individuals to honestly talk with one another. What invariably gets in the way of clear, honest communication is the presence of diversity of language and cultural backgrounds of all such parties to such conversation.

Also one has to be cognizant of the motivating factors behind such conversations, whether such purpose is to do business together or to understand each other better, religiously, physically and/or spiritually.

When we look at the state of ethics in this world, one cannot hide the fact that there is at every level and corner of this world a sense of disarray and disrepair caused by ceaselessly selfish acts of both individuals and groups. Let me explain. In order for us to grow together we need to be aware and alert of each other's needs. Only when such understanding is crystal clear can we hope to proceed with the arduous and challenging task of optimally relating to each other. Unfortunately, what is actually happening in the world is the reverse of this ideal process of communication. The individual, corporation or nation first thinks of all it priorities and then works out a way of relating with the other individual, corporation or nation. Therefore, there is no proper communication or relationship. The more powerful nation or corporation gets the upper hand in such relationships. The world as we see it now is in a constant state of war between the strong and the weak. The strong represent the haves of this world; the weak represent the have-nots. The stronger, more financially capitalized and agile company tends to dominate world markets and creates disharmonious relationships with its customers and the world at large. Surely, when Green Peace and other world- minded individuals and organizations protest at G-7 meetings, these protests represent some cause and reason.

I am not a member of the Green Peace organization nor do I belong to any other activist groups. But I know one thing for sure and that is the fact that the time has come when big and small nations, big and small corporations and corporations and lawmakers sit down and do something to clean up the mess. And what is this mess? It is the mess of unbridled exploitation of energy and financial resources. It is the filthy and unconscionable act of throwing up greenhouse gases to make a profit at any cost. It is actions made by groups of executives to rip off the public by financial misrepresentations and distortions. This nonsense needs to stop right now.

Although what is happening now ethically is very negative we must realize that even this cloud has a silver lining. Maybe the Lord has wanted all this to happen to bring us all together in a spirit of compromise, adjustment and peace.

The philosophy behind a global crisis points to a deeper and honest understanding of all the problems being created today as a result of a lack of concern for others. This philosophy also calls for all parties responsible for such "pollution" to sit together and talk earnestly with a view to solving such problems immediately and instantaneously. Corporations must talk to their customers, nations must talk with other nations, and people must talk with other people to overcome cultural gaps. We must all try hard to communicate and act together to save the world. This is not a Utopian vision. It is the truth. The World is decaying and dying slowly but surely. But this is not the end of Life or Existence.

We need to step back and look at the problems we have created and come back with a humble positive mind to undo all the wrongs of the past. This is absolutely possible given the depth and breadth of human intelligence. We have had the power to advance technologically; to send a man to the moon; to create numerous and marvelous scientific advancements and even to prolong life itself. Why can the human mind not go one step forward and solve this bigger problem it has created through poor communications and deplorable personal and business ethics?

In the solution to this problem lies our philosophical and real advancement. And the message is simple. To live together in this marvelous and wonderful world, we must understand why we seek to dominate others, why we seek to use unethical actions as an excuse to get ahead in our lives and how we can come together and all win together by respecting everyone's right to live, whether it is a poor man living in a slum in India or an African afflicted with AIDS.

The burning need today is for the human to work together with his fellow human to bring about good in the world. Good ethics, good conduct and proper action always starts and ends with the human being. Are we really ready to make this great inner change? On the answer to this question lies the hope and salvation of Mankind.

Work together honestly, help others and co-operate harmoniously and the World will always be there to supply all our needs.

Keep fighting and building walls, misrepresent constantly, continue expressing unethical behavior and feed greenhouse gases to the atmosphere and our world will cease to exist, as we know it. The choice is yours.

It is the author's fervent prayer, that we can make decisive and positive change at the individual, corporate and national level to make this world a better place for our children and us.

May this book be a small opening to get us into the vast expanse of universal consciousness, where everything is possible.

CHAPTER 3
PSYCHOLOGY OF A CRISIS

The current global financial and credit crisis had its intimate roots in the manifestation of human greed. How else can you explain the massive fraud, misrepresentation and cruel exploitation of financial players in the worldwide system? This greed was amplified by the superiority and secrecy of prevailing knowledge. Let me explain. Firstly, we need to put the blame where it is due. The blame primarily rests in the hands of the large US commercial and investment banks, along with other influential mega players, like US hedge funds, the US insurance leadership under AIG Insurance and US mortgage related outfits like mortgage brokers, mortgage originators, mortgage re-sellers, and etcetera.

These large players engaged in severe and unconscionable gambling on an unprecedented scale. Their investment behavior had all the hallmarks of engaging in activities with unlimited upside potential and no downside investment risk. The commercial banks that sold home loans to the investment bank for further sale had no risk. They took the loan off their balance sheet the moment they sold it to the investment banks. There was zero risk for them. In an environment of low interest rates and rising home prices and availability of capital they lent billions of dollars to sub-prime borrowers, and immediately resold these loans to investment banks after making a substantial profit.

The investment banks then repackaged the loans into different Tranches (credit tranches) and sold it to institutional investors, foreign governments, and foreign banks through the mechanism of direct sales. They also had no skin in the game and could engage in shifting billions of dollars of risk all over the world. The differentiating factor for these investment package sales and what made them easily saleable was the paucity of information. This paucity of information was created by the employment of advanced financial engineering techniques. The securitization process was so complicated and devious that no one, save the investment banks themselves, knew exactly what was inside these loans. In such absence of information the investment community surrendered their collective intelligence and judgment to the well known US rating agencies. They believed that these rating agencies had exercised due diligence in analyzing and assessing the risk worthiness of these tranches of sub-prime and other mortgage loans. But the rating agencies themselves failed to exercise financial prudence in evaluating the appropriate risk of these investment vehicles. Such rating agencies erroneously labeled most of these real estate loans, packaged collaterized loans and other asset-backed mortgages as AAA never anticipating in their mathematical valuation models that the real estate market would show such significant downward correction. Huge banks and institutions all over the world bought these securities trusting the declared risk ratings provided.

However and very mysteriously none of these sophisticated investors paid attention to the inherent conflict of interest between the rating agencies and issuers of debt (which was being evaluated by the agencies). The non-palatable fact was that the that the issuers of debt like investment banks paid these rating organizations for their services---- one wonders how and why most of these securities were labeled AAA.

The financial crisis became serious when investors had no way of determining where the toxic assets were and therefore could not professionally value any specific investment. Since the toxic assets were everywhere, there was an immediate loss of investor confidence causing a lack of trust and confidence in the market. This led to the credit crisis and the deplorable market condition today.

Another important psychological factor, which involved the manipulation of other financial investors by these large banks and insurance companies basically, revolves around the issue of ethics. These large players exhibited very poor ethics in their business dealings with others as they decided to maximize profit at any cost with no regard to the values and needs of others.

Therefore, greed, a superiority based on having exclusive and protected knowledge about loans securitization (knowledge which the investment public did not have), and a poor sense of ethics all contributed to this financial mess the world is in now.

Let us now turn our attention to the issues surrounding the need for proper ethical behavior on part of these large financial institutions.

To understand ethical behavior one needs to look closely at human psychology. Human psychology is a fascinating subject. How and why we act and the results there from can fill thousands and thousands of pages of psychological material. Looking at our psychology in terms of ethics, we must first step in and understand our motivation factors. Abraham Maslow, a psychologist I respect a great deal, came up with a hierarchy of human needs pyramid. He believed that every action we took had its roots in our quest to fulfill a dominant need or desire. However, we tended to focus on first fulfilling basic needs, like the need for food, water and shelter. After we achieved this, we moved on to our safety and physiological needs. Then we spent our energy in meeting with our self-esteem needs and so on........

What does an understanding of Maslow's hierarchy of needs have to do with the psychology of ethics? I believe it has a lot to do with a deeper understanding of this subject matter. Depending on which part of the world you live in and your current economic and political situation, you may be forced to behave in certain ways. If you live in India in a slum, your day-to-day life may involve struggling to get enough bread, water and salt for your family. With a lack of abundant jobs in your community accompanied by the ever-increasing financial demands from your family, you may be forced to lie, cheat and steal to survive.

On the other hand, if you live in the vast profitable expanse of North America, you may not have the same sense of economic urgencies as a poor East Indian.

You probably are paying for a home and have a decent job and worthwhile material comforts. What causes you to lie and cheat and steal?

Coming back to Maslow's pyramid, you are probably attempting to fulfill your needs and desire to get rich quicker than at your usual normal pace. This invariably is what happened to the executives who went to jail when associated with Enron Corporation in the US. These executives were rich; they enjoyed positions of power and influence. However, that was not enough for them. In order to get richer faster they took shortcuts. However, these shortcuts created end results, which were devastating to the lives of thousands of employees at Enron Corporation. Many of these employees lost their entire jobs and life savings and retirement pensions.

So, if you live in a developed economy, you may decide to cheat, lie and steal to get up the corporate ladder faster or to make a fast buck period... There is no other motivating factor to be unethical here.

How do we change this human psychology of survival in India and other developing economies and the preponderance of greed in North America, Europe and most of the developed world??

This is a very difficult question to answer. And in the proper answer and implementation of such answer lies the solution to the ethical dilemmas all around this world.

In order to stem and control the ethical issues, a host of national and international regulations have sprung up.

The Sarbanes-Oxley Act in the US was passed into law soon after the Enron scandal. The United Nations has recommended model corporate governance standards after reviewing all the worldwide problems in the corporate ethics field.

Therefore, we have two sides of a coin, both of which can help solve the problem.

Educate the people; make them more aware of what they are doing wrong; present the social penalties for wrongful action [set up a strong judiciary and police system to monitor ethical performance and develop the societal laws to discourage ethical abuse. Bring the citizens into the picture by large page ads. Show them the cost of unethical behavior to their livelihood and to the nation and world at large. Ask them to become whistleblowers, if they notice or suspect unethical activity at any personal, private, business or corporate level. Give them a monetary reward for spotting and reporting on potentially criminal unethical activity. In India, the Income tax department gives a percentage of the department's recovery of unpaid taxes to the ordinary citizen, who spots and reports someone not paying his fair share of taxes. Why can we not make this a model policy on a worldwide scale? Get the common man to report on unethical behavior. Neither government nor the entire United Nations can effectively police this problem with bad ethics on a consistent basis without the aid of the common man.

The solution to the unethical dilemma philosophically is to pull all stops out and get everyone involved in solving the problems.

Successful solution of this problem at a personal, societal, and judicial/police level will result in better allocation of world resources and a more efficient and productive world. Each and every human being has a responsibility to make the world a better place to live in. This is the first step in solving this problem and removing this curse from this world.

In closing, the challenge in solving the global financial and credit crisis is to be able to understand the driving psychological factors behind this problem: unbelievable greed, an information superiority in terms of the development of exotic financial instruments like securitization and a blatant expression and abuse of personal and business ethics.

All these three psychological factors caused the major problem the world is in now.

CHAPTER 4

PSYCHOLOGY OF A CRISIS REVISITED

I feel at this juncture that it makes sense to understand what happened and caused this global crisis. A clear understanding of the problems (on a psychological level) should hopefully prevent this type of crisis from re-occurring in the future. As I had indicated in the last chapter the crisis was caused by massive greed, information manipulation and poor ethics by the large financial houses in the United States. On closer examination, greed, which is the predominant cause of this behavior, has a deep and interconnected relationship with ethics. Poor ethics represents itself in the manifestation of greed and therefore I have attached this chapter for perusal, study and discussion. All I am talking about in this chapter is definitions, understanding and expression of both personal and business ethics; it is my hope that this understanding will help governments and other responsible financial authorities in setting up checks and balances in the system to catch irresponsible, fraudulent and unethical behavior so that such a crisis can never reoccur in the future. It is with this understanding that I am paying particular attention to the subjects surrounding personal and business ethics. Let us now move forward to an understanding of both personal and business ethics.

Wikipedia Encyclopedia defines Ethics as, "Ethics is a major branch of philosophy, which encompasses right conduct and good life. It is significantly broader than the common conception of analyzing right and wrong. A central aspect of ethics is 'the good life,' the life worth living or life that is satisfying, which is held by many philosophers to be more important than moral conduct. The major problem is the discovery of the summun bonum, the greatest good."

Some of the core issues in the study of ethics are:

1. Justice
2. Value
3. Right
4. Duty
5. Virtue
6. Equality
7. Freedom
8. Trust
9. Free will
10. Consent
11. Moral responsibility

Now that the Wikipedia definition is established, let us move along with details on the described components of ethics.

1. JUSTICE

Personal ethics involves the application of justice. In your dealings with others, are you following the code of law established in your community?

Are you dealing fairly and justly with your neighbor and friend? In your business relationships involving your customers are you seeking to provide the best behavior in consonance with the legal codes?

2. VALUE

In terms of value, are you offering a product or service, which represents an ultimate storehouse of value? Is the price of the product commensurate with its quality and embedded service promises? In terms of personal relationships with family and friends, is your relationship one, which embodies the application of the highest standard of value?

3. RIGHT

Do your personal and business actions involve doing something, which is generally regarded as being right? Or are your actions in a gray area---- you are acting legally but have exhibited improper moral behavior. You understand that the law expects certain minimum standards of moral behavior, but that you may be in fact doing something legal and yet something immoral (not right).

4. DUTY

In every situation and interaction with others, are you discharging your duty to the relationship fully and wholly, with no regard to the amount of time, attention or energy expended by you in this process?

5. VIRTUE

The best way of expressing the application of virtue is by quoting from the Bible. The Holy Bible: New Revised Standard Version quotes in Galatians 5:22–23: virtue being:

"Love, joy, peace, patience, kindness, generosity, faithfulness, gentleness and self–control."

The central question the reader must ask himself is if he exercising the above virtues in his dealings with others.

6. EQUALITY

In your everyday relationships, do you approach matters respecting other's right to live and think freely? In business matters, where you seek to influence others, are you approaching your customer with a fair and level sense of equality? Or are you trying to exploit the relationship because of your special and unique status, resources and power?

7. FREEDOM

Are your actions conducted in an environment of personal freedom? And are you dealing with others while respecting their freedom to agree or disagree with your proposition?

Do you accept another's option to accept or reject your ideas and proposition, thereby exercising their personal freedom even if this means your idea or acceptance being put at risk?

8. FREE WILL

When interacting with others, are you conducting your affairs armed with complete self- knowledge of your actions and behaviors? Is your conduct a result of an exercise of free will unabated and uninfluenced by peer or pressure groups? Are you doing what you believe is the best possible thing for your loved one, friend or customer? In short, are you exercising free will all the time?

9. CONSENT

In your everyday actions, are you making sure that you take the consent of all affected parties in your relationships? Or are you taking their involvement in the relationship as granted?

10. MORAL RESPONSIBILITY

Are you aware of your moral responsibilities in communications with others? Are you taking the time to understand and study the impact of your behavior and business interactions with others? Are you enhancing someone else's life? Or are you merely ripping them off?

RELATIONSHIPS BETWEEN ETHICS AND MORALS

Coming back to definitions from Wikipedia, the following further clarifications are provided in terms of the relationships between a study of ethics and morals. Further, there is a good definition of personal ethics. Here are the definitions:

"Ethics and morals are respectively akin to theory and practice. Ethics denotes the theory of right action and the greater good, while morals indicate their practice. Personal ethics signifies a moral code applicable to individuals, while social ethics means moral theory applied to groups. Social ethics can be synonymous with social and political philosophy, in as much as it is the foundation of a good society or state. Ethics is not limited to specific acts and defined moral codes, but encompasses the whole of moral ideals and behaviors, a person's philosophy of life."

ETHICS AND THE WISE GREEK PHILOSOPHERS

Several Greek philosophers, countless centuries back, had a basic awareness of what ethical action was. According to Socrates, knowledge, which had an intimate connection with human life, was the most important type of knowledge.

Socrates propounded the system of "self-knowledge" as the most important knowledge center. Awareness was the key to good self-knowledge.

If a person was aware of the impact of his actions on him and the society at large and had the capacity and capability of distinguishing right from wrong, society would comprise of more wiser citizens and less crime would be committed. Happiness and harmony would result as a direct effect of such enlightened awareness and action.

Another great Greek philosopher, Aristotle envisaged a system of ethics under the heading of the term," self-realizationism." What he meant by this term was that all individuals were born with certain specific and unique talents.

If individuals acted according to their built in nature and used their God-given talents, they would be more content and complete. As a result man should live with moderate virtue. This is normally difficult since this implies doing the right thing, to the right person, at the right time, to the proper extent, in the correct fashion, for the right reason.

To close this chapter, an intimate awareness and knowledge of personal ethics is a starting point and foundation for all human relationships. If one can understand and accept these values, then individuals can work together more fairly.

Business relationships will improve as a result and the incidence of exploitation will decrease. Also, if individuals approach their personal lives with such high standards, then ultimately this will result in better family and community relationships. Everything starts and ends with the individual.

To create a lasting and permanent change in the world ethically, the individual will need to take the first steps in understanding and modifying his behavior for the greater social good. He will need to understand that he is linked with his family, community, business and world around him. Good actions at all levels will create stellar relationships at all levels of existence. This will make the community and world a better and more harmonious place to live in---- a world in which people learn to share and celebrate differences and not a world where talent, money and power control future results.

BUSINESS ETHICS

Business Ethics may be defined as, "a form of the art of applied ethics that examines ethical principles and more or ethical problems that can arise in a business environment." Put simply, business ethics has to do with the ethical value of decisions made by businesses in their quest for profits. Let us now look at the various issues corporations face as they react and interact with all the different people they do business with.

GENERAL ETHICAL CONSIDERATIONS

The following are some of the areas, which create perceptions of unethical or ethical behavior on part of the corporation:

AREA 1

FUNDAMENTAL OBJECTIVES OF BUSINESS

On a very fundamental basis, one needs to ask why the corporation exists in the first place. If we review the Anglo-American model, which is prevalent in the United Kingdom, the United States and Canada, we understand the predominant and primary reason for doing business from the corporation's perspective is to maximize value for their shareholders. If corporations engage and act on this narrow view at the detriment of relationships with all the other stakeholders, like suppliers, customers and competitors, to name a few, then this process of shareholder maximization at the expense of all other interested parties could be generally viewed as unethical behavior.

AREA 2

CONTRIBUTION TO CORPORATE SOCIAL RESPONSIBILITIES

Another way of assessing the quality of ethics in a corporation is to examine their corporate social responsibility mission. If the corporation talks about such responsibilities but never gets off ground zero to take an active interest and involvement in social causes, then this again can be viewed as unethical activity.

AREA 3
INTER-COMPANY RELATIONSHIPS
How companies behave with each other, particularly when they are in neck-to-neck competition defines their ethical role. When a company sees its competitor as getting weak and exercises an aggressive hostile takeover bid or when a corporation pays someone to spy on its competitors (industrial espionage) determines its outlook to business and ethics in general.

AREA 4
POLITICAL CONTRIBUTIONS AND LOBBYING EFFORTS
The extent of political contributions and the capital expended on lobbying for continuation of existing products and addition of new ones provides the ethical flavor of a company. For example, a tobacco company paying a lobbyist in Washington to get generous advertising exposures for cigarettes can be viewed as a highly unethical action.

A) ACCOUNTING INFORMATION ETHICS

Here are some examples of unethical accounting information use.

Creative accounting scams
The behavior of Enron Corporation in the US is a very good example of how hiding liabilities and misreporting income created a massive problem for everyone who was associated with this company.

Briberies and kickbacks

When corporations bribe government officials in order to seek government contracts, this constitutes anti-competitive behavior and results in misallocation of societal resources. Insider trading refers to an executive or other interested party having information in advance of public knowledge. For example, if a company is going to start selling a new product after receiving governmental approval, a fact which could increase its stock price. The manufacturing vice-president of this company has this information in advance and seeks purchase of his company shares in advance, knowing that once this announcement is made the share price will rocket upwards and he can make a quick profit. This definitely constitutes unethical behavior.

B) HUMAN RESOURCE MANAGEMENT AND UNETHICAL BEHAVIOR

Human resources ethics deals with all relationships between an employer and an employee. In such relationships, the employer usually has an upper hand. When we view how the corporation is treating its employees, we then get an idea of the extent of ethical or unethical behavior on part of the corporation.

Here are some examples of corporate behavior in this field:

(i)Discrimination issues surrounding age, gender, race, religion, and disabilities among other factors.

(ii) Factors dealing with representation of employees like actions involving union busting, etcetera

(iii) Actions involving infringement of employee privacy without specific permission and authorization by concerned employee like video, Internet and telephone surveillance of employees and drug testing.

(iv) Occupational safety and employee health issues.

C)   MARKETING AND SELLING ETHICS

Several issues abound on unethical use of marketing strategies, techniques and plans of action. These areas cover the following:

(i)   Price fixing, price discrimination and price skimming

(ii)   Unethical marketing strategies like the Ponzi scheme, Spam electronic marketing, pyramid schemes and planned obsolescence techniques.

(iii)   Dangerous and unethical advertising content in the form of subliminal advertising and misrepresentation of product properties.

(iv)   Unethical exploitation of children through specially designed advertisements.

(v)   Unethical representation of products and services by salespeople representing a corporation.

D) PRODUCTION ETHICS

The ethics of production has to do with the processes used to produce a product and how ethically a corporation engages in such processes. Here are some of the concerns in the production area:

  (i) Defective, addictive and inherently dangerous products and services (like tobacco, alcohol, weapons manufacturing and bungee jumping)
  (ii) Production processes causing industrial waste into our rivers and general environmental pollution through greenhouse gases, etcetera.
  (iii) Problems arising out of new technologies like genetically modified food.
  (iv) The business of product testing ethics such as animal testing of products.

E INTELLECTUAL PROPERTY ETHICS

Intellectual property rights are intangible in nature. They are concerned with who has the rights to develop an idea.

Here are some areas of concern:
(1) For example, if an author writes a new book and finds most or all his ideas plagiarized, then this constitutes an intellectual property right infringement.
(2) Issues dealing with patent infringement.
(3) Issues dealing with copyright and trademark infringement.

SIGNIFICANCE OF BUSINESS ETHICS

Since most businesses in the world are in corporate form, how such businesses behave and interact becomes crucial. Here are some of the reasons for the importance of the study of business ethics:

1. There is progressively greater power and influence exerted by corporations on the daily lives of people.
2. Big businesses have the potential power to positively assist or negatively destruct the communities they serve.
3. Businesses have the ability to effect the environment and their immediate communities positively or negatively.
4. With greater pressure being exerted by stakeholders like suppliers, other competitors, it becomes real important to understand how and when corporations should respond to such pressures and what constitutes acceptable behavior in this department.

GLOBALIZATION & ITS IMPACT
ON BUSINESS ETHICS

When corporations move away from their normal place of doing business into a new territory or country, several new issues come to the forefront. These are basically legal, accountability and cultural issues. Since the legal framework of doing business shifts when one moves from say, a developed nation to a developing economy, what rules of conduct are OK? The country of incorporation rules of the corporation? The rules of the emerging nation, where it seeks to do trade and investments? Who is going to police the business actions of the corporation now? What about cultural issues? How is the corporation to adapt to a totally different cultural expectation surrounding their products or services? And what about accountability issues? Since the corporation does not really report on a daily basis to anyone, and since it does not have to be held accountable on numerous fronts, how does it serve its accountability responsibilities?

Several of these areas are gray areas. By this I mean, there is no definite standard of conduct here. And this is where most of the misunderstandings and mistrust lies for such multinational corporations.

The United Nations, with a view, to setting up some standards for international trade, business and conduct has suggested the achievement of 8 Millennium Development goals by 2015.

On the United Nations website, "www.undp.org", the following goals are listed:

Goal 1: Eradicate extreme poverty and hunger

Goal2: Achieve universal primary education

Goal 3: Promote gender equality and empower women

Goal 4: Reduce child mortality

Goal 5: Improve maternal health

Goal 6: Combat HIV/AIDS, malaria and other diseases

Goal 7: Ensure environmental sustainability

Goal 8: Develop a global partnership for development

Why am I talking about the United Nations goals? And what does this have to do with business ethics? Simply those since corporations are now becoming multinational in character and have the power to gain and profit from exposure to opportunities all over the world that this opportunity also entails a responsibility on their part. If you are taking from the world then you must also give back to it. And what better way to give back than to assist the United Nations fulfills its eight major goals for the world. Therefore, if corporations are to be seen as truly caring and concerned global players, they must design and execute their strategies with a view to achieving one or more of these eight goals. Merely paying lip service or designing slick website content on their commitment to world issues is not enough. The message to them is: "Put your money where your mouth is. You simply cannot exploit the world masses. Now is the time to pay back for all your profits and success. Prove that you are really a caring corporate citizen."

This is why the corporation's role in helping the UN will go a long way in improving their credibility and enhancing their reputation as a caring, concerned world player.

THE CASE FOR SUSTAINABILITY

Right through the world, time boundaries apart, more and more people are questioning the ethical behavior of corporations as they plunder and rape the natural resources of this world. Corporate ethical standards are now being applied to include the role of the corporation in respecting and nourishing the resources around it. Issues like pollution creation, the dumping of greenhouse gases, the issues surrounding product recyclability are all creating a framework, where a corporation will be forced to work environmentally and ecologically creatively to preserve the natural balance of the world. The corporation will need to prove that it is indeed a corporate citizen of the world and cares not only for the goal of making profits but also in playing its part in keeping the balance in Earth between companies and their natural environments.

THE TRIPLE BOTTOM LINE INITIATIVE

Triple bottom line is a phrase coined by John Elkington in 1994. It refers to the triple responsibility of a corporation to take care of the 3 P's: People, Planet and Profit. People in this equation refer to the social responsibilities of corporations.

Planet refers to the environmental responsibilities, including the cause of sustainability by companies. Profit represents what most corporations are in business for anyway.

Triple bottom line actions represent a new way of defining a corporation's responsibility. Instead of a corporation merely maximizing revenue for its shareholders, it now is called to contribute equally to a clean and sound ecological environment and to take positive steps to support all stakeholders. A stakeholder refers to anyone, who is effected directly or indirectly by the actions of the firm.

The stakeholder theory suggests that the firm should be used as vehicle for satisfying and coordinating stakeholder interests, instead of solely maximizing shareholders profit. In real and practical terms these are some of the actions and initiatives to be taken by a firm to satisfy the triple bottom initiative of People, Planet and Profit.

In order to serve the People/Human Capital initiative a firm needs to have fair and beneficial practice towards labor and the community at large.

In order to ably serve the Planet/Natural capital initiative it needs to benefit the natural order as much as possible by conducting a life cycle assessment of all products manufactured.

This is done to calculate the actual and true environmental cost of growth and harvesting of raw materials to manufacture to distribution to eventual disposal by the end user.

All processes to optimize the ecological and environmental impact of production are taking into consideration by such company. In order to serve the profit initiative the corporation must make a real contribution financially and economically to all the markets it serves.

CONCLUSION

The global financial crisis has shown the ruthless and exploitive of large financial institutions and their leaders. To a great extent, these corporations and their senior management stand guilty in violation of most personal and business ethics principles elucidated in this chapter. From Bernard Madoff and his 50 billion dollar Ponzi scheme to defraud investors to a president of an investment bank who invested more than one million dollars on his office furniture, these examples represent the reasons why this global crisis is like no other. And to come out of this mess will require the coordinated and co-operative effort of all world nations and world people. It is simply too big a problem to be solved by any one country or any group of people. Understanding this massive violation of personal and business ethics should provide a guideline to everyone to measure their personal and business behavior according to a higher ethical standard. We are all in this mess and we all need to work together to develop a higher ethical consciousness---- this consciousness and understanding will work wonders to accelerate the solution of the problem.

CHAPTER 5

BACKGROUND ON PAST GLOBAL FINANCIAL CRISES

Before we start this book in earnest, we need to understand certain definitions and occurrences pertaining to global financial crises. We would also be better served if some theories on causes and consequences of financial disasters were elaborated. This will help put Part 2 in proper context and afford a panoramic view of the subject matter.

TYPES OF FINANCIAL CRISES
BANKING CRISES

When a bank suffers a sudden rush of withdrawals by depositors, this is called a *bank run*. Since banks lend out most of the cash they receive in deposits, it is difficult for them to quickly pay back all deposits if these are suddenly demanded, so a run may leave the bank in bankruptcy, causing many depositors to lose their savings unless they are covered by deposit insurance. A situation in which bank runs are widespread is called a *systemic banking crisis* or just a *banking panic*. A situation without widespread bank runs, but in which banks are reluctant to lend, because they worry that they have insufficient funds available, is often called a credit crunch.

A credit crunch also arises if a bank hoards cash because they see the existence of unquantifiable risk in the marketplace.

As banks drastically reduce the amount of credit available, this results In shortage of capital available for borrowing by small and medium sized business and by customers---- creating a credit crisis. Examples of bank runs include the run on the Bank of the United States in 1931 and the run on Northern Rock in the United Kingdom in 2007. The collapse of Bear Stearns in 2008 has also sometimes been called a bank run, even though Bear Stearns was an investment bank rather than a commercial bank.. The U.S. Savings and loan of the 1980s led to a credit crunch which is seen as a major factor in the U.S. recession of 1990–1991.

Speculative bubbles and crashes

Economists say that a financial asset (stock, for example) exhibits a *bubble* when its price exceeds the present value of the future income (such as interest or dividends that would be received by owning it to maturity *3 If most market participants buy the asset primarily in hopes of selling it later at a higher price, instead of buying it for the income it will generate, this could be evidence that a bubble is present. If there is a bubble, there is also a risk of a *crash* in asset prices: market participants will go on buying only as long as they expect others to buy, and when many decide to sell the price will fall.

However, it is difficult to tell in practice whether an asset's price actually equals its fundamental value, so it is hard to detect bubbles reliably. Some economists insist that bubbles never or almost never occur. *4

Well-known examples of bubbles (or purported bubbles) and crashes in stock prices and other asset prices include the Dutch tulip mania, the Wall Street crash of 1929, the Japanese property bubble of the 1980s, the crash of the dot-com bubble in 2000-2001, and the now-deflating United States housing bubble. *5 *6

International financial crises

When a country that maintains a fixed exchange rate is suddenly forced to devalue its currency because of a speculative attack, this is called a *currency crisis* or *balance of payments crisis*. When a country fails to pay back its sovereign debt, this is called a *sovereign default*. While devaluation and default could both be voluntary decisions of the government, they are often perceived to be the involuntary results of a change in investor sentiment that leads to a sudden stop in capital inflows or a sudden increase in *capital flight*.

Several currencies that formed part of the European Exchange Rate Mechanism suffered crises in 1992-93 and were forced to devalue or withdraw from the mechanism.

Another round of currency crises took place in Asia in 1997–98. Many Latin American countries defaulted on their debt in the early 1980s. The 1998 Russian financial crisis resulted in a devaluation of the ruble and default on Russian government bonds.

Wider economic crises

A downturn in economic growth lasting several quarters or more is usually called a *recession*. An especially prolonged recession may be called a *depression*, while a long period of slow but not necessarily negative growth is sometimes called economic stagnation. Since these phenomena affect much more than the financial system, they are not usually considered financial crises *per se*. But some economists have argued that many recessions have been caused in large part by financial crises. One important example is the Great Depression, which was preceded in many countries by bank runs and stock market crashes. The subprime mortgage and the bursting of other real estate bubbles around the world are widely expected to lead to recession in the U.S. and a number of other countries in 2008.

Nonetheless, some economists argue that financial crises are caused by recessions instead of the other way around. Also, even if a financial crisis is the initial shock that sets off a recession, other factors may be more important in prolonging the recession.

In particular, Milton Friedman and Anna Schwartz argued that the initial economic decline associated with the crash of 1929 and the bank panics of the 1930s would not have turned into a prolonged depression if it had not been reinforced by monetary policy mistakes on the part of the Federal Reserve,*7 and Ben Bernanke has acknowledged that he agrees. *8

CAUSES AND CONSEQUENCES OF FINANCIAL CRISES

Strategic complementarities in financial markets

It is often observed that successful investment requires each investor in a financial market to guess what other investors will do. George Soros has called this need to guess the intentions of others " reflexivity" * 9 Similarly, John Maynard Keynes compared financial markets to a beauty contest game in which each participant tries to predict which model *other* participants will consider most beautiful. *10

Furthermore, in many cases investors have incentives to co-ordinate their choices. For example, someone who thinks other investors want to buy lots of Japanese yen may expect the yen to rise in value, and therefore has an incentive to buy yen too. Likewise, a depositor in Indy Mac Bank who expects other depositors to withdraw their funds may expect the bank to fail, and therefore has an incentive to withdraw too. Economists call an incentive to mimic the strategies of others *strategic complementarity. *11*

It has been argued that if people or firms have a sufficiently strong incentive to do the same thing they expect others to do, then *self-fulfilling prophecies* may occur. *12 For example, if investors expect the value of the yen to rise, this may cause its value to rise; if depositors expect a bank to fail this may cause it to fail. *13 Therefore, financial crises are sometimes viewed as a vicious circle in which investors shun some institution or asset because they expect others to do so. *14

Leverage

Leverage, which means borrowing to finance investments, is frequently cited as a contributor to financial crises. When a financial institution (or an individual) only invests its own money, it can, in the very worst case, lose its own money. But when it borrows In order to invest more, it can potentially earn more from its investment, but it can also lose more than all it has. Therefore leverage magnifies the potential returns from investment, but also creates a risk of bankruptcy. Since bankruptcy means that a firm fails to honor all its promised payments to other firms, it may spread financial troubles from one firm to another.

The average degree of leverage in the economy often rises prior to a financial crisis. For example, borrowing to finance investment in the stock market (margin buying) ") became increasingly common prior to the Wall Street Crash of 1929.

Asset-liability mismatch

Another factor believed to contribute to financial crises is *asset-liability mismatch*, a situation in which the risks associated with an institution's debts and assets are not appropriately aligned. For example, commercial banks offer deposit accounts which can be withdrawn at any time and they use the proceeds to make long-term loans to businesses and homeowners. The mismatch between the banks' short-term liabilities (its deposits) and its long-term assets (its loans) is seen as one of the reason bank runs occur (when depositors panic and decide to withdraw their funds more quickly than the bank can get back the proceeds of its loans). *13 Likewise, Bear Stearns failed in 2007-08 because it was unable to renew the short-term debt it used to finance long-term investments in mortgage securities.

In an international context, many emerging market governments are unable to sell bonds denominated in their own currencies, and therefore sell bonds denominated in US dollars instead. This generates a mismatch between the currency denomination of their liabilities (their bonds) and their assets (their local tax revenues), so that they run a risk of sovereign default due to fluctuations in exchange rates. *15

Uncertainty and herd behavior

Many analyses of financial crises emphasize the role of investment mistakes caused by lack of knowledge or the imperfections of human reasoning. Behavioral finance studies errors in economic and quantitative reasoning. Psychologist Torbjorn K A Eliazonhas also analyzed failures of economic reasoning in his concept of 'œcopathy'. * 16

Historians, notably Charles Kindleberger, have pointed out that crises often follow soon after major financial or technical innovations that present investors with new types of financial opportunities, which he called "displacements" of investors' expectations. * 17 & 18   Early examples include the South Sea Bubble and Mississipi Bubble of 1720, which occurred when the notion of investment in shares of company stock was itself new and unfamiliar, *19 and the Crash of 1929, which followed the introduction of new electrical and transportation technologies. *20 More recently, many financial crises followed changes in the investment environment brought about by financial deregulation, and the crash of the dot com bubble in 2001 arguably began with "irrational exuberance" about Internet technology.*21

Unfamiliarity with recent technical and financial innovations may help explain how investors sometimes grossly overestimate asset values.

Also, if the first investors in a new class of assets (for example, stock in "dot com" companies) profit from rising asset values as other investors learn about the innovation (in our example, as others learn about the potential of the Internet), then still more others may follow their example, driving the price even higher as they rush to buy in hopes of similar profits. If such "herd behavior" causes prices to spiral up far above the true value of the assets, a crash may become inevitable. If for any reason the price briefly falls, so that investors realize that further gains are not assured, then the spiral may go into reverse, with price decreases causing a rush of sales, reinforcing the decrease in prices.

Regulatory failures

Governments have attempted to eliminate or mitigate financial crises by regulating the financial sector. One major goal of regulation is transparency: making institutions' financial situation publicly known by requiring regular reporting under standardized accounting procedures. Another goal of regulation is making sure institutions have sufficient assets to meet their contractual obligations, through reserve requirements, capital requirements, and other limits on leverage.

Some financial crises have been blamed on insufficient regulation, and have led to changes in regulation in order to avoid a repeat.

For example, the Managing Director of the IMF, Dominique Strauss-Kahn, has blamed the financial crisis of 2008 on 'regulatory failure to guard against excessive risk-taking in the financial system, especially in the US'.[22] Likewise, the New York Times singled out the deregulation of credit default swaps as a cause of the crisis.[23]

However, excessive regulation has also been cited as a possible cause of financial crises. In particular, the Basel II Accord has been criticized for requiring banks to increase their capital when risks rise, which might cause them to decrease lending precisely when capital is scarce, potentially aggravating a financial crisis.[24]

Fraud

Fraud has played a role in the collapse of some financial institutions, when companies have attracted depositors with misleading claims about their investment strategies, or have embezzled the resulting income. Examples include Charles Ponzi's scam in early 20th century Boston, the collapse of the MMM investment fund in Russia in 1994, the scams that led to the Albanian Lottery Uprising of 1997, and, allegedly, the collapse of Madoff Investment Securities in 2008.

Many rogue traders that have caused large losses at financial institutions have been accused of acting fraudulently in order to hide their trades.

Fraud in mortgage financing has also been cited as one possible cause of the 2008 subprime mortgage crisis; government officials stated on Sept. 23, 2008 that the FBI was looking into possible fraud by mortgage financing companies Fannie Mae and Freddie Mac, Lehman Brothers, and insurer American International Group.[25]

Contagion

Contagion refers to the idea that financial crises may spread from one institution to another, as when a bank run spreads from a few banks to many others, or from one country to another, as when currency crises, sovereign defaults, or stock market crashes spread across countries. When the failure of one particular financial institution threatens the stability of many other institutions, this is called *systemic risk*.[26]

One widely-cited example of contagion was the spread of the Thai crisis in 1997 to other countries like South Korea. However, economists often debate whether observing crises in many countries around the same time is truly caused by contagion from one market to another, or whether it is instead caused by similar underlying problems that would have affected each country individually even in the absence of international linkages.

Recessionary effects

Some financial crises have little effect outside of the financial sector, like the Wall Street crash of 1987, but other crises are believed to have played a role in decreasing growth in the rest of the economy. There are many theories why a financial crisis could have a recessionary effect on the rest of the economy. These theoretical ideas include the 'financial accelerator', 'flight to quality' and 'flight to liquidity', and the Kiyotaki-Moore model. Some 'third generation' models of currency crises explore how currency crises and banking crises together can cause recessions.[27]

THEORIES OF FINANCIAL CRISES

World systems theory

Recurrent major depressions in the world economy at the pace of 20 and 50 years have been the subject of empirical and econometric research especially in the world systems theory and in the debate about Nikolai Kondratiev and the so-called 50-years Kondratiev waves. Major figures of world systems theory, like Andre Gunder Frank and Immanuel Wallerstein, consistently warned about the crash that the world economy is now facing.

World systems scholars and Kondratiev cycle researchers always implied that Washington Consensus oriented economists never understood the dangers and perils, which leading industrial nations will be facing and are now facing at the end of the long economic cycle which began after the oil crisis of 1973.

Minsky's theory

Hyman Minsky has proposed a post-Keynesian explanation that is most applicable to a closed economy. He theorized that financial fragility is a typical feature of any capitalist economy. High fragility leads to a higher risk of a financial crisis. To facilitate his analysis, Minsky defines three types of financing firms choose according to their tolerance of risk. They are hedge finance, speculative finance, and Ponzi finance. Ponzi finance leads to the most fragility.

Financial fragility levels move together with the business cycle. After a recession, firms have lost much financing and choose only hedge, the safest. As the economy grows and expected profits rise, firms tend to believe that they can allow themselves to take on speculative financing. In this case, they know that profits will not cover all the interest all the time. Firms, however, believe that profits will rise and the loans will eventually be repaid without much trouble. More loans lead to more investment, and the economy grows further.

Then lenders also start believing that they will get back all the money they lend. Therefore, they are ready to lend to firms without full guarantees of success. Lenders know that such firms will have problems repaying. Still, they believe these firms will refinance from elsewhere as their expected profits rise. This is Ponzi financing. In this way, the economy has taken on much risky credit. Now it is only a question of time before some big firm actually defaults. Lenders understand the actual risks in the economy and stop giving credit so easily. Refinancing becomes impossible for many, and more firms default. If no new money comes into the economy to allow the refinancing process, a real economic crisis begins. During the recession, firms start to hedge again, and the cycle is closed.

Coordination games

Mathematical approaches to modeling financial crises have emphasized that there is often positive feedback[28] between market participants' decisions (see strategic complementarity). Positive feedback implies that there may be dramatic changes in asset values in response to small changes in economic fundamentals. For example, some models of currency crises (including that of Paul Krugman) imply that a fixed exchange rate may be stable for a long period of time, but will collapse suddenly in an avalanche of currency sales in response to a sufficient deterioration of government finances or underlying economic conditions.[29][30]

According to some theories, positive feedback implies that the economy can have more than one equilibrium. There may be an equilibrium in which market participants invest heavily in asset markets because they expect assets to be valuable, but there may be another equilibrium where participants flee asset markets because they expect others to flee too.[31] This is the type of argument underlying Diamond and Dybvig's model of bank runs, in which savers withdraw their assets from the bank because they expect others to withdraw too.[13] Likewise, in Obstfeld's model of currency crises, when economic conditions are neither too bad nor too good, there are two possible outcomes: speculators may or may not decide to attack the currency depending on what they expect other speculators to do.[14]

Herding models and learning models

A variety of models have been developed in which asset values may spiral excessively up or down as investors learn from each other. In these models, asset purchases by a few agents encourage others to buy too, not because the true value of the asset increases when many buy (which is called "strategic complementarity"), but because investors come to believe the true asset value is high when they observe others buying.

In "herding" models, it is assumed that investors are fully rational, but only have partial information about the economy.

In these models, when a few investors buy some type of asset, this reveals that they have some positive information about that asset, which increases the rational incentive of others to buy the asset too. Even though this is a fully rational decision, it may sometimes lead to mistakenly high asset values (implying, eventually, a crash) since the first investors may, by chance, have been mistaken.[32][33][34] In "adaptive learning" or "adaptive expectations" models, investors are assumed to be imperfectly rational, basing their reasoning only on recent experience. In such models, if the price of a given asset rises for some period of time, investors may begin to believe that its price always rises, which increases their tendency to buy and thus drives the price up further. Likewise, observing a few price decreases may give rise to a downward price spiral, so in models of this type large fluctuations in asset prices may occur. Agent-based models of financial markets often assume investors act on the basis of adaptive learning or adaptive expectations.

References

1. ^ Charles P. Kindleberger and Robert Aliber (2005), *Manias, Panics, and Crashes: A History of Financial Crises*, 5th ed. Wiley, ISBN 0471467146.
2. ^ Luc Laeven and Fabian Valencia (2008), 'Systemic banking crises: a new database'. International Monetary Fund Working Paper 08/224.
3. ^ Markus Brunnermeier (2008), 'Bubbles', in *The New Palgrave Dictionary of Economics*, 2nd ed.
4. ^ Peter Garber (2001), *Famous First Bubbles: The Fundamentals of Early Manias*. MIT Press, ISBN 0262571536.
5. ^ "Episode 06292007". *Bill Moyers Journal*. PBS. 2007-06-29. Transcript.
6. ^ Justin Lahart (2007-12-24). "Egg Cracks Differ In Housing, Finance Shells", *WSJ.com*, *Wall Street Journal*. Retrieved on 13 July 2008. "It's now conventional wisdom that a housing bubble has burst. In fact, there were two bubbles, a housing bubble and a financing bubble. Each fueled the other, but they didn't follow the same course."
7. ^ Milton Friedman and Anna Schwartz (1971), *A Monetary History of the United States, 1867-1960*. Princeton University Press, ISBN 0691003548.
8. ^ '1929 and all that', *The Economist*, Oct. 2, 2008.
9. ^ 'The Theory of Reflexivity', speech by George Soros, April 1994 at MIT.

10. ^ J. M. Keynes (1936), *The General Theory of Employment, Interest and Money*, Chapter 12. (New York: Harcourt Brace and Co.).

11. ^ J. Bulow, J. Geanakoplos, and P. Klemperer (1985), 'Multimarket oligopoly: strategic substitutes and strategic complements'. *Journal of Political Economy* 93, pp. 488–511.

12. ^ R. Cooper and A. John (1988), 'Coordinating coordination failures in Keynesian models.' *Quarterly Journal of Economics* 103 (3), pp. 441–63. See especially Propositions 1 and 3.

13. ^ *a b c* D. Diamond and P. Dybvig (1983), 'Bank runs, deposit insurance, and liquidity'. *Journal of Political Economy* 91 (3), pp. 401–19. Reprinted (2000) in *Federal Reserve Bank of Minneapolis Quarterly Review* 24 (1), pp. 14–23.

14. ^ *a b* M. Obstfeld (1996), 'Models of currency crises with self-fulfilling features'. *European Economic Review* 40 (3-5), pp. 1037–47.

15. ^ Eichengreen and Hausmann (2005), *Other People's Money: Debt Denomination and Financial Instability in Emerging Market Economies*.

16. ^ Torbjörn K A Eliazon (2006) [1] – Om Emotionell intelligens och Œcopati (ekopati)

17. ^ Kindleberger and Aliber (2005), op. cit., pp. 54–58.

18. ^ 'Of manias, panics, and crashes', obituary of Charles Kindleberger in *The Economist*, July 17, 2003.

19. ^ Kindleberger and Aliber (2005), op. cit., p. 54.

20. ^ Kindleberger and Aliber (2005), op. cit., p. 26.
21. ^ Kindleberger and Aliber (2005), op. cit., p. 26 and pp. 160-2.
22. ^ Strauss Kahn D, 'A systemic crisis demands systemic solutions', *The Financial Times*, Sept. 25, 2008.
23. ^ 'Don't blame the New Deal', *New York Times*, Sept. 28, 2008.
24. ^ Gordy MB and Howells B (2004), 'Procyclicality in Basel II: can we treat the disease without killing the patient?'
25. ^ 'FBI probing bailout firms', CNN Money, Sept. 23, 2008.
26. ^ George Kaufman and Kenneth Scott (2003),'What is systemic risk, and do bank regulators retard or contribute to it?' *The Independent Review* 7 (3).
27. ^ Craig Burnside, Martin Eichenbaum, and Sergio Rebelo (2008), 'Currency crisis models', *New Palgrave Dictionary of Economics*, 2nd ed.
28. ^ 'The widening gyre', Paul Krugman, *New York Times*, Oct. 27, 2008.
29. ^ P. Krugman (1979), 'A model of balance-of-payments crises'. *Journal of Money, Credit, and Banking* 11, pp. 311-25.
30. ^ S. Morris and H. Shin (1998), 'Unique equilibrium in a model of self-fulfilling currency attacks'. *American Economic Review* 88 (3), pp. 587-97.
31. ^ Darryl McLeod (2002), 'Capital flight', in the Concise Encyclopedia of Economics at the Library of Economics and Liberty.

32. ∧ A. Banerjee (1992), 'A simple model of herd behavior'. "Quarterly Journal of Economics" 107 (3), pp. 797–817.
33. ∧ S. Bikhchandani, D. Hirshleifer, and I. Welch (1992), 'A theory of fads, fashions, custom, and cultural change as informational cascades'. "Journal of Political Economy" 100 (5), pp. 992–1026.
34. ∧ V. Chari and P. Kehoe (2004), 'Financial crises as herds: overturning the critiques'. "Journal of Economic Theory" 119, pp. 128–150.

CHAPTER 6

TIMELINE OF GLOBAL FINANCIAL CRISIS
OF 2007–2009

The global crisis, which started in the United States in 2007, created one of the most difficult economic and financial moments. However, the crisis by its nature was global in effect. This was due to the fact that the entire world financial system was networked, with the US as its epicenter. Seismic disturbances at the center of the crisis, the United States reverberated all across the world through a system of financial shocks, effecting not only stock markets but also the credit markets. And in time, the crisis jumped from being a financial problem to an economic problem. This transition in nature of crisis, resulting in world recession, increasing unemployment and plummeting consumer confidence is the stage the world is in the month of March 2009. To provide a bird's eye view of this crisis, it seems best to look at not only the starting point of the crisis in 2007 but look at all the preliminary indicators which lead up to the start and the current position we are in early 2009.

Therefore, I would like to continue Part 2 of this Book with a timeline of the crisis. Here are the chronological points, which created the bubble effect we are in now.

Edward Harrison in his brilliant exposition on the "Credit Crisis Timeline," indicated a series of events, which happened, leading up to the great financial panic of 2007. Here is the chronological list of crisis points:

PRE-PANIC PHASE

2007 02 08 -----HSBC to boost loan-loss provisions on bad mortgages.

2007 02 08 -----Sub-prime Mortgage Bond Risks Surge, Index Suggests.

2007 02 22 -----HSBC announces departure of two top executives at US business.

2007 03 04-------US triggers $ 11 billion HSBC fallout

2007 03 05 -----New Century leads drop in shares of Mortgage lenders.

2007 03 12 ----- DR Horton warns of huge losses.

2007 03 12----- New Century shares are suspended.

2007 03 21-----Short sellers who predicted sub-prime rout see more declines.

2007 04 02-----New Century Financial in Chapter 11 move.

2007 05 30---- Kensington agrees to 283 million pound buyout.

PRELUDE TO PANIC PHASE

2007 06 23 -- $3.2 billion move by Bear Stearns to rescue fund.
2007 07 30----IKB cuts profit forecast amid rout in US mortgages.
2007 07 31---American Home can't fund mortgages, shares plummet.
2007 08 02 - - Accredited may face bankruptcy, merger in doubt.
2007 08 06 -- American Home files for bankruptcy.
2007 08 08 - Fund of German Bank WestLB stops payouts.

START OF THE FINANCIAL CRISIS

The financial crisis of 2007-2009 began in July 2007 when a loss of confidence by investors in the value of securitized mortgages resulted in a liquidity crisis in the US--- this prompted a substantive infusion of capital by the Federal Reserve, the European Central Bank and the Bank of England into their respective markets. The TED spread, an indicator of perceived credit risk in the general economy spiked up in July 2007, remaining volatile for the next year and finally spiking up again in September 2008, reaching a record high of 4.65% in October 2008. In September 2008 the crisis deepened as stock markets crashed worldwide.

Before we discuss the start of the current financial and credit crisis in the third quarter of 2007, let us first try to understand what a financial crisis means in layman language. The term," financial crisis," is applied broadly to a variety of situations in which some financial institutions or financial assets suddenly lose a large part of their value. In the nineteenth and early twentieth century, many financial crises were associated with banking panics, and many recessions coincided with these panics. Other situations that are often called financial crises include stock market crashes and the bursting of other financial bubbles, currency crises and sovereign defaults. Many economists have offered theories about how financial crises develop and how they could be prevented. There is little consensus, however, and financial crises are still a regular occurrence around the world.

Let us now look at the start of the current financial crisis of 2007-2009. The sub-prime crisis was the first indicator of things going wrong in the US economy. Although the process of sub-prime lending was well recognized and employed by commercial and investment banks in the US, the problem became acute when hundreds of thousands of US homeowners labeled as," sub-prime risks" stopped paying on their mortgages. A sub-prime risk is a below average credit customer, who does not have the wherewithal to effectively and efficiently pay his mortgage debt on his home, given his current assets, income and expenses.

The United States saw several investment banks and commercial banks supporting the securitization of sub-prime mortgage loans. The banks had found an easy way of attracting a lot of fees in originating, packaging and transferring the debts attributable to sub-prime mortgages.

A stage was reached in the history and evolution of the mortgage market in the US, where sub-prime or poor creditworthy clients, encountered difficulties paying their mortgages. This was because many banks had teaser interest rates, which were very low and increased the number of sub-prime borrowers. These teaser rates were set to re-adjust a few years down the road and when such interest rates increased, the sub-prime borrower could not afford the higher payment, which went with the new re-set interest rate (higher interest rate). This resulted in thousands and thousands of sub-prime borrowers defaulting on their loan obligations to banks. As these defaults increased astronomically, the investor community suddenly woke up to the fact that they were being misled fraudulently by investment and commercial banks. Sub-prime mortgages, which were blended with other mortgages, in many cases, acquired an AAA credit rating by the major US ratings agencies. These gave investors an extra feeling of financial security when undertaking investments. When investors realized that the AAA rating in a sub-prime was not an indicator of real credit risk of a sub-prime mortgage, they were shocked and dismayed.

Numerous small and large investors exited these types of investments to a point that even financial institutions playing this game could not get refinancing. The sub-prime crisis developed into a full-blown credit crisis. Since investors were not sure how to ascertain the risk value of any pool of investments and since no one knew how many toxic assets resided in any specific portfolio, the investors just stopped investing. Things became so bad that even the inter-bank lending market was affected. One bank would not lend bank money for even a week---- such behavior was not seen for so many years in the past. The credit shrinkage created the liquidity crisis, as no one would lend to another. The global financial system, which was based on credit and trust between different players, had suddenly broken down. What happened first was the sub-prime crisis, which quickly developed into a credit crisis, which sparked liquidity issues. This was followed by a stock market collapse. US housing was the first trigger for the global crisis and this transformed into a credit and liquidity crisis. This precipitated into a stock market crisis. And to make things worse, the financial crisis spilt into the real world economy. The economy responded to the financial disaster by going into recession--- an economic process, which caused diminishing production, higher levels of national employment and rapidly eroding consumer confidence.

The book will take you through all the stages of this financial and credit disaster. This chapter serves as a starting point to develop an understanding of this huge and complex problem, which is no longer restricted to the US but is a global problem of the greatest magnitude since the Great Depression.

Let us now look at developing financial incidents since the start of the crisis in August 2007. Here is another time line of sequential activities in financial markets:

- August 2007 – Liquidity crisis emerges
- February 2008– Nationalization of Northern Rock
- March 2008–Collapse of Bear Stearns
- March 2008–Federal takeover of Fannie Mae and Freddie Mac
- June 27, 2008 – Bear market of 2008 declared
- September 2008–Bankruptcy of Lehman Brothers
- September 2008–Full blown global financial crisis
- September 2008–Merrill Lynch sold to Bank of America Corporation
- September 2008–Partial nationalization of Fortis Holding
- October 2008–Large losses of financial markets worldwide
- October 2008–Passage of EESA in the US
- October 2008– Iceland's major banks nationalized
- November 2008–China creates a stimulus plan
- November 2008–DJIA reaches low point of 7507 points

- December 2008 –The Australian Govt. seeks another stimulus package
- December 2008–Madoff Ponzi scheme scandal erupts
- January 2009 – President Obama proposes federal spending bill of around 1 trillion dollars to remedy financial crisis
- January 2009–Lawmakers propose massive bailout of failing US banks
- January 2009–US House of Representatives passes above bill
- January 2009–Government of Iceland collapses
- February 2009–Canada passes early budget & 40 billion dollar stimulus
- February 2009– President Obama signs 787 billion dollar American Recovery and Reinvestment Act of 2009 into law
- February 2009–Australia enacts second economic stimulus package
- February 2009–Eastern Europe financial crisis starts
- February 2009–The Bank of Antigua is taken over by the E. Caribbean
  Bank after Sir Allen Stanford is accused by US of 8 billion dollar investment fraud
  February 27,2009–DJIA and S & P 500 Indexes reach 12 year lows
- March 6, 2009 –UK Govt. takes controlling interest in Lloyds Bank

CHAPTER 17

THE REAL ESTATE BUBBLE & US SUB-PRIME CRISIS

A sub-prime loan refers to a loan provided to an individual or family with less than average credit. Several of these individuals have either spotty or poor credit histories. Some have inadequate income to service their mortgage debt. This chapter discusses the sub-prime loan crisis in America.

HISTORICAL BACKGROUND

The US has recently witnessed a great run up on residential house prices. Between the period of 1997 and 2006, American home prices increased by approximately 124%.

Anyone and everyone connected with the real estate industry joined this party. Joining the bandwagon were the mortgage bankers, mortgage loan origination agents, the mortgage brokers, the rating agencies and most important new homebuyers. With a booming house market accompanied with liberal standards for lending money, several million borrowers were enticed to purchase homes. To sell the process of financing homes, most banks offered an incentive interest rate, which was an introductory low rate of interest.

This rate of interest would get reset one, two or more years after the initial loan was granted. In order to accelerate loans and profit there from, banks started closing their eyes to the details and due diligence normally required in the loan assessment process. Loans were granted left, right and center. Money was flowing into borrowers' hands at unprecedented speeds. And then the bubble burst.

HOW DID THE CRISIS START?

The crisis started when these homeowners could not pay their monthly loan obligations on their newly financed homes. This usually happened when the interest rate was readjusted at a future date. At that time, the borrower, due to his poor loan record or low total annual income could not service the mortgage debt. But this was only the tip of the iceberg. The bigger problem was exacerbated by the banks, which sold these loans to third parties through a novel system of financial engineering called securitization. What the banks did was create synthetic notes out of these obligations. They packaged these loans as securities. Typical securities were collaterized debt obligations (CDO's) or Mortgage Backed Securities (MBS). Since banks did not want to hold on to loans, which they knew were sub-par and sub-prime, they sold these notes or debts to third parties by repackaging them. These CDO's and MBS have landed up in the hands of other investors, mutual funds and international investors.

As house prices started spiraling downwards in the US, the equity guaranteed in the MBS evaporated and investors were left with mortgage notes, which had less value, since the collateral representing the debt was reducing value day-to-day.

With heightened media coverage of this process, more and more investors stayed away from purchasing these MBS's resulting in a liquidity and confidence crisis in such instruments. Welcome to the sub-prime crisis, fueled by greed and avarice, with a total disregard for truth, disclosure and transparency in business dealings.

THE HOUSING SECTOR CRISIS

Housing Prices started plummeting downwards in 2007 and start of 2008. Projections indicated future house price decreases in 2008. As banks and other investors started losing money on bad sub-prime debts, the banks got very cautious on lending money and offered loans to only the best customers, credit wise. Less money lent, meant fewer investments in the real estate industry, which meant slower national economic growth. As banks started giving fewer loans to individuals and businesses, this resulted in reduced economic investment across the board resulting in lower GDP and a crisis of confidence.

RELATIONSHIP BETWEEN HOUSING CRISIS & SUB-PRIME SCANDAL

The sub-prime crisis unveiled a very serious ethical issue, which is, "Who is responsible for lending money to people who cannot afford in the first place to repay their loan? And secondly," Who was to blame for this crisis?"

In terms of responsibility for lending money, I would place the blame on many players in the lending game, starting with unconscionable banks, (ready and willing to make a fast buck) to unethical mortgage brokers and mortgage underwriters who knew from the start that they were recommending or processing inadequate credit documentation. And last but not the least were the slick realtors, ready and willing to make a buck out of the ever expanding real estate trade, who now found it easy to find prospects and fit them into houses, even though such prospects could ill afford the types of mortgages they were applying for.

In terms of the second question, all the above players were responsible for the crisis in varying proportions. But the commercial and investment banks well aided by the large financial brokerage houses exacerbated this problem by packaging and selling these notes not only in the US but overseas.

I will now list some of the fallouts in the banking and brokerage industry as a result of this crisis. Several of the large brokerage houses like Merrill Lynch took significant write downs of assets as a result of lost value of sub-prime securities.

Other banks, which took a big hit, were UBS, Credit Suisse, Deutsche Bank among others. Here is a statement of damage as a result of this crisis.

SOME US BUSINESSES FILING FOR BANKRUPTCY
1. New Century Financial
2. American Home Mortgage
3. Americus.

WRITE DOWNS ON VALUE OF SOME LOANS (MBS AND CDO)

1. Citigroup- Investment Bank loss of $24.1 billion US
2. Merrill Lynch-Investment Bank loss $22.5 billion US
3. UBS AG -Investment Bank Loss $18.7 billion US
4. Morgan Stanley -Investment Bank Loss $10.3 billion US)
5. Bank of America -Bank Loss $ 5.28 billion US
6. MBIA-Bond insurance Loss $ 3.3 billion US
Note: All above losses are approximate in value

Here is some background on how individual nations and their financial institutions have got impacted by the sub-prime crisis.

SINGAPORE

Overseas-Chinese Banking Corp. (OCBC) indicated that fourth quarter profits for the last quarter of 2007 fell 16 % as it wrote down investments connected to US sub-prime mortgages. OCBC joined its other banking rival, DBS Group Holdings in writing down more than 85% of investments linked to sub-prime mortgages.

SWITZERLAND

Credit Suisse discovered pricing errors on bonds in 2008- -- these were anticipated to cut first quarter profit by about 1 billion US dollars. The bank took $2.85 billion dollars of write downs in asset backed securities after an internal review found mismatched markings, which were attributable to a group of traders.

As one can see the crisis spread like wildfire throughout the world. Banks in Europe were also affected dramatically due to their investments in mortgage-backed paper linked to sub-prime notes.

ETHICAL ISSUES

Several questions remain unanswered as a result of the sub-prime crisis. These are:

1. Why did banks close their eyes to sub-prime customers?

2. Why were mortgage brokers not honest in advising clients of the risks of taking mortgage loans with interest reset periods, particularly when this did with their customer not being able to make future payments based on their current asset and income picture?

3. How did mortgage underwriters approve such shady loans, when prima facie, there was either no or inadequate financial history to justify such loans being approved?

4. Why did realtors breach their ethics and due diligence responsibilities in allowing potential purchasers to buy properties they were not inherently qualified for?

5. Why have governments stayed super quiet and not made active steps to solve the problems caused by this erring industry?

6. And what about consumers themselves? What made a potential homeowner lie, or misrepresent his financial status to buy a home? Why did the sudden rush for future profits (if markets went up) and the accompanying greed cloud his judgment?

This and numerous other ethical questions have not been answered fully and the verdict is out to present us with an answer regarding the severe breach of trust by institutions and their agents on defrauding the public.

CHAPTER 18

FIRST MANIFESTATION OF
STOCK/REAL ESTATE/BANKING BUBBLE

As the real estate bubble burst in the US, this was accompanied by a banking crisis of unbelievable proportions. As seen in the last chapter, banks were over-leveraged in acquisition of securitization risks and by taking on too much bad subprime risk on their books. As the real estate market crashed, banks held mortgages, which were worth 20,30 or 40 per cent below their initial levels of value. These banks had no credible asset security in the form of the house mortgage, since house prices had crashed. Also intermediaries like investment banks who had repackaged these loans found that these securitized loans on their books were worth very little. The banking and real estate crisis caused tremendous erosion of public confidence in the US. It was not surprising that the stock markets in the US would be affected soon or later.

In September 2008 the Dow Jones reached a low of 7507 and things got worse in the next few months and in February 2009 both the Dow Jones and S&P 500 index reached 12 year lows. It was not until the first two weeks of March 2009 that there was some positive momentum in US stock markets.

International investors had long subscribed to a theory that Asian stock markets were decoupled from American stock markets.

Therefore in 2007 and early 2008 millions of dollars of capital found their way into Asian stock markets. However, this theory was totally unfounded. Asian stock markets lost more value than their American counterparts in 2008. Although there was a certain sense of decoupling in economic realities between the rich Asian countries and the US, this divergence did not show up in their respective stock market performance. On the contrary, it showed how all countries are linked through the financial network and that one should never take any such theory for granted. Numerous investors lost millions of dollars on the Asian trade. In short, the stock market decimation continued with unabated breath all over the world, starting with the US markets and then spreading to Europe and even to Asia.

NORTHERN ROCK CRISIS IN THE UK

Northern Rock Building Society was formed in the United Kingdom in 1965---- this was a result of the merger of Northern Counties Permanent Building Society and Rock Building Society. Northern Rock was one of the top five mortgage lenders in the United Kingdom in terms of gross lending. The bank also dealt with savings accounts, loans and insurance.

In 2006, the bank had moved into sub-prime lending via a deal with the now ill-fated Lehman Brothers of the US. Although the mortgages were sold under Northern Rock's brand through intermediaries, the risk was being underwritten by Lehman Brothers.

On 14 September 2007, the Bank sought and received a liquidity support facility from the Bank of England. This was due to the problems it experienced in the credit markets.

When news of this got out in the United Kingdom, customers in fear of losing their life savings, started queuing outside their branches to withdraw money. This was a typical bank run faced by Northern Rock.

As a result of the run and due to the fact that no one was able to take over the bank, Northern Rock was taken into state ownership on February 22, 2008. The bank is managed at "arm's length" by the government through UK Financial Investments Limited.

The Government had invested billions of pounds in the form of capital to prop up Northern Rock to maintain its financial stability. Northern Rock had made a commitment to repay the government debt In a period to three to four years. However by the end of March 2009 the Bank was well ahead of its goal, owing only around 9 billion pounds of the loan, reducing it from around 27 billion pounds at the end of 2007.

The good news is that the public starting reacquiring confidence in the bank, knowing that the government stood behind all their savings deposits. New public deposits followed into Northern Rock. In February 2009 Northern Rock announced an offering of almost 14 billion pounds of new mortgages over the next two years as part of their new business plan.

MORAL OF THE NORTHERN ROCK CRISIS

Northern Rock was a profitable bank with good risk management controls. However, they depended greatly on raising money in wholesale markets. This funding would then be utilized to lend money to consumers in the form of mortgages. As a result of the US sub-prime crisis, no one was willing to invest money in Northern Rock bonds or give them financing in wholesale markets. So, due to no fault of their own, they were mercilessly cut off from funding markets. With the bank run on Northern Rock, this organization lost almost 2 billion pounds in customer withdrawals in two days. The bank had nowhere else to go but to the UK government for debt assistance. The moral of this story is that bad things happen to good organizations just because of problems in some other part of the world. It is creditable to see them back on track so soon, something, which cannot be, said of the belabored US banking industry as of March, 2009.

CHAPTER 19

THE COLLAPSE OF BEAR STEARNS

BACKGROUND

Bear Stearns was founded as an equity-trading house in 1923 with $500,000 in capital. This corporation served other companies, institutions, governments and individuals. In 1985 it went public. The company specialized in corporate finance, mergers and acquisitions, institutional equities and fixed income sales, trading and research, private client service, derivative, foreign exchange and futures sales and trading, asset management and custody service. The company employed more than 15,000 employees and was headquartered in New York City.

FINANCIAL HISTORY

As of November 30, 2006 the company had a total capital of around 67 billion dollars and total assets of approximately 350 billion dollars The April 2005 issue of Institutional Investor ranked Bear Stearns as the seventh largest securities firm in terms of total capital. As of November 30, 2007 the company had notional contract amounts of approximately 13 trillion dollars in derivate financial instruments of which 1.85 trillion dollars were listed futures and option contracts.

In addition, they had 28 billion dollars in "Level 3 assets on its books at the end of fiscal 2007 versus a net equity position of only around 11 billion dollars. These 11 billion dollars supported 395 billion dollars in assets, a leverage ratio of around 35:1. This highly leveraged balances sheet, consisting of many illiquid and potentially worthless assets lead to rapid erosion of lender and investor confidence, which finally evaporated. Now Bear Stearns was forced to call the New York Reserve to stave off the looming cascade of counter party risk, which would ensue from forced liquidation.

BEAR STERN FUNDS BAIL-OUT

On June 22, 2007 Bear Stearns pledged a collaterized loan of up to 3.2 billion dollars to bail out one of its funds, the Bears Stearns High Grade Structured Credit Fund. This and another hedge fund were backed primarily by subprime loans. During the week of July 16, 2007 Bear Stearns disclosed that the two subprime hedge funds had lost nearly all of their value amid a rapid decline in the market for subprime mortgages.

On November 15, 2007 it was reported that the firm was writing down a further 1.2 billion dollars in mortgage related securities and that Bear Stearns would face its first loss in 83 years.

Matthew Tannin and Ralph R. Cioffi both former managers of hedge funds at Bear Stearns were arrested June 19, 2008.

They are facing criminal charged and are suspected of misleading investors about the risks involved in the sub-prime market. Tannin and Cioffi have also been names in lawsuits brought by Barclays bank who claim they were one of the many investors misled by the executives.

GOVERNMENT BAIL OUT AND SUBSEQUENT SALE TO JPMORGAN CHASE

On Tuesday, March 11, 2008 a bank run began on the securities and banking firm, Bear Stearns. While Bear Stearns was not a regular deposit taking bank, it typically financed its long term investments by selling short term bonds(asset backed commercial paper). This method of financing made Bear Stearns vulnerable to panic on part of its bondholders. And panic is what ensued. Rumors started in Wall Street among their competitors that Bear Stearns was insolvent and not in a position to make good on its obligations. The result of this market panic is that within two days, Bear Stearns's capital base dwindled from 17 billion dollars to 2 billion dollars in cash. Bear Stearns told government officials that bankruptcy now appeared to be the only choice.

On March 14, 2008 JPMorgan Chase in conjunction with the Federal Reserve Bank of New York provided a 28 day emergency loan in order to prevent a market crash that would surely have happened if Bear Stearns was allowed to go insolvent. Conditions deteriorated at Bear Stearns to a point that it was sold for 2 dollars per share to JPMorgan chase on March 16, 2008.

However a shareholder outrage resulted in JPMorgan chase paying 10 dollars per share instead of 2 dollars announced earlier. What a humbling defeat for an old well-known investment bank, which heralded a stock market price of 172 dollar a share as late as January 2007.

MORAL BEHING THIS REAL LIFE STORY

Large investment banks made huge bets in the sub-prime mortgage market. This was done with an intention of lining the corporate pockets and increasing the bottom line profit. Combined with senior executives who engaged in unethical activity and were arrested, this is a story of how greed and unethical behavior brought one of the largest US firms to its knees. In the process, one realizes that no one can protect oneself completely. A little less greed, a better corporate governance system and stronger investment risk management systems would have been able to avoid this collapse. However, in the absence of these elements the final result was destruction and sale of this company and massive shareholder price destruction.

CHAPTER 20

COLLAPSE OF INDYMAC BANK

The story I would like to share with you is the collapse of Indy Mac Bank, the third biggest bank failure in American history.

BACKGROUND

Indy Mac Bank was founded as Countrywide Mortgage Investment in 1985 by David Loeb and Angelo Mozilo as a means of collaterizing Countrywide Financial loans too big to be sold to Freddie Mac and Fannie Mae. Countrywide spun off Indy Mac as an independent company.

According to the Office of Thrift Supervision (OTS), in the nine months before it went into receivership, Indy Mac incurred significant losses, severely depleting capital and jeopardizing the institution's continued financial viability. Indy Mac specialized in Alt-A mortgage loans, a type of loan where a borrower did not need to furnish all necessary information on income and expenses as is typically required on a normal application form for a home mortgage. In late 2007, Indy Mac Bank could not securitize and sell its Alt-A mortgages due to a decline in the secondary market for non-agency mortgage loans. Indy Mac moved 10.7 billion dollars of loans intended for sales to the category, "held for investment, in the fourth quarter of 2007.

On June 27, 2008 Senator Charles Schumer's office released (to the press) a letter sent to various bank regulatory agencies questioning the financial viability of Indy Mac Bank. The result of the public disclosure by Senator Schumer, who sits on both the Senate Finance Committee and the Senate Banking Committee was an eleven-day bank run on Indy Mac bank, resulted in a withdrawal of more than 1.3 billion dollars. But this run represented only part of the overall financial, liquidity and solvency problem at Indy Mac Bank.

CAUSES OF INDYMAC BANK FAILURE

Indy Mac Bank had some other bigger problems. It was heavily invested into Alt-A mortgages. As the market for sub-prime mortgages (like Alt-A mortgages) tanked, there was no demand for them in the marketplace. All sources of liquidity and refinancing dried up at Indy Mac Bank. With numerous mortgage defaults, the amount of non-performing loans increased on its balance sheet. This and the non-refinancing position of Alt-A mortgages accompanied with the liquidity crisis caused by the 1.3 billion dollar bank run were contributory issues to its demise.

On July 11, 2008 citing liquidity concerns, Indy Mac bank was placed into conservatorship by the FDIC. (Federal Deposit Insurance Corporation). With 32 billion dollars in assets. Indy Mac is the third biggest bank failure in US history.

Indy Mac Bank Bancorp filed for Chapter 7 bankruptcy on August 1,2008.In August 2008, the FDIC mentioned that Indy Mac's failure would probably cost more than 8.9 billion dollars, compared with the previous estimated range (of cost) of between 4 and 8 billion dollars.

MORAL OF THE STORY

Going back to the Indy Mac Bank failure, customers were insured for up to $100,000 dollars. However, the FDIC mentioned that the bank had about 1 billion dollars of "potentially uninsured deposits." This is with respect to deposits held by about 10,000 depositors. The FDIC mentioned that it would begin contacting uninsured customers on July 14, 2008.

Given the current financial mess and what may be inadequate insurance coverage for customers with larger deposits in banks, investors must under no circumstances deposit more than $100,000 in any one bank, however great this temptation may be in terms of banking and planning ease. FDIC expects future bank failures to cost more and has hiked bank fees, which need to be paid by banks into an insurance fund, which pays off all creditors within limits in event of a bank going bankrupt.

The moral of the story is to stay away from small regional and community banks that are involved in dubious trading and investment activities. An astute investor must check if the bank has FDIC coverage, either by calling FDIC or checking at the FDIC website. There is a temporary FDIC insurance guarantee of up to 250,000 dollars---- but this is effective only till December 31, 2009 and may or may not be renewed. Therefore, in the interest of safety do not invest more than 100,000 dollars per bank.

CHAPTER 21

THE LEHMAN BROTHERS FIASCO

BACKGROUND

Lehman Brothers was one of the largest investment banking houses in the US. Through several centuries, they were recognized as a financial icon in the international marketplace. Lehman Brothers was indeed a global financial services firm, which did business in investment banking, equity and fixed income sales, research and trading, investment management, private equity and private banking. The firm's worldwide headquarters were in New York City, with regional headquarters in London and Tokyo, as well as offices all over the world. To give you a true perspective into how big and strong this organization was prior to its bankruptcy, one needs to see it as a 150-year-old global investment bank, with over sixteen thousand employees in the US and around the world and with over 15 billion dollars in annual revenue.

CAUSES OF BANKRUPTCY

Lehman Brothers filed for Chapter 11 Bankruptcy protection on September 15, 2008. The bankruptcy of Lehman Brothers is the largest bankruptcy filing in US history with Lehman holding over 600 billion dollars in assets.

In 2008, Lehman Brothers was carrying an extremely large position in US sub-prime mortgages. They were well known packagers of sub-prime mortgages, which then got sold over the world to numerous international investors. In addition to packaging and selling these products, Lehman decided to actually own a lot of these mortgage and other derivative securities. Huge losses were accrued in their lower-rated mortgage backed securities throughout 2008. For a better understanding of what lower rated mortgaged back securities is, these refer to a " tranche" of securities backed by mortgages provided to subprime/lower credit quality clients. In the second fiscal quarter of 2008, Lehman reported losses of around 3 billion dollars and was forced to sell around 6 billion dollars of assets to ensure liquidity and its financial survival. In the first half of 2008, as a result of all these investment losses, the stock price of Lehman's lost 73% of its value. Things went from bad to worse and on September 10, 2008, Lehman announced a loss of 3.9 billion dollars and their intent to sell off a majority stake in their investment management business, which included Neuberger Berman. September 15,2008 was the last day of existence of Lehman Brothers. Lehman filed for bankruptcy at the US Bankruptcy Court, Southern District of New York (Manhattan). As part of the liquidation process, part of the Lehman business was acquired by a giant Japanese securities organization--- Nomura Holdings.

Nomura, on September 22, 2008 announced it agreed to acquire Lehman Brothers franchise in the Asia Pacific region, including Japan, Hong Kong and Australia.

Nomura also announced its intention the next day to acquire Lehman's investment banking and equities businesses in Europe and in the Middle East. The Lehman's tower in New York City was sold to Barclays bank. But there was still the question of how to liquidate the other assets and what kind of pain this would generate to the creditors and shareholders of Lehman. Timothy Geithner, then President of the Federal Reserve Bank of New York, did not support any additional capital into Lehman Brothers (with a view to stabilizing their long-term financial situation). Therefore, Lehman Brothers were on their own and at the mercy of the court appointed liquidators.

EFFECTS OF LEHMAN BANKRUPTCY

The bankruptcy of Lehman Brothers was the "straw, which finally broke the camel's back." Now the financial crisis entered its full-blown stage. The refusal of US governmental authorities to support Lehman capital-wise or with back stop provisions created a massive flight of investor confidence from financial institutions and investment banks in the US and severely affected all financial markets, including the commercial paper market, the bond market, the sub-prime market and finally led up to a total credit crisis in the early part of 2009.

These were some of the firm's directly impacted by the bankruptcy of Lehman:

1. The institutional cash fund run by the Bank of New York, Mellon.
2. About 2.5 billion dollar in losses by Japanese banks and insurers.
3. Around 1.5 billion dollars loss to Freddie Mac as a loss of counter party guarantee positions.
4. Numerous US hedge funds with undeclared and unknown losses.

MORAL OF THE STORY

Poor handling of the Lehman Brothers situation was indeed a very dangerous and costly mistake made by the US government. The government bailed out Bear Stearns, but found it in their wisdom to let Lehman Brothers go under. They failed to realize how important Lehman Brothers was in the global financial system and how letting this giant fail would cause permanent and irreparable consequences to the financial system.

In March 2009, when Ben Bernanke, was talking to the country on CBS 60 minutes, he acknowledged the government's mistake in not supporting Lehman Brothers and said that although some people thought this was a good decision he knew it wasn't.

The moral of the story for an ordinary investor is not to be hyped up by all the great news surrounding any one financial institution.

The need for overall diversification of assets is critical. Investors being brainwashed by Lehman's credit rating and solid reputation, who trusted all or a major portion of their assets here were hurt beyond repair. In financial markets and in investment, the caveat, "buyer be aware," holds good. It is always better to get a lower return than a very high promised return by risking all your assets with one financial institution.

CHAPTER 22

CONTROVERSY BEHIND FREDDIE MAC AND FANNIE MAE

ORIGINS

The Federal National Mortgage Association also known as Fannie Mae was formed in 1938. This was a period right through the Great Depression---- times when private banks and lenders were unwilling to finance house mortgage debt. This was due to the complete collapse of the housing market. The need for Fannie Mae was to do two things predominantly:

1. Firstly to provide funding to local banks using federal money---- the money then got used to financing home mortgages.

2. Secondly, cheaper interest rates would allow more families to afford homes and this would be a good social cause.

In time, what developed was a secondary mortgage market. Fannie Mae, who had a special financial support mechanism from the Government, dominated this market. Special lines of credit were established for Fannie Mae, which could be drawn down as and when required.

Since Fannie Mae had an explicit guarantee on funds borrowed in the open market, they were able to borrow money from the international market at comparatively low interest rates. Fannie Mae's profit was the spread between their cost of borrowings and the interest rate earned on their mortgage portfolio.

In 1968, due to fiscal pressures, President Lyndon Johnson privatized Fannie Mae--- this was done to remove it from the national budget. At this point of time, Fannie Mae became a Government sponsored entity--- a GSE. It now created profit for its shareholders, also enjoying exemption from local and state taxes in addition to their implied Government backing.

In 1970, another GSE was born--- this was called Federal Home Mortgage Corporation or Freddie Mac. Fannie Mae and Freddie Mac control around 90% of the secondary mortgage market in the US. The combined debt of these two government-sponsored enterprises is around 45% of the current national debt---- their importance to a possibility of systemic risk is great.

ACCOUNTING ERRORS

In 2003 and 2004, Fannie Mae was mired in an infamous accounting scandal. Its top executives earned around 110 million dollars and they were found "cooking" the books. The Justice Department and the SEC investigation revealed accounting errors in an amount of around 11 billion dollars--- this resulted in the termination of its three senior most executives. $400 million dollars of fines were paid but funnily, though, no one went to jail. The investigation further revealed that the motivation behind these accounting anomalies were the intention of these senior executives to maximize their bonuses and to deceive investors.

GSE's & THE GLOBAL FINANCIAL AND CREDIT CRISIS

Fannie Mae and Freddie Mac are the only two constituents of the Fortune 500 group of companies that are not obligated to inform the public of any potential financial difficulties (they may experience). In the event of financial collapse and insolvency, the US taxpayer would probably land up holding the outstanding debt.

The real problem with these two GSE's occurred when they started shifting their financial operations from their original mandate--- one of supporting other banks and financial lenders in the secondary mortgage market. They started buying and holding the same securities they created and sold to investors. The more they created the more they bought.

Since they had a free rein to borrow funds from the market on an international market and domestically, and enjoying the implicit US government guarantee, they borrowed vigorously and aggressively. Their borrowing resulted in a bloated balance sheet. These two GSE's got to a position where they guaranteed or held more than 6 trillion dollars in mortgage-associated securities.

Due to unbridled expansion, investment in sub-prime mortgages and poor internal risk management controls, the share prices of these two GSE's tumbled. Also, there was accompanying high asset depreciation on their balance sheet, since the mortgages on their books were worth a fraction of their original value. Things got so bad that on September 7, 2008 the government took over both Fannie Mae and Freddie Mac. Both companies were put into conservatorship, similar to a condition reflective of Chapter 11 bankruptcy.

In justifying the Government capital infusions into these GSE's (to support their financial survival) Paulson, the Treasury Secretary of the US, said," Fannie Mae and Freddie Mac are so large and so interwoven in our financial system that a failure of either of them would cause great turmoil in our financial markets here at home and around the globe."

To put their astronomic losses into perspective, Freddie Mac had a 25.3 billion dollar loss in the third quarter of 2008 and a 23.9 billion dollar loss in the fourth quarter of 2008. Fannie Mae lost 25.2 billion in the fourth quarter of 2008. Freddie Mac has asked for a capital infusion of 30.8 billion dollars from the Treasury to survive into 2009 while Fannie Mae has asked for 15.2 billion dollars from Treasury.

MORAL OF THE STORY

The Freddie Mac and Fannie Mae experience tells us what is seriously wrong with the financial system in America. Although these enterprises were set up with a lofty ideal, there was no proper risk management control over their financial activities, either inside them boardrooms or by external responsible authorities like the government. Allowing these companies not to report any internal financial difficulties was a disastrous policy plan.

With no proper governmental control, the senior executives had a blank check---a situation they exploited to the best of their ability. With an implicit government guarantee and freedom to invest when and as they felt fit, these executives perpetrated accounting fraud, hiding the real financial results from the public till they were caught between 2003 and 2004. But now the damage was done. The enterprises continued to go downhill, causing taxpayers billions of dollars of loss.

The moral of this story is that never again should the US government give such carte-Blanche authority to any financial institution. And never again should there be such lax risk management and asset monitoring processes in place. The government is responsible to the public and it must revamp the financial system—this revamping must apply to all financial institutions, including all government-sponsored enterprises. There must be clarity and transparency in all financial dealings.

Only then is there a possibility of preventing the major mistakes made in the US---- this is the only hope of repeating the financial and credit disaster of 2007.

CHAPTER 23

THE COLLAPSE OF WASHINGTON MUTUAL

The collapse of Washington Mutual marked the largest bank failure in US history. Seattle based Washington Mutual, also known as "WaMu" with assets of 307 billion dollars collapsed as a result of poor investments in the sub-prime mortgage market.

BACKGROUND

Washington Mutual was incorporated as the Washington National Building Loan and Investment Association on September 25,1989. Before it went into receivership, it was the sixth largest bank in the United States. As of June 30,2008, WaMu had total assets of US $307 billion with 2239 retail branch offices operating in 15 states, with 4932 ATM's and 43,198 employees.

HISTORY

WaMu Chairman and CEO Kerry Killinger had pledged in 2003, "We hope to do to this industry what Wal-Mart did to theirs, Starbucks did to theirs, Costco did to theirs and Lowe's-Home Depot did to their industry. And I think if we've done our job, five years from now you're not going to call us a bank."

It appears from his statement above, that Killinger was trying to develop WaMu into a people's bank of sorts--- catering to lending to lower and middle-class customers that other banks deemed risky. WaMu adopted this approach through the use of sub-prime mortgages and credit card sales, which made it easy for the least creditworthy borrowers to get financing, whether this was to purchase a home or make frivolous purchases at the local shopping mall. The bank extended this lending strategy to big metropolitan cities in the US including Chicago, New York and Los Angeles. WaMu encouraged sales agents to pump in loans while disregarding borrowers' income and assets. WaMu set up a system of dubious legality that enabled real estate agents to collect fees of more than $10,000 for bringing in borrowers. As WaMu was selling many of its loans to investors, it did not worry about potential defaults on its loan books, since the risk was being transferred to other interested investors in the marketplace. This lending strategy generated a net income of 1 billion dollars in 2005 through the home loan business of WaMu.

ENTER THE SUB-PRIME MESS

Such high profits of 1 billion dollars in 2005 were not sustainable. With the problems in the subprime mortgage, customers en masse started defaulting on their mortgage loan obligations.

In 2006, this delinquency showed up in a net income loss of 48 million dollars in their home division. 2007 and 2008 were more disastrous years, as inter-bank lending froze and credit markets were in bad shape. It was not possible for WaMu to raise new capital by selling their mortgages since no one was interested in purchasing these toxic assets. The losses at WaMu, the share price decimation and the attendant unfavorable publicity started the next big chain of events---- a massive run on the bank. Between 15th to the 25th of September, 2008 there was a bank run------customers withdrew 16.7 billion dollars from the bank. On September 25,2008 the Office of Thrift Supervision was forced to shut down Washington Mutual. WaMu Chief Executive, Alan H. Fishman was flying from New York to Seattle on the day the bank was closed, and eventually received a 7.5 million dollar sign-on bonus and cash severance of 11.6 million dollars after being CEO for 17 days.

EFFECTS OF CLOSURE

Washington Mutual was sold to JPMorgan Chase for around two billion dollars and the new bank assumed most of the liabilities of Washington Mutual. However, senior unsecured debt was not covered under the terms of the sale. The net result was that all shareholders were wiped out in addition to the unsecured debt holders, subordinated debt holders and preferred stock holders.

MORAL OF THE STORY

The moral of this story is not to invest in any US bank stocks at all, given the current global banking mess. Even preferred share investments in banks, which may carry a fixed declared interest rate are very risky in terms of US bank investments. In March 2009, the Government forced all preferred share holders of Citigroup to either convert to common equity of Citigroup or risk not earning any dividend income on their preferred share investments. A move of this magnitude decimated the income of millions of people, who over the years had been led to believe that Citigroup would always be profitable and would be able to generate a dividend, which dividend could be used for income generation purposes.

The second moral of WaMu's collapse indicates that one must avoid investment in any US bank debt through the medium of corporate bonds. The Washington Mutual story indicated, with clarity, that even bond investments in US banks were not safe since the sale of WaMu to JPMorgan Chase, precluded the assumption of debt of certain unsecured bond debt, unsubordinated debt and preferred share holder obligations.

CHAPTER 24

THE DEMISE OF THE INVESTMENT BANKING INDUSTRY AND WALL STREET

This chapter provides a broad introduction to investment banks and how they have fared in this great financial and credit crisis. Before we start, a definition of an investment bank is in order. A great definition of an investment bank, as expressed in www.investorglossary.com is: "An investment bank is an institution that performs a variety of financial services for corporations, individuals, and the government. The primary function of an investment bank is to raise capital for growing companies and the government by issuing equity and debt securities. In essence, the role of an investment bank is to operate as an agent between companies in need of funding and the public markets. The chief difference between an investment bank and a retail bank is that an investment bank does not accept deposits or originate loans. An investment bank also offers advisory and strategic services related to mergers, acquisitions and corporate structuring. Today, a typical investment bank may offer risk management and broker dealer services as well. An investment bank is also known as an underwriter."

Prior to the global financial and credit crisis of 2007 the following were the top tier Investment banks, headquartered in the US:

1. Merrill Lynch
2. Bear Stearns
3. Lehman Brothers
4. Morgan Stanley
5. Goldman Sachs
6. JP Morgan (which has merged with chase, known as JPMorgan Chase)

The global financial crisis saw the demise of Bear Stearns, which was purchased by JPMorgan Chase for around 2 billion dollars. Lehman Brothers collapsed and its assets were pieced up and sold to foreign corporations, like Nomura Holdings of Japan, who swallowed up the Asian and European businesses and Barclays who purchased parts of the US businesses. Merrill Lynch was sold to Bank of America. Therefore, effectively, only three players existed as investment banks post September 1, 07. On September 21, 2008 the Federal Reserve Board sent a press release approving the applications of Goldman Sachs and Morgan Stanley to become bank holding companies. This last move effectively converted any surviving investment banks into bank holding companies--- the motivation behind this move on part of the now ex-investment banks was the opportunity to receive public deposits and funding from the Government (funding was normally reserved for commercial banks and not for investment banks in the past).

129

This also meant that along with JPMorgan Chase, which was already a banking entity as a result of its merger with Chase, all investment banks lost their investment bank status and became regular commercial banks, while maintaining their investment banking operations.

TARP (TROUBLED ASSET RELIEF PROGRAM) RECIPIENTS

The TARP program was put into place by the then Secretary of Treasury, Henry Paulson as a process of freeing up credit for the markets and assisting banks deal with their troubled non-performing assets. Here is a list of some of the recipients:
1. JPMorgan Chase ----- $25 billion
2. Goldman Sachs ------ $10 billion
3. Merrill Lynch --------$10 billion
4. Morgan Stanley -------$10 billion

USE OF TARP MONEY

Unfortunately, a lot of TARP money, was not used out for the purpose for which it was provided, i.e. to provide more credit to individuals, corporations and businesses. John Thain, the disgraced CEO of Merrill Lynch in a telephone call with analysts said," We will have the opportunity to redeploy that. But at least for the next quarter, it's just going to be a cushion."(Thain was referring to use of the new TARP funds received as a bailout package from the Government).

Roger Freeman, an analyst with Barclays Capital, the firm which acquired parts of the US businesses of Bear Stearns said in a conference call, about the use of the TARP funds, " My expectation is that it's quarters off, not months off, before you see that capital being put to work"...

Such comments indicate that numerous ex-investment banks are not very serious about performing the government mandate and are merely using these funds to temporarily prop up their balance sheet and add to reserves.

MORGAN STANLEY AND THE GLOBAL CRISIS

During the financial and credit crisis in 2007 on, and around the time of collapse of Bear Stearns, a well watched index measuring the risk of failure among large Wall Street dealers had climbed above its previous high. There was a great amount of nervousness in the investor environment about the financial viability of investment banks. This contagion effect hit the likes of Morgan Stanley. The attack on Morgan Stanley's share price was so great that the shares lost 24% in one day alone. Facing a total lack of investor confidence, the boss at Morgan Stanley, John Mack held talks with several potential partners, including Wachovia, a commercial bank and Citic of China. On September 21, 2008 it was reported that the Federal Reserve allowed Morgan Stanley to change its status from investment bank-to-bank holding company.

On September 29,2008 it was announced that Mitsubishi UFJ Financial Group, Japan's largest bank would take a stake of 9 billion dollars in Morgan Stanley equity. Mitsubishi UFJ effectively purchased 21% of Morgan Stanley stock on October 14, 2008.

GOLDMAN SACHS AND THE GLOBAL CRISIS

Goldman Sachs has also attracted a lot of negative press in the past few months. The global financial crisis has not spared this large investment firm. It has also suffered from share price volatility and negative investor sentiment. Certain circumstances worked in the favor of Goldman Sachs----notable among those was the investment of five billion dollars by billionaire investor, Warren Buffet. Buffet's Berkshire Hathaway agreed to invest five billion dollars around 24th September 2008. In addition, Goldman also said it would raise 2.5 billion dollars in a public offering of common shares.

Ex-investment banks like Goldman Sachs have been criticized in the press and by investors for a flawed investment-banking model, which places over reliance on funding through capital markets. In addition there is a known public disdain for their vast leverage and unknown risk taking activities in derivative markets, among others. The infusion of capital from Buffett helped Goldman Sachs prop up its capital base and balance sheet at a time when all investment banks were under extreme pressure.

However, certain contentious issues appear to come up associated with Goldman Sachs.

The Mail Online, a UK news agency, reported on October 30/2008 the following release:

"Goldman Sachs is on course to pay its top City bankers multimillion pound bonuses---despite asking the US government for an emergency bail-out. The struggling Wall Street Bank has set aside 7 billion pounds for salaries and 2008 year-end bonuses, it emerged yesterday. Each of the firm's 443 partners is on course to pocket an average Christmas bonus of more than 3 million pounds. As Washington pours money into the bank, the cash will immediately be channeled to Goldman's already well-heeled employees. News of the firm's largesse will revive the anger over the 'rewards for failure" culture endemic in the world of high finance. The same bankers who have brought the global economy to its knees seem to be pocketing the same kind of rewards they got during the boom years."

On March 15, 2009 AIG released where its funds from the Government TARP program were allocated. Goldman Sachs was identified as recipient of $13 billion of taxpayer TARP funds. Although the payout was in terms of a legitimate contract entered into between AIG and Goldman Sachs, several moral issues appear. Are these sophisticated financial players, who take on such great risks, allowed to insure their risks?

From a business point of view it is fair game. But from a broad societal perspective, should these culprits who have milked and exploited the financial system in every way imaginable not be forced to pay back for some of the damages they have inflicted on the lives of everyone and the resultant disarray in the financial architecture of the world system? Several questions arise now and the verdict is still out.

MORAL OF THE STORY

The moral of this story is the vindication by the market that the investment-banking model is dead. Gone are the days when investment bankers could command million dollar bonuses whole transferring and insuring risk to third parties. This over dependence on the capital markets and the creation of sophisticated instrument of leverage are gone. No one and I mean no one is going to trust these bankers again.

As an ordinary investor, I would suggest you stay clear of any business with these ex-investment banks, unless you desperately need them to raise capital for your company. And even if you use them, verify all their recommendations. Ask them to write down their presentations in writing and have experienced financial counselors review their presentation to appraise you of all opportunities and risks in any proposed investments. Always ask for a prospectus for any proposed investment. Remember this is the law---you have a right to a prospectus as a potential investor. Better still make no equity or preferred share or bond investments in any of these ex-investment banks.

CHAPTER 25

THE CITIGROUP FIASCO.

BACKGROUND

Citibank is a major international bank, founded in 1812. Citibank is the consumer banking arm of financial services giant, Citigroup, one of the largest companies in the world. Citibank has operations in more than 100 countries and territories around the world. In addition to standard banking services, Citibank offers insurance, credit card and investment products. Their online services division is among the most successful in the field, having more than 15 million users.

As a result of the global financial and credit crisis, and due to huge losses In the value of its sub-prime mortgage assets, Citibank was rescued by the US government. On November 23, 2008 in addition to initial aid of 25 billion dollars, a further 25 billion dollars was invested with the corporation, together with guarantees for risky assets amounting to 306 billion dollars.

HISTORY

Citi reported losing over 8 billion dollars several days after Merrill Lynch announced that it too had been losing billions from the subprime mortgage crisis in the U.S. On April 11, 2007, the parent Citi announced huge staff cuts.

On November 4, 2007 Charles Prince quit as chairman and chief executive of Citigroup, following crisis meetings with the board in New York.

On January 16, 2009 Citigroup announced that it was splitting into two companies. Citicorp will continue with the traditional business while CitiHoldings Inc. will own the more risky investments, some of which will be sold to strengthen the balance sheet of the core business.

CITIBANK AND THE SUB-PRIME MORTGAGE CRISIS

Citibank committed major risk management errors during the financial crisis starting in 2007. Their entire risk assessment system was flawed. The poor risk management system failed to properly assess and monitor risk. Although the company used elaborate mathematical models to gauge risk in different geographical markets, it never built two important variables in such models. Those variables, which should have been taken into consideration for proper risk evaluation, were:

    a) The possibility of a national housing downturn, involving losses of over 15% in value in price and

    b) The prospect that millions of mortgage holders, particularly sub-prime risks would default on their mortgage obligations.

As a result there was no forward contingency planning.

And when the real estate bubble burst, the downward valuation of sub-prime mortgages (in an ever declining real estate market along with cash flow damage due to delinquencies in mortgages) caught the risk managers with their pants down.

CITIBANK GOES OUT WITH THE BEGGAR BOWL

With a view to add to its capital base, Citibank went on a fishing expedition to attract international capital. Citi was successful in raising funds from the following sources:

1. The Kingdom of Abu Dhabi in the United Arab Emirates, invested 7.5 billion dollars in 2008. The investment was in convertible bonds that pay 11 per cent interest.
2. Sovereign funds of Kuwait
3. Government of Singapore through its investment authority.
4. Saudi Prince Alwaleed.

However, with all the recent moves announced by the Government to stop paying dividends to preferred shareholders, all of the above investors face massive losses in revaluation and reinvestment of their investments as they are forced to exchange their bond or preferred share positions for common equity.

CITIBANK AND THE SHADOW BANKING SYSTEM

Citibank was the bank, which invented structured investment vehicles or SIV's. These SIV's are an integral part of the shadow banking system. This shadow banking system consists of non-bank financial institutions that, like banks, borrow short, and in liquid forms, and lend or invest long in less liquid assets. The difference in interest/returns earned by this investment exercise is the bank's profit. This investment process undertaken by banks is ably assisted by the use of credit derivative instruments, which allow normal commercial banks to evade normal banking regulations, such as those related to specifying ratio of capital reserves to debt. Many "shadow bank-like" institutions have emerged in American and European markets, between 2000 and 2008.

The shadow banking system is comprised of SIV's, conduits, money funds, monolines, investment banks, hedge funds and other non-bank financial institutions. These institutions are subject to market risk, credit risk and especially liquidity risk, since their liabilities are short-term while their assets are more long term and illiquid. This can create a problem in that they are not depository institutions and do not have direct or indirect access to their central banks lender of last resort support. Therefore, during periods of market illiquidity, they could go bankrupt if unable to refinance their short term liabilities. This shadow banking system has been blamed for aggravating the subprime mortgage crisis and helping to transform it into a global credit crunch.

In a June 2008 speech, US Treasury Secretary, then president of the New York Federal Reserve Bank placed significant blame for the freezing of credit markets on a run on the entities in the parallel banking system, also called the shadow banking system. These entities became critical to the credit markets underpinning the financial system, but were not subject to the same regulatory controls. This means that disruptions in credit markets would subject them to rapid deleveraging, selling their long term assets for pennies on the dollar.

Noble laureate Paul Krugman described the run on the shadow banking system as the "core of what happened."

"As the shadow banking system expanded to rival or even surpass conventional banking in importance, politicians and government officials should have realized that they were re-creating the kind of financial vulnerability that made the Great Depression possible--- and they should have responded in extending regulations and the financial safety net to cover these new institutions. Influential figures should have proclaimed a simple rule: Anything that does what a bank does, anything that has to be rescued in crises the way banks are, should be regulated like a bank. He referred to this lack of controls as "malign neglect."

CITIBANK AND THE US GOVERNMENT BAILOUT PLAN

With deteriorating reserves and lowered capital, Citibank needed support to prevent it from collapsing. In 2008 and 2009, Citibank was the recipient of direct and indirect support from the US Government. Direct support came in the form of bailout funds and indirect support came from back-stopping systems set up.

These were the levels of funding support received from the government:

1. An initial amount of 25 billion dollars as part of the 700 billion dollar bill passed by Congress in October 2008.
2. An additional 20 billion dollars from the US Treasury.
3. The US Treasury and the FDIC backstop of losses against more than 300 billion dollar in troubled assets. Citi would take the first 29 billion dollars in losses sustained plus 10% of additional losses, for a maximum total of 57 billion dollars.

MARKET REACTION TO CITI FINANCIAL POSITION

Citi has performed miserably as it continues to write down losses from its normal operations and its investments I in the shadow banking system. As of the end of Novemebr,2008 Citi has 2 trillion dollars in assets on its balance sheet and more than 1.2 trillion dollars in " off balance sheet" investments.

Citi's credit card business is performing terribly. It has 182 million open credit card accounts and its global card division lost $1.59 billion in the third quarter of 2008. All of this led to extreme share price volatility and at one point in March 2009, Citi stock price was below $1.

NATIONALIZATION OF CITI

Currently with all the preferred and equity shares owned by the US Treasury as a result of the bailouts done, the US Government owns around 40 per cent of Citi. However, day-to-day management operations are still being directed by senior management headed by Mr. Pandit, its current CEO. I believe this ceding of management control to the current board of directors, including the incumbent CEO is a big mistake on part of the US Treasury. Citi needs to be temporarily nationalized and all management decisions need to be executed by a professionally appointed team of government appointed executives. As credit starts flowing and the financial system stabilizes, it can be sold to other interested commercial entities. The decision not to nationalize and allow current management to continue business, as usual, is one of the most critical mistakes made by the US Treasury and one which may mean that either Citi will never recover financially or that more taxpayer money be used in the future for ongoing cash bailouts, leading to a very slow economic and financial recovery accompanied by waste of US taxpayer resources.

IMPLICATION FOR CITI SHAREHOLDERS AND BOND HOLDERS

Citi shareholders have lost a lot of money. The share price is very low, and as time goes, and more and more funding is received from the Government, it looks like the share price could go back to less than one dollar. In any situation like this, the shareholders usually get zeroed out. Also, currently, preferred shareholders will stop receiving dividends and need to consider the option of transferring their preferred shares for common equity, which could lead to further losses for these investors.

INSIDE SPECULATION BY CITI SENIOR MANAGEMENT

Four Citigroup executives who bought the banks stock in March 2009 generated a 2.2 million profit in nine days, regulatory filings show. One of the executives, director Roberto Hernandez bought 6 million shares at an average price of $1.25.

Latin America Chief Executive Officer, Manuel Medina-Mora bought 1.5 million shares on March 3 at an average price of $1.24. Other buyers included Vice-Chairman Lewis Kaden with 100,000 shares and Controller John Gerspach with 65,000 shares.

MORAL OF THE STORY

The global financial crisis has several financial institutions like Citigroup to blame. If one wants to looks at the causes and effects of this crisis all one has to do is examine the conduct of Citigroup and its greedy and avaricious executives. From developing SIV's in a parallel shadow banking system with no regulatory controls to speculation on the stock market making millions of dollars on insider information and knowledge of the bank, their actions reek of mischief, deceit, deception and fraud. I would like to close with reporting Citi's Chief Executive Officer's compensation for 2008. Mr. Vikram Pandit made 10.8 million dollars. In this culture of paying bonuses irrespective of firm success or failure, how are we going to turn this mess around? Or are we directly or indirectly using government bailout money to subsidize and finance the very key executives who caused and/or supported this financial mess? The large bonuses being paid on Wall Street and to banking executives raises some serious ethical issues.

To control this financial abuse, what is required is complete and immediate control and temporary or permanent nationalization of Citi---- a complete government sponsored exercise which grants immediate credit to ordinary people and businesses and a zero tolerance policy of excessive wastes in bonuses and a moratorium against alleged or suspected insider trading of shares for the next one year or more till the situation stabilizes.

The only authority which can take this step is the US Treasury with the blessing of the US president. I sincerely hope President Obama and Timothy Geithner make the hard decisions to improve permanently future damage, which will happen if strong controls are not put into place today. Slimy executives will find some way of making money, whether it is by awarding themselves multimillion dollar bonuses through their crony friends on the board or through conspiring to make profits with insider information on the stock market.

AUTHORS NOTE*****: Chapter 25 and Chapter 26 must be read together, since there are great links between Merrill Lynch and Bank of America. Merrill Lynch was sold to Bank of America and a lot of the problems in Merrill Lynch simply got transferred to Bank of America.

CHAPTER 26

BALANCE SHEET PROBLEMS AT MERRILL LYNCH

BACKGROUND

Merrill Lynch and Company, Inc. is a global financial services firm, which was acquired by Bank of America under emergency and distressed circumstance. Merrill Lynch provides capital markets services, investment banking and advisory services, wealth management, asset management, insurance, banking and related financial services worldwide. Merrill Lynch is headquartered in New York City and occupies the entire 34 stories of the Four World Financial Centre building in Manhattan. Merrill Lynch has a very profitable wealth management unit equipped with thousands of financial advisors. It also has a 49 per cent stake in Black Rock, which is a world-renowned asset manager.

HISTORY

Merrill Lynch was founded in 1914. Merrill Lynch rose to prominence on the strength of its brokerage network, which amounted to more than 15,000 brokers in 2006. The firm went public in 1971 and has since become a multinational corporation with over US 1.8 trillion in client assets, operating in more than forty countries around the world.

Mr. Stanley O'Neal was appointed as CEO in 2001. Mr. O'Neal pushed Merrill into risky investment relationships. After a large 8.4 billion write-down and his unauthorized merger approach to Wachovia Bank, he lost confidence of the board and was pitched out in November 2007. John Thain, then president of the New York Stock Exchange replaced him on December 1, 1997.

Mr.Thain inherited a shaky portfolio of assets at Merrill. This was amply demonstrated when Merrill on January 17,2008 reported a 9.83 billion fourth-quarter loss incorporating a 16.7 billion write down of assets associated with sub-prime mortgages.

PROBLEMS AT MERRILL

To understand the balance sheet problems at Merrill, we need to go back a few years. We are in Manhattan, the premier financial center in the world. And we are in the year of our Lord, 2006. The staff at Merrill is jubilant. The firms gamble to invest in the mortgage business has been paying off very well this year. Revenue is high and earnings are higher too; shares have appreciated by at least 40 per cent. Merrill has now gone into the business of manufacturing and selling mortgage securities, including Alt-A loans.

Merrill has also started trafficking in complex derivative products tied to mortgage and other debt. They have also got heavily involved in currency and interest rate derivatives, i.e. products which bet on a specific direction of movement of currencies and interest rates.

146

You win if you make the right call, you lose big time if you miss the future direction. With numerous wrong way bets associated with the subprime crisis, Merrill was left with more than 70 billion dollars of eroding mortgage debts.

The losses of around 8.4 billion dollars in Stanley O'Neal's reign were contributive to his demise and John Thain the next CEO had to deal with a portfolio filled with toxic assets--- although no one called or understood them as toxic in those days.

John Thain, in order to raise much needed capital sold Merrill's commercial finance business to General Electric and also sold off a lot of Merrill's shares to Temasek Holdings, a fully owned subsidiary of the Government of Singapore. These two deals raised over 6 billion dollars. However, the capital decimation continued on Merrill's balance sheets. In July 2008 Thain announced a 4.9 billion dollar loss for the fourth quarter from defaults and bad investments in the ongoing mortgage crisis. To give you a perspective on the huge losses in Merrill, for a one year period between July 2007 and July 2008, Merrill lost 19.2 billion dollars---- this calculates to a daily loss of around 52 million dollars.

Two weeks later, the company announced the sale of select hedge funds and securities in an effort to reduce their risk exposure to mortgage-related investments. Temasek Holdings of Singapore agreed to purchase the funds and increase its total investment in Merrill to 3.4 billion dollars.

Losses mounted in Merrill in the third quarter and fourth quarter of 2008. On September 14, 2008 Bank of America announced it was in talks to purchase Merrill and this sale finally went through. The Wall Street Journal reported that Merrill was sold to Bank of America for 0.8595 shares of Bank of America common stock for each Merrill common share or about US 50 billion dollars, calculated at a price of 29 dollars per share.

MORAL OF THE STORY

Here is another story of high class greed in corporate America. Financial companies of great reputation and success chose to ever-accelerate their revenue and earnings. And in order to do so, they got involved in exotic financial instruments like Collaterized debt obligations, other credit derivative products and overleveraged in the mortgage-backed securities market. When things were great and markets normal, they made a ton of money. But with deteriorating subprime market conditions, they took huge losses. The scope of the investments was so huge in the failed markets that the losses were unsustainable.

So, in the end all the Harvard school graduates and the MBA and PhD's in quantitative finance were helpless in saving the company. They had made a conscious risk management decision to tamper with highly volatile and risky derivative products and when the market tanked their corporate fortunes evaporated.

The situation was so bad in terms of the deceleration of assets in Merrill's balance sheet that they themselves succumbed to their greed and excesses---- they got sold to a relatively stronger financial institution.

In terms of the moral of this story for an average investor, it is again a reiteration of the fact that one should not get caught up in the hype and reputation surrounding a successful financial institution. All investment decisions made should be scientific and based on your objectives, risk tolerance and with a view to minimizing your investment acquisition/management costs All proposals made by financial advisors should be thoroughly dissected and understood in term of risks and benefits and second and third opinions extracted before any investment decision is made. It is very easy to commit vast sums of capital through a financial advisor, only to realize at the end, that you have been left carrying an empty bag. Your hard-earned money is yours. Be wary and careful in its investment. And, as I keep saying again and again, a small but predictable return is better than an outlandish expectation, whether this is a self- imposed expectation or hype due to a sales pitch from a financial advisor, which has been made to appeal to your sense of greed.

Do understand that greed and fear have nothing to do with your hard-earned money. You need to stay away from these two emotional elements of insatiable greed and irrational fear, if you are to make and keep any worthwhile fortune in your balance sheet.

CHAPTER 26

FINANCIAL PROBLEMS AT BANK OF AMERICA

BACKGROUND

Bank of America Corporation based in Charlotte, North Carolina, is the largest financial services company in the world, largest bank by assets, second largest commercial bank by assets. Bank of America is the number one underwriter of global high-yield debt, and the third largest underwriter of global equity and the ninth largest adviser of global mergers and acquisitions. Its market capitalization in February 09 was around 19 billion dollars with total asset of around 2.88 trillion dollars as of September 08.

HISTORY

Bank of America went into acquisition mode after 2001. In 2004, it acquired FleetBoston Financial for 47 billion dollars in cash and stock. On 30 June 2005, it purchased credit card giant, MBNA for 35 billion dollars in cash and stock. On September 14, 2007 Bank of America won approval from the Federal Reserve to acquire ABN AMRO N.A. and Lasalle Bank Corporation from Netherlands ABN AMRO for 21 billion dollars. A Dutch court blocked the sale until it was late approved in July.

The acquisition was completed on July 1,2007. On August 23, 2007 Bank of America announced a two billion dollar repurchase agreement for Countrywide Financial. The purchase of preferred stock was arranged to provide a return on investment of 7.25% and provided the option to purchase the common stock at 18 dollars per share. Following the initial investment on January 11,2008, Bank of America announced that they would buy Countrywide Financial for 4.1 billion dollars.

ACQUISITION OF MERRILL LYNCH

The acquisition of Merrill Lynch started a host of problems at Bank of America. On September 15, 2008 Bank of America (BOA) announced its intentions to purchase Merrill Lynch for an all-stock deal of 50 billion dollars. Prior to this point time, BOA had received 25 billion dollars of TARP money to deal with its troubled toxic assets. After the Merrill Lynch acquisition deal was approved by the shareholders of BOA, two important situations erupted. Firstly, Merrill disclosed larger losses than expected in Q4 of 2008, losses which were not known nor disclosed to BOA shareholders and secondly, Merrill approved a multi-billion dollar bonus package to several key executives.

In fact, after all this information was revealed the press noted that the CEO of BOA wanted to back down from his offer to buy Merrill but was persuaded to go ahead with the deal by the Government.

After he relented, the government provided an additional 20 billion dollars in TARP(Troubled Asset Relief Program) money to BOA in addition to significant backstopping funds. This amounted to a guarantee of 118 billion dollars in potential losses to the company as a result of among other things, the purchase of Merrill. All of these matters made the investor lose confidence in stock price of BOA and future return possibilities. The BOA share decimation, which followed, resulted in a major loss of over 80 percent of share price and a call from some shareholders for the firing of Ken Lewis, the current CEO of Bank of America. Some of the reasons cited for the firing of the CEO were a lack of disclosure of real costs of acquisition of Merrill and poor risk management control, among other factors.

MORAL OF STORY

Here is another story of things gone really wrong. A large financial organization announces in a few days after initial discussion, that it will purchase a weaker competitor, Merrill Lynch. Merrill is tethering on the edge of potential bankruptcy and without exercising due diligence the larger and more stronger competitor, Bank of America, decided to buy a wounded victim of the subprime and mortgage crisis. In terms of disclosure, this is a classic case of inappropriate disclosure. Large debts and billion dollar bonus payouts are not disclosed to shareholders of BOA, resulting in share price decimation and loss of investor confidence.

The moral of this story is that things have really gone wrong in America. Large financial corporations with deep pockets aided with political influence make decisions not in favor of the shareholders of the general public. And what follows is a series of accusations, each one blaming the other for wrongdoing. In the meantime, ordinary investors get hammered by loss of hard-earned wealth in share investments. Where is the end in sight? I frankly do not know.

From a personal investment point of view, as I have said earlier, do not invest in stocks and/or bonds of any US banks till the financial system stabilizes. Also, if you need any wealth management recommendations from these huge companies, take everything down in writing, including the risks, costs and benefits of any proposed investments. Consult a second or third opinion before you commit your hard-earned capital through these institutions. Be very very careful with your investments. This is your hard-earned money. Do not lose it. It will be hard to earn it back if you make poor and unsound investment decisions today.

CHAPTER 28

EUROPE AND THE BANKING CRISIS

As the financial crisis erupted in the US, its waves of negativism and pain spread across the world. The connection between the US and the rest of the world was through the massive securitization process. Investment banks, through this securitization process, manufactured and distributed synthetic mortgage, derivative and other asset-backed securities to the leading banks and financial institutions in Europe. Everyone was making money for a while till the subprime mortgage crisis hit. And when it hit and derivative investment values plunged--- as a result the numerous European banks, who were holding this paper, suffered massive losses.

BNP: INABILITY TO VALUE MORTGAGE RELATED ASSETS

The first perception of this European crisis hit in Paris. Banque Nationale de Paris (BNP), a well-known and highly respected French bank got hit with a loss of several million dollars. On 9 August 2007, BNP Paribas announced that it could not fairly value the underlying assets in three funds as a result to exposure to US subprime mortgage lending markets.

SOCIETE GENERALE AND ROGUE TRADER

In early 2008, it was reported that Jerome Kerviel, a 31 year old trader, who worked in Societe Generale's Delta One products team in Paris was responsible for a colossal loss of over seven billion dollars. SocGen's Delta One business includes ETF's, swaps, program trading, index and quantitative trading. BBC news reported that, "The bank said the fraud was based on simple transactions, but concealed by sophisticated and varied techniques."

TROUBLE AT UK BANKS

Losses stemming from sub-mortgage positions were greater in the United Kingdom than in most other parts of Europe. In fact most of the UK banks were involved in irresponsible risk taking in sub-prime investments in the US. This was accomplished through massive purchases of securitized products from the US investment banks--- such purchase was motivated to increasing their investment yields. HSBC was the first well publicized banking case, where the bank lost around 10 billion dollars in the residential US market. The losses were so bad that in early 2009 HSBC announced it was exiting all major businesses in the US, save the credit card business and a few other minor, insignificant businesses. Other British banks like Royal Bank of Scotland, Lloyds Bank and Barclays also suffered massive losses. Royal Bank of Scotland was effectively nationalized by the British Government.

In early 2009 Lloyd's senior management lost control of the bank and were taken over by the UK government. Barclays refused to take bailout money, instead attracting overseas inventors----however, there capital reserves are precariously low and there is a possibility of management collapse unless they can sell their " I-shares" business and increase their Tier 1 ratio as a result.

CRISIS IN GERMANY

The worldwide subprime investment losses did not spare German banks. One of the largest German banks, lost billions of dollars in this crisis. Smaller banks went under. Of particular interest is the story involving IKB Deutsche Industriebank, which is a bank based in Dusseldorf, Germany. It specialized in lending to small and medium sized businesses. In August 2007, it had to be bailed out due to bad losses in investments arising from the US subprime market.

To control the effects to the German banking sector resulting from fallout from IKB and other affected smaller and medium sized banks, numerous commercial German banks, including Deutsche and Commerzbank, formed a rescue fund to bail out such groups. The funds used to bailout IKB amounted to around 3.5 billion Euros (app. 4.20 billion US dollars as of March 2009). Although IKB stock depreciated precipitously, the bank avoided default, and the rescue is credited with having spared the German economy drastic fallout from the subprime crisis.

In February 2008, the German Government announced that IKB would require another rescue package to remain liquid, largely because peer banks were reluctant to invest further in the bank. The rescue package announced in mid-February 2008 was an amount of 1.5 billion Euros.

DUTCH AND BELGIAN BANKS IN TROUBLE

Other banks in Europe had their problems, too. Some notable problems experienced were with the Fortis and Dexia banking groups and with Ing bank of the Netherlands. Ing Bank got bailed out with a capital infusion of approximately 10 billion dollars from the Government of the Netherlands.

SWITZERLAND BANKING ISSUES

Switzerland has two major banks, UBS and Credit Suisse. Both banks took big hits as a result of their exposure to subprime mortgage exposure. UBS was bailed out by the Swiss government while Credit Suisse obtained financing form sovereign funds and other international investors.

A SPECIAL CONGRATULATORY NOTE TO GORDON BROWN

Of all politicians in Europe, Gordon Brown is the smartest and wisest. Through this banking and subprime crisis he has exhibited extraordinary leadership in coming in terms with the financial problems in Britain.

Through comprehensive bailout programs he has taken a different route than the US. He has gone in and forcefully and decisively nationalized banking companies, effectively removing old management and dictating policies to new government appointed management. The focus is on increasing consumer and business lending and doing everything possible to stimulate the economy. Although his moves have shown limited success in the early stages, the United Kingdom will show the best results long-run under the guidance and scholarly direction of Gordon Brown.

BANKING CRISIS IN EASTERN EUROPE

Eastern Europe is home to several West European banks. In the boom years of the past decade, several W. European banks from Austria and Switzerland, among other countries, set up shop here. Loans were provided to individuals and businesses in foreign-denominated currencies like the Euro, Swiss franc and US dollar. What compounded the problem was the devaluation of the local currencies in question. Take the case of a homeowner in Poland. The Polish zloty has lost more than one-third of its value against the euro in recent months. The Polish homeowner could not now pay his regular home mortgage since it cost him fifty percent more in his local currency to pay it every month. His income was in Polish zloty but his mortgage obligations were in a foreign currency. This loan crisis has enveloped numerous European countries as their individuals and businesses are in default mode.

This is the beginning of a wider crisis in Eastern Europe, in which numerous banks have been affected. The problem calls for an international bailout, similar to the US bailout but none of the developed countries of the EU are willing to finance this bailout. The problem has got worse since the IMF has already invested billions in dollars of capital in bailing out Hungary, Ukraine, Latvia, Belarus, Iceland and Pakistan.

The London office of Morgan Stanley has issued a report indicating that Eastern Europe has borrowed a total of more than 1.7 trillion dollars abroad from mainly W. European banks. It is also known from the press that around 500 billion dollars of these loans are due for renewal in 2009.

The problem needs systematic and planned coordination in support from both member nations of the EU and the IMF. It is foolish to make statements like the one made by the German Minister of Finance who said recently(in reference to the East European crisis), when asked about supporting these E. European economies, "claiming it was not Germany's problem."

MORAL OF THE STORY

The world has indeed become a small global village. The international financial network is so closely interlinked and intertwined that when the US sneezes, the Europeans get a cold and the Asians fall sick. This is because financial instruments have been internationalized. Through cross-border capital movements, financial products have started bearing the same flavor in diverse countries. A securitized product manufactured in an investment bank in the US gets sold to a European bank, who may later resell it to a bank in India or Australia. When the value of such product depreciates, the effect is felt worldwide. The networking effect can help or create disaster as small nations may not be able to economically have the resources to fight the discord and negativism caused by plunging asset values, imported from abroad.

The real challenge today is to have a set of global financial rules and regulations which all countries accept. Also, there is a dire need for a universal financial regulator, who is in charge of policing all kinds of investments, financial institutions, investment banks and unregulated capital investing entities like hedge funds. Unless such systems are set up, we are in for more financial crises in the future.

CHAPTER 29

THE BOND RATING AGENCIES AND THEIR DEBACLE

Credit rating agencies play a very important role in the selection and maintenance of investments. Such agencies assess the creditworthiness of a corporation's debt issue in terms of a bond rating provided. Some of the largest credit rating agencies in the US are Standards and Poor, Fitch, Moody's, and A& M Best Company. These credit rating agencies played an important role in the sub-prime crisis. They have been highly criticized for understanding the risk involved in mortgage-backed securities.

IMPACT ON SUB-PRIME CRISIS

Credit rating agencies are now under scrutiny for giving investment grade ratings to securitization transactions (CDO's and MBO's), based on subprime mortgage loans. By providing higher debt ratings than was the actual risk value of such investments, they misled the investment public into believing they were entering into safe investments, which in effect were sometimes toxic. This resulted in poor investor judgment and higher risk leading to principal loss in instances.
It is not clear how involved the rating agencies in fraudulently circulating ratings.

However, there is a lot of doubt in the marketplace about their objectivity in assigning ratings. For example, it is reported that one email between colleagues at a major credit rating agency, Standards and Poor's states, "Ratings agencies continue to create and <sic> even bigger monster--- the CDO market. Let's hope that we are all wealthy and retired by the time this house of cards falters." Part of the problem is the obvious conflict of interest in the rating exercise. The investment banks, who produce and distribute these derivative products, for which ratings are assigned, are the paymasters to the rating agencies. It follows that an AAA or AA rating would help the investment bank peddle more financial products to far corners of the world. How sure can we be that there is no conspiracy or complicity in falsely and deceitfully releasing high investment grade for their issuers, who also happen to be their paymasters? No one really knows. However, the conflict of interest is clear.

RATING ACTIONS DURING CRISIS

As a result of public and investor uproar during this crisis, the rating agencies took their jobs more seriously, resulting in hundreds of credit downgrades as a result of new credit research undertaken. Now they conducted a detailed and descriptive reexamination of many of the issues they had rated in the past.
In this process of reexamination, rating agencies lowered the credit ratings on 1.9 trillion dollars in mortgage backed securities from Q3 2007 to Q2 2008.

As of July 2008, Standards and Poor downgraded 902 tranches of US residential mortgage securities and CDO's of asset backed securities (ABS) that had been originally rated AAA out of a total of 4083 tranches originally rated AAA.

NEW GOVERNMENT REGULATIONS

With a view to stop this abuse of power and misreporting of credit information, the US Securities and Exchange Commission on June 11, 2008 proposed far reaching rules designed to address perceived conflicts of interest between rating agencies and issuers of structured securities. The proposals would among other things, prohibit a credit rating agency from structuring the same products that they rate, and require the public disclosure of the information a credit rating agency uses to determine the rating of a structured product, including information on the underlying assets.

MORAL OF THE STORY

In a wealthy capitalistic nation like the US, there are great opportunities to make money. However, in an enforcement system which is weak and poorly policed, these opportunities to make money or in the other extreme, the risks of losing money are both amplified. In the process, the big and strong banking corporations find ways of making money at any cost.

Although they do not necessarily break the law, their actions border on the illegal and smell of poor ethics and lack of concern for the investment community and general public.

In terms of an investor, the end effect can be disastrous. How does an ordinary investor make decisions based on inadequate risk information? This is what happened in the subprime crisis where the investment banks not only fooled the ordinary US investor but also succeeding in duping other large banks and rich investors in Europe and all over the world. The moral of such story is twofold: from the investor point of view, take credit ratings with a pinch of salt; always verify creditworthiness from other credible sources. Secondly, it is time for government in all countries to work cooperatively in a joint effort to monitor the credit rating agencies. Not only have new rules to be put in place to control their negative conduct, but in addition, government auditors are required to go in and make flash audits on the staff at these rating agencies and analyze if they are doing an accurate job of reflecting accurate credit involving different types of debt. What is required most urgently is an internal affairs department external to the credit rating agency. We desperately need a police to watch over the accepted credit police to bring back a semblance of law, order, and accuracy in credit reporting. Only in this policed manner can the public be protected and a semblance of decency, honesty and fair reporting is restored to this wild and unpredictable marketplace.

CHAPTER 30

CREDIT DERIVATIVES

This Chapter discusses some basic concepts pertaining to derivative products--- which brought the international financial system to its knees. A huge amount of these derivatives were invested in off line balance sheet portfolios of major commercial and investment banks--- the end result of the credit crisis through wholesale employment of such derivatives is well evident to all. What turned out as a way of diversifying risk became a money destructive machine in the hands of greedy, selfish and deceitful bankers, who with the assistance of their quant specialists in finance designed and sold billions of dollars of these products worldwide, causing worldwide pain and financial negativism.

Here follows a simple and straightforward explanation on credit derivatives. In finance, a **credit derivative** is a derivative whose value derives from the credit risk on an underlying bond, loan or other financial asset. In this way, the credit risk is on an entity other than the counterparties to the transaction itself.[1] This entity is known as the *reference entity* and may be a corporate, a sovereign or any other form of legal entity which has incurred debt.[2] Credit derivatives are bilateral contracts between a buyer and seller under which the seller sells protection against the credit risk of the reference entity.[2]

The parties will select which credit events apply to a transaction and these usually consist of one or more of the following:

- bankruptcy (the risk that the reference entity will become bankrupt)
- failure to pay (the risk that the reference entity will default on one of its obligations such as a bond or loan)
- obligation default (the risk that the reference entity will default on any of its obligations)
- obligation acceleration (the risk that an obligation of the reference entity will be accelerated e.g. a bond will be declared immediately due and payable following a default)
- repudiation/moratorium (the risk that the reference entity or a government will declare a moratorium over the reference entity's obligations)
- restructuring (the risk that obligations of the reference entity will be restructured).

Where credit protection is bought and sold between bilateral counterparties this is known as an unfunded credit derivative. If the credit derivative is entered into by a financial institution or a special purpose vehicle (SPV) and payments under the credit derivative are funded using securitization techniques, such that a debt obligation is issued by the financial institution or SPV to support these obligations, this is known as a funded credit derivative.

This synthetic securitization process has become increasingly popular over the last decade, with the simple versions of these structures being known as synthetic CDOs; credit linked notes; single tranche CDOs, to name a few. In funded credit derivatives, transactions are often rated by rating agencies, which allows investors to take different slices of credit risk according to their risk appetite.

Credit default products are the most commonly traded credit derivative product[3] and include unfunded products such as credit default swaps and funded products such as collateralized debt obligations (see further discussion below).

The ISDA[4] reported in April 2007 that total notional amount on outstanding credit derivatives was $35.1 trillion with a gross market value of $948 billion (ISDA's Website). As reported in The Times on September 15th, 2008, the "Worldwide credit derivatives market is valued at $62 trillion". [5]

Although the credit derivatives market is a global one, London has a market share of about 40%, with the rest of Europe having about 10%.[3] The main market participants are banks, hedge funds, insurance companies, pension funds, and other corporates.[3] ·Credit derivatives are fundamentally divided into two categories: funded credit derivatives and unfunded credit derivatives.

An **unfunded credit derivative** is a bilateral contract between two counterparties, where each party is responsible for making its payments under the contract (i.e. payments of premiums and any cash or physical settlement amount) itself without recourse to other assets. A **funded credit derivative** involves the protection seller (the party that assumes the credit risk) making an initial payment that is used to settle any potential credit events. The advantage of this to the protection buyer is that it is not exposed to the credit risk of the protection seller [6].

Unfunded credit derivative products include the following products:

- Credit default swap (CDS)
- Total return swap
- Constant maturity credit default swap (CMCDS)
- First to Default Credit Default Swap
- Portfolio Credit Default Swap
- Secured Loan Credit Default Swap
- Credit Default Swap on Asset Backed Securities
- Credit default swaption
- Recovery lock transaction
- Credit Spread Option
- CDS index products

Funded credit derivative products include the following products:

- Credit linked note (CLN)
- Synthetic Collateralized Debt Obligation (CDO)
- Constant Proportion Debt Obligation (CPDO)
- Synthetic Constant Proportion Portfolio Insurance (Synthetic CPPI)

Key unfunded credit derivative products

Credit default swap

The credit default swap or CDS has become the cornerstone product of the credit derivatives market. This product represents over thirty percent of the credit derivatives market [2]. A credit default swap, in its simplest form (the unfunded single name credit default swap) is a bilateral contract between a *protection buyer* and a *protection seller*. The credit default swap will reference the creditworthiness of a third party called a reference entity: this will usually be a corporate or sovereign. The credit default swap will relate to the specified debt obligations of the reference entity: perhaps its bonds and loans, which fulfill certain pre-agreed characteristics. The protection buyer will pay a periodic fee to the protection seller in return for a *contingent payment* by the seller upon a *credit event* affecting the obligations of the *reference entity* specified in the transaction.

The relevant credit events specified in a transaction will usually be selected from amongst the following: the bankruptcy of the reference entity; its failure to pay in relation to a covered obligation; it defaulting on an obligation or that obligation being accelerated; it agreeing to restructure a covered obligation or a repudiation or moratorium being declared over any covered obligation.

If any of these events occur and the protection buyer serves a credit event notice on the protection seller detailing the credit event as well as (usually) providing some publicly available information validating this claim, then the transaction will settle. This means that, in the case of a physically settled transaction, the protection buyer can deliver an amount of the reference entity's defaulted obligations to the protection seller, in return for their full face value (notwithstanding that they are now worth far less). In the case of a cash settled transaction, a relevant obligation of the reference entity will be valued and the protection seller will pay the protection buyer the full face value of the reference obligation less its current value (i.e. compensating the protection buyer for the decline in the obligation's creditworthiness). Credit default swaps have unique characteristics that distinguish them from insurance products and financial guaranties. The protection buyer does not need to own an underlying obligation of the reference entity. The protection buyer does not need to suffer a loss.

Since the reference entity is not a party to agreement between the protection buyer and seller, the seller of protection has no inherent recourse to the reference entity in the event of default and no right to sue the reference entity for recovery. However, if the transaction were to be physically settled the seller of protection could derive a right to take action against the reference entity on the basis of the loan or securities acquired during the settlement process. The product has many variations, including where there is a basket or portfolio of reference entities, although fundamentally, the principles remain the same. A powerful recent variation has been gathering market share of late: credit default swaps which relate to asset-backed securities [7].

Total return swap

A total return swap (also known as *Total Rate of Return Swap*) is a contract between two counterparties whereby they swap periodic payments for the period of the contract. Typically, one party receives the total return (interest payments plus any capital gains or losses for the payment period) from a specified reference asset, while the other receives a specified fixed or floating cash flow that is not related to the creditworthiness of the reference asset, as with a vanilla Interest rate swap. The payments are based upon the same notional amount. The reference asset may be any asset, index or basket of assets.

The TRS is simply a mechanism that allows one party to derive the economic benefit of owning an asset without use of the balance sheet, and which allows the other to effectively "buy protection" against loss in value due to ownership of a credit asset.

The essential difference between a *total return swap* and a *credit default swap* is that the credit default swap provides protection against specific credit events. The total return swap protects against the loss of value irrespective of cause, whether default, widening of credit spreads or anything else i.e. it isolates both credit risk and market risk.

Key funded credit derivative products

CREDIT LINKED NOTES

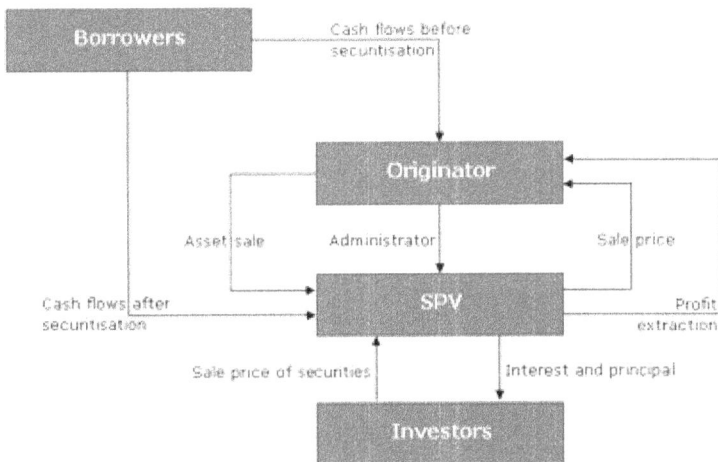

In this example, coupons from the bank's portfolio of loans are passed to the SPV which uses the cash flow to service the credit linked notes. A credit linked note is a note whose cash flow depends upon an event, which may be a default, change in credit spread, or rating change. The definition of the relevant credit events must be negotiated by the parties to the note. A CLN in effect combines a credit-default swap with a regular note (with coupon, maturity, redemption). Given its note like features, a CLN is an on–balance–sheet asset, in contrast to a CDS.

Typically, an investment fund manager will purchase such a note to hedge against possible down grades, or loan defaults. Numerous different types of credit linked notes (CLNs) have been structured and placed in the past few years. Here we are going to provide an overview rather than a detailed account of these instruments. The most basic CLN consists of a bond, issued by a well-rated borrower, packaged with a credit default swap on a less creditworthy risk.

For example, a bank may sell some of its exposure to a particular emerging country by issuing a bond linked to that country's default or convertibility risk. From the bank's point of view, this achieves the purpose of reducing its exposure to that risk, as it will not need to reimburse all or part of the note if a credit event occurs. However, from the point of view of investors, the risk profile is different from that of the bonds issued by the country. If the bank runs into difficulty, their investments will suffer even if the country is still performing well. The credit rating is improved by using a proportion of government bonds, which means the CLN investor receives an enhanced coupon. Through the use of a credit default swap, the bank receives some recompense if the reference credit defaults.

There are several different types of securitized product, which have a credit dimension. CLN is a generic name related to any bond whose value is linked to the performance of a reference asset, or assets.

This link may be through the use of a credit derivative, but does not have to be.

- <u>Credit-linked notes</u> **CLN**: Credit-linked note is a generic name related to any bond whose value is linked to the performance of a reference asset, or assets. This link may be through the use of a credit derivative, but does not have to be.
- <u>Collateralized debt obligation</u> **CDO**: Generic term for a bond issued against a mixed pool of assets – There also exists CDO-squared (CDO^2) where the underlying assets are CDO tranches.
- <u>Collateralized bond obligations</u> **CBO**: Bond issued against a pool of bond assets or other securities. It is referred to in a generic sense as a **CDO**
- <u>Collateralized loan obligations</u> **CLO**: Bond issued against a pool of bank loan. It is referred to in a generic sense as a **CDO**

CDO refers either to the pool of assets used to support the CLNs or, confusingly, to the **CLN**s themselves.

Collateralized debt obligations (CDO)

Collateralized debt obligations or CDOs are a form of credit derivative offering exposure to a large number of companies in a single instrument. This exposure is sold in slices of varying risk or *subordination* – each slice is known as a <u>tranche</u>.

In a cash flow CDO, the underlying credit risks are <u>bonds</u> or <u>loans</u> held by the issuer. Alternatively in a synthetic CDO, the exposure to each underlying company is a <u>credit default swap</u>. A synthetic CDO is also referred to as CSO. Other more complicated CDOs have been developed where each underlying credit risk is itself a CDO <u>tranche</u>. These CDOs are commonly known as CDOs-squared.

Risks

Risks involving credit derivatives are a concern among regulators of financial markets. The <u>US Federal Reserve</u> issued several statements in the Fall of 2005 about these risks, and highlighted the growing backlog of confirmations for credit derivatives trades. These backlogs pose risks to the market (both in theory and in all likelihood), and they exacerbate other risks in the financial system. One challenge in <u>regulating</u> these and other derivatives is that the people who know most about them also typically have a vested <u>incentive</u> in encouraging their growth and lack of regulation. (The incentive may be indirect, e.g., academics have not only consulting incentives, but also incentives in keeping open doors for research.)

Notes and references

1. ^ *Das, Satyajit (2005)*. Credit Derivatives: CDOs and Structured Credit Products, 3rd Edition. *Wiley.* ISBN 978-0-470-82159-6.
2. ^ *a b* *"PLC Finance Practice Note: Credit Derivatives by Edmund Parker".* http://www.mayerbrown.com/london/article.asp?id=4234&nid =1575.
3. ^ *a b c d* *"British Banker Association Credit Derivatives Report" (PDF).* http://www.bba.org.uk/content/1/c4/76/71/Credit_derivative_r eport_2006_exec_summary.pdf.
4. ^ *"ISDA".* http://www.isda.org.
5. ^ http://business.timesonline.co.uk/tol/business/industry_sector s/banking_and_finance/article4761839.ece
6. ^ *Dominic O'Kane. "Credit Derivatives Explained" (PDF). Lehman Brothers, posted at Simon Fraser University.* http://www.sfu.ca/~sp6048/Reading/LEH%20O'Kane%20Credit% 20Derivatives%20Explained%200301.pdf. Retrieved on 2008-07-02.
7. ^ *"Documenting credit default swaps on asset backed securities, Edmund Parker and Jamila Piracci, Mayer Brown".* http://www.mayerbrown.com/london/article.asp?id=3517&nid =1575.

177

CHAPTER 31

THE GREAT CREDIT CRISIS OF 2007-2009

The New York Times in its Saturday, March 21, 2009 business section commented on the credit crisis as follows, "In the fall of 2008, the credit crunch, which had emerged a little more than a year before, ballooned into Wall Street's biggest crisis since the Great Depression. As hundreds of billions in mortgage related investments went bad, mighty investment banks that once ruled high finance have crumbled or reinvented themselves as humdrum commercial banks. The nation's largest insurance company and largest savings and loan both were seized by the government. The channels of credit, the arteries of the global financial system, have been constricted, cutting off crucial funds to consumers and businesses small and large." The nation's largest insurance company, which failed, was AIG while the nation's largest savings and loan organization was Washington Mutual.

The credit crisis had a tremendous impact on almost everyone. This impact included individuals, corporations and small and medium size businesses. As we all know, credit is the lifeblood of our financial system. Once credit stops or gets impeded in any shape, form or manner, it result in a seizure in the financial system.

Some of the first symptoms of this malaise are reduced production of goods and services, which is followed by retrenchment and higher unemployment.

This is what happened in this financial and credit crisis. First, banks stopped lending to each other, instead choosing to hoard cash, which even included the cash provided as bailout money from the Government. This hoarding process not only happened in the US but also in Europe, where banks were nervous about general business conditions and were afraid of losing more money than they had.

The credit crisis which followed the banking and financial crisis was when problems got accentuated. In spite of numerous fiscal initiatives by the US government and from the European Central Bank and the Bank of England and Bank of Japan, there was no loosening of credit. All credit markets including the commercial paper market, the student loan and credit-card securitized loan market and of course the asset-backed mortgage market all remained frozen.

It has been said that unless credit is restored in the financial system along with a stability in the banking system, that there will be no possibility to upward economic growth anywhere in the world. I fully subscribe to this view.

The credit crisis poses as one of the greatest challenges we face collectively as world citizens and I pray that the banking and credit crisis is resolved soon, so that we can get a greater semblance of trust and confidence in our financial architecture and financial system.

CHAPTER 32

CRISIS IN THE INSURANCE INDUSTRY

BACKGROUND

Although the main thrust of the crisis has been directed in the global banking industry, the insurance sector around the world has not been spared. This is because insurance companies have various assets on their balance sheets--- and, of late, has mimicking the investment portfolios of commercial and investment banks. One area where there has been a lot of investment is in corporate bonds and as their values have plummeted so has the balance sheet contracted at insurance companies. There are different kinds of insurance entities--- the life insurance sector and the non-life (property, casualty) sector, in addition to the re-insurance sector. The life insurers in the US and the rest of the world have been hit harder than the non-life insurance companies.

THE FACTS

The worst and most tragic outcome of the financial crisis was the downfall of American International Group (AIG). Before its decimation and collapse, AIG was the largest insurance company in the world and widely respected in international investment circles.

What brought down AIG was reckless and unconscionable trading at their "Financial unit" in London. A group of reckless traders took big bets on derivative trades, which went sour. The actual risk exposure amounted to billions of dollars and created such a massive financial problem for AIG that they had to be bailed out by the US government for 80 billion dollars as of March 09. The situation surrounding AIG is so serious that an entire chapter has been devoted to understanding what happened there. Other important losses in the international insurance industry were:

1. The Yamato Life Insurance Company, a small insurer in Japan was the first insurer victim of the global financial crisis. Australia's non-life insurers reported an aggregate underwriting loss of about 740 million dollars in 2008.

2. Aegon, a large European insurer in the Netherlands reported a total loss of Euro 1.1 billion and were bailed out by their largest shareholder, Association Aegon, and funded by the Dutch Government.

3. In 2009, the full extent of the British insurers' investment in corporate bonds was revealed. Industry expert, Ned Cazalet, indicated that a total of 137 billion dollars were invested by UK insurers as a whole in corporate bonds. As everyone knows, the corporate bond market has tanked in the UK as investors demand higher yields, resulting in ever lower prices of bonds.

4. A.M. Best and Company, a prominent insurance credit rating agency, indicated the following in regard to the health of Canadian insurers, "Canadian life insurers are experiencing mounting pressures as the global financial crisis hampers their ability to maintain a conservative capital base as well as sustain the favorable revenue and earnings stream recorded in recent years." This was a report released in March 2009.

5. Further deterioration in profit performance has been seen with some of the top Canadian life insurers. Manulife, the largest Canadian insurer and No. 2. Canadian life insurer, Great West Life Company, both reported their first quarterly losses in at least a decade. These were Q4 2008 losses. Sun life said that their profits fell 77 per cent as the overall industry suffered from debt write-down and plunging stock prices.

6. In 2009, Moody's downgraded the "insurance financial strength" of Manulife from Aa1 to Aa3. "Moody's based its decision to downgrade Manulife, on the company's weakened financial flexibility and capitalization, caused by the decline in equity markets globally," said Peter Routledge, vice president and senior credit officer, in a release.

7. A.M. Best Company lowered its outlook for Canada's life insurance industry to "negative" from "stable" due to the impact of the economic downturn. A.M. Best further said that it may downgrade credit ratings and financial strength grades as the insurers face "mounting pressures" from a worldwide financial crisis that affects their ability to maintain capital and increase earnings in the future.

SITUATION IN THE US INSURANCE INDUSTRY

PR Newswire reported on January 7/2008, " While some long-term trends look favorable for the life insurance industry, short-term challenges will occupy the attention of senior management for the next two or three years due to the impact of the financial crisis, according to a new report by Conning Research and Consulting, Inc.
Further, Terence Martin, analyst at Conning Research and Consulting notes," The financial crisis has hit the life insurance industry hard. Our projected results for 2008 indicate a drop in ending surplus plus AVR of about 75 billion dollars to 237 billion dollars--- a 24% decline from 2007. The volatile equity markets and interest rates are challenging the investment and hedging skills of insurers. Several large insurance companies, particularly individual annuity companies, have seen significant decreases in assets and surplus, resulting in an urgent need to raise capital at a time when capital markets are constrained."

In a Bloomberg news release on March 19/2009, there was a report on Prudential Financial Inc, the second biggest US life insurer, which had recently received a downgrade from Moody's Investors on costs tied to its retirement products. Prudential fell $6.16 or 25% to $18.76 at 4.15 pm in the New York Exchange composite trading, the most since the company went public in 2001. The Bloomberg report further went on to say, "Life insurers, which guarantee minimum returns on retirement products called variable annuities, have suffered as a decline in stocks backing the policies forced them to set aside more capital to fund potential future payouts. Assets in US variable annuities fell 13 per cent industry wide in the three months ended December 31, a trade group said yesterday."

GENERAL EXPLANATIONS

A life insurance company provides death benefits and other guarantees several decades into the future. In order to fund these obligations, the insurance companies normally invest in both the equity market and the bond market. They may also take positions in the real estate mortgage market. These assets then comprise the left side of their balance sheet. With the financial crisis, equity values and bond and real estate values all got hammered. This meant that insurance companies took big losses on their balance sheet.

Another area where they got hit big time was in the retirement products area. Variable annuities were a very hot product pre-global financial crisis. Some of these variable annuity products contained a minimum interest rate guarantee. A retiree could choose to invest his retirement capital in such an annuity, picking where he wanted to invest his capital.

However, irrespective of the performance of his chosen retirement portfolio, there would be a minimum guarantee of say, 6 per cent, by the company. The insurance company was providing an income floor to the investor. What they were saying was that they would pay the greater of 6% or actual returns on his investment portfolio. When things were going well, while the market was stable and stocks were going up, an insurance company did not have to allocate any capital from its reserves to pay for such risk-laden guarantees. However, with the way the markets have tanked now, the real value of portfolios held by insurance companies are down 50 to 60 per cent down, but insurance companies must guarantee both the principal and the interest loss of, say 6 per cent. In this case, the insurance company must find capital from its other operational and revenue centers in the balance sheet to make good on the income guarantee or otherwise default and go insolvent, which is an option no insurance company wants to invoke. A lot of losses in the insurance company balance sheet and profit-and -loss statement have come from funding these guarantees in their variable annuity guaranteed interest retirement products.

MORAL OF THE STORY

There must be a public understanding that insurance companies act no different than commercial banks and investment banks when it comes to investment of capital. Some insurance companies have got burnt in the sub-prime mortgage investment area, otherwise have got into derivative products and others have experienced unhedged losses in stock and currency markets. As an investor, first and foremost, before giving a dime to either a life insurance or non-life company, check their financial strength ratings from A.M.Best and Company, a well known insurance strength rating agency. Then look thoroughly at any product you purchase, particularly if the product is a variable retirement annuity. Believe me there may be a lot of hidden fee in these products. You must demand a prospectus for such investment products— -- it is the law and your right to receive same. Be very careful in selecting the best product available. It would always help to pay a few hundred dollars and get a second opinion of a life insurance product though an accredited financial planner. Fee-based only financial planners are good because their compensation is not tied to a particular insurer or specific insurance products; this gives them the ability to objectively present what are the best products given your financial and risk tolerance situation. In that sense, there is no conflict of interest here. Use a financial planner. Do your independent research. Then make your move.

The second moral of this story is not to run in a rush and cancel your existing life insurance or annuity policy. This could be a move which could cost you thousands of dollars in the long run. And then there is the issue of insurability. If you are not in good health, you would pay an increased premium in the form of a medical rating on any new life insurance policy.

And even if you are in good health, your premium would be higher since you are now older than you were when you bought your existing policy. Think long and hard before you make any substantive changes to your insurance and retirement coverage's.

In closing, an investor must be super-careful of the products pitched by insurance companies. Do your home work and research and only purchase products from companies whose claim paying abilities are in the top 5 per cent with the highest strength and claims paying abilities. This information is easily available from A.M. Best and Company.

CHAPTER 33

SUPER-CRISIS IN THE US INSURANCE INDUSTRY

-THE FALL OF A GIANT (AIG)

BACKGROUND

Prior to the global financial and credit crisis, AIG International Group, Inc. was the world's number one international insurance and financial services organization, with operations in more than 130 countries. AIG companies served commercial and individual customers through a very extensive and complex network. AIG was involved in the sale of life insurance, property and commercial interest and retirement products. According to the 2008 Forbes Global 2000 list AIG was the 18th largest public company in the world.

HISTORY

AIG was founded in Shanghai, China in 1919 by Cornelius Vander Starr. Starr was the first Westerner in China to sell insurance to the Chinese people. He continued to be involved with AIG till the corporation was forced to leave China--- this leave coincided with the advance of Mao Zedong, as the Chinese commander led the People's Liberation Army on Shanghai. Starr was involved in US insurance activities, too, through AIG.

In 1962 Starr gave Maurice Greenberg the opportunity to lead AIG activities in the US. On September 16, 2008 AIG suffered a liquidity crisis following the downgrade of its credit rating.

AIG FINANCIAL PRODUCTS LONDON

AIF Financial Products Corporation (AIGFP), based in London, U.K., is a subsidiary of American International Group. AIGFP is considered a key company in the global financial crisis of 2007-2009. Joseph Cassano and Thomas R. Savage helped start the group in 1987. AIGFP focuses principally on over-the-counter derivatives markets and acted as principal in nearly all of its transactions involving capital markets offerings and corporate finance, investment and financial risk management products. From 1987 to 2004, AIGFP contributed over 5 billion dollars to AIG's pre-tax income. During that period AIG's market capitalization increased from 11 billion dollars to 181 billion dollars, and its stock price increased from $ 4.50 per share to $62.34 per share.

AIG Financial had a unit running from London, which was most responsible for the damage which brought the company down. The London based subsidiary of AIG which almost bankrupted the US bond insurance giant was not regulated by Britain's Financial Services Authority.

Reporters at ABC network claim trader Joseph Cassano led a team into risking half a trillion dollars, investing in toxic investments, which quickly lost their value amid the subprime crisis. "AIG financial products were the core, the hottest point of the global financial crisis. It was the epicenter." Peter Koenig, an investigative reporter told ABC's Good Morning America. When the US housing market slumped, they had to come up with a half a trillion dollars, the reporters claimed, but due to a regulatory loophole they only had a couple of million to cover their losses. The Serious Fraud Office is investigating the activities of AIG's London office.

AIG's trading in credit derivatives led to enormous losses. These losses at AIGFP division essentially bankrupted the entire worldwide AIG operation and forced the US government to bail out the insurer.

BAIL OUT BY US GOVERNMENT

The US Federal Reserve to prevent AIG's collapse, and in order for AIG to meet its obligations to post additional collateral (as a result of downgraded credit rating) to credit default swap trading partners, announced the creation of an 85 billion dollar facility. This facility was secured by the assets of AIG subsidiaries, in exchange for warrants for a 79.9% equity stake, including the right to suspend dividends to previously issued common and preferred stock. Two further bailouts were provided to AIG to a total of around 170 billion dollars as of March 16, 2009.

FURTHER LOSSES AT AIG

AIG posted a Q4 2008 loss of 61.7 billion dollars. This brought AIG total loss to end of 2008 at 100 billion dollars. Most observers and the government itself have conceded that AIG is too big and crucial to the global financial system to fail. Not supporting them with bailouts could cause several counterparty failures risks all across the world and has systemic importance in preventing a global financial meltdown. To illustrate the importance of AIG in the global financial system, one must realize that AIG is insurer for more than 100,000 companies' worldwide, including municipalities and retirement plans in its client list. This insurance and guarantor effect influences the lives of 100 million Americans, in some form or another, whether it is protection through a car or life insurance policy or as a source of retiree funds.

AIG AND FOREIGN BANK PAYOUTS

When the government enquired about where the AIG bailout money went, it was realized that several foreign banks became intended beneficiaries of TARP money. Some of these beneficiaries were:

Deutsche Bank of Germany: $ 11.8 billion

Barclay's PLC of Britain: $ 8.5 billion

Also there were some US banks who were beneficiaries.

These banks had earlier got TARP funds as stand-alone banks in the US. In addition they received money as insurance proceeds, under credit default swaps from AIG. These companies were:

Goldman Sachs $12.9 billion

Merrill Lynch $ 6.8 billion

News of these indirect bailout beneficiaries created a hue and cry in the US. Was it the role of the Federal Reserve to bail out foreign powers? And such foreign powers, being knowledgeable as they were, did contribute to this crisis. Should they not have to share some burden of this global financial mess? The verdict is still out on this ethical and moral dilemma. In the meantime, AIG's position is that these payments were contractual obligations and they had to be paid, irrespective of where the money went.

AIG AND THE EMPLOYEE RETENTION BONUS ISSUE

When AIG initially announced that they were going to pay executive bonuses over 150 million dollars for 2008, a year in which the corporation had losses of around 100 billion dollars, there was a public outrage. How could a corporation, which was a recipient of taxpayer money, use some of these funds to pay bonuses in a year of very poor financial performance? The CEO, Mr. Liddy, of AIG was grilled in a US Senate committee meeting in March 2009.

In this meeting of March 18/09, when Liddy was questioned about the 164 million dollar retention bonuses, he explained these as not being performance bonuses but incentive earnings linked to specific performance inside the AIG Financial Products division. He mentioned that each of the executives was involved in reducing risk and unwinding positions in this department. The bonuses were negotiated as an incentive for bringing down overall risk exposure of AIG.

He suggested that the overall risk exposure had been decreased by about one trillion dollars and the incentive income of 164 million dollars was provided as an indication of executive's ability to drive down risk by removing and disassociating from very risky positions. He also mentioned that this was a very difficult job and one which required great skills and expertise and that he could not consider canceling this retention bonus since it was contractual in nature and that canceling or reducing it would result in some or all of the concerned executives leaving the company, which could result in unraveling of even higher risk exposure in their absence. He felt it was better to pay the bonuses and employ the skills of the available talent, then risk a bigger risk calamity in their absence. What he was saying, in simple words, was that the executives in charge were competent folks and had good handling of the positions in their allocated portfolio and that the best solution for taxpayers and for everyone would be to unwind these trades as soon as possible.

In terms of a plan to return to profitability and to return over 80 billion dollars in bailout plan he suggested that he had a plan but the eventual success of the plan would be based on how soon the markets recovered. Conditions at the present were depressed and market values extraordinarily low and therefore there could be no thought of selling any assets currently. However, as soon as the overall risk in the financial units were scaled down and markets returned to normal, he would sell some of this units and pay back the government loan/bail out money.

FURTHER CONTRADICTIONS OF BONUS POOL

In March, 2009 it became aware to the public that 165 million dollars of bonuses were to be paid out to a government bailed out organization, i.e. AIG. This created great uproar in the US. President Obama vowed to find a legal way of stopping this bonus payout. Later AIG disclosed that an amount of around 50 million dollars was already paid out to certain recipients. Bloomberg through a news release on 21 March, 2009, at its business site, www.bloomberg.com, indicated that the office of the Attorney General of Connecticut said the insurer was going to pay a total of 218 million dollars in bonuses. The documents received at Connecticut showed that 418 people received bonuses from $1000 to 6.4 million dollars. At least 73 people made $1 million or more, and there were seven people who made $4 million or more.

As it has been hard to find a legal way of stopping payment of these bonuses, Congress has passed a bipartisan bill creating a 90 percent bonus tax on all employs of TATP recipient organizations receiving more than 5 billion dollars in aid, when such employees earn more than $250,000 income per year. This bill has passed Congress and is due to go to Senate for a vote and possible approval in the third week of March, 2009.

MORAL OF THE STORY

Several issues including some moral and ethical ones arise with respect to the AIG crisis. These are:

Issue 1

How could such a large, successful insurer have a regulatory lapse in its assessment of risk coverage in its London Financial unit? Why were there no adequate policing arrangements here? How did a few people have so much power to make billions of dollars of trades, a volume of derivative trading, which had the potential and which in fact bankrupted the giant insurer?

Issue 2

How long will the "too big to fail" doctrine hold good? With 100 billion dollars in losses in 2008 and over 150 billion in TARP money and no end in sight, is there not a better solution to this financial crisis inside AIG than to continue throwing good money after bad?

Issue 3

When a corporation is not making a profit, is there a moral and ethical right for such corporation to pay out over 200 million dollars in profit for performance to some key executives? Where do these excesses stop???? What is it going to take to stop this insatiable executive greed? Better corporate governance? Legislation in Congress? Or a combination of both? How do we stop these bonus payments in the future, whether you call these executive bonuses or retention bonuses?

For an investor, it is critical that he spreads out his risks in the form of obtaining insurance coverage's. This process must involve not relying on one company for financial/insurance coverage, even if that company has a AA or AAA financial strength and superior claims paying ability as rated by AM Best and Company. The financial situation is so challenging now, that all investors must re-visit their insurance portfolio and determine if it is possible to spread their insurance risk among four or five top quality insurers. This way, if one goes down you have four others to get some funding support for your retirement or business or whatever other reason you may buy insurance for.

CHAPTER 34

THE BANKRUPTCY OF ICELAND

BACKGROUND

Iceland is one of the most beautiful countries in Europe. It boasts a population of 300,000 citizens. From very simple beginnings, it developed into a financial and economic powerhouse in the 1990's. The United Nations publishes a study called the "Human Development Index" every year. This study tracks the best countries in the world in terms of a multi-faceted index, which takes into account numerous factors. In the last report published in 2008, tracking national developments to 2006, they listed Iceland as the best country in the world with Norway trailing in second place. For those of you who are not familiar with the Human Development Index, this index represents a multifaceted factor, which looks at among other things, national per capita income, human mortality performance, health services education and so on. Iceland had a higher per capita income than the U.S. prior to this financial crisis. Iceland had really pulled off a veritable economic miracle. Here was a country with the highest number of cell phone users per house. It was also one of the few countries in the world, which offered free education and free health care services to its citizens.

Iceland also offered government mandated generous leaves plus an excellent pension system. These were the happiest people on earth. But their happiness was not destined to last forever.

HISTORY

In the early 90's there was social and political unrest in Iceland. There was a national mood to diversify industrially and internationally with a view to further building the economy. Leading this change was Mr. David Oddsson, who became prime minister in 1991. He promised to bring an end to the "boom- and- bust" cycles tied to a predominantly fishery industry. He also solidly believed in privatization of industry like the domestic banking industry. He sold off numerous domestic companies, fetching two billion dollars as a result. His next target was the nationalized banks. In a 2004 speech, Mr. Oddson remarked, "The crucial factor was the iron grip that the Icelandic state had on all business activity through its ownership of the commercial banks." All the commercial banks were sold. In time and with some consolidation, there evolved three major banks in Iceland. And here is where the tragic mistake was made. The banks were given too much power accompanied with too much laxity in regulation---- a repeat of the US financial history with banks. The three banks got really big in assets. They did so by borrowing in foreign currency in international markets. They took Euros, Swiss francs, dollars, and numerous other exotic currencies.

In order to build their portfolios, they lent money to local Icelandic people in foreign currencies----this allowed a lower rate of monthly interest paid compared to taking a loan in the local Icelandic currency, the " kruner". This assumption was   true as long as the kruner did not depreciate against the target foreign currency. They also lured international investors by offering very high rates of interest in kruner, their local currency. In this way there were able to attract billions of dollars in capital.

To illustrate how large the banks had grown the country's largest bank, Kaupthing Bank, had assets of just 208 billion kruner. By mid-2008 the assets had gone up 3000% to around 6.5 trillion kroner. In early 2008, the three main banks of Iceland had a capitalization of 75% of the entire Icelandic stock market. In terms of earning revenues, these banks had large overseas operations. This was due to the reason that they could ill afford to earn low profits and revenues out of a mere 300,000 inhabitants in Iceland. And then the bubble burst. Welcome to the 2008-2009 financial crisis and the newest fatal target--- Iceland.

THE BANKING CRISIS

The 2008-2009 Icelandic financial crises was a major ongoing economic crisis in Iceland that involved the collapse of all three major banks following their difficulties in refinancing their short-term debt and a run on deposits in the United Kingdom.

Relative to the size of its economy, Iceland's banking collapse was the largest suffered by any country in economic history. This financial crisis had serious consequences for the Icelandic economy---the national currency fell sharply in value and foreign currency transactions were virtually suspended for weeks. The capitalization of the stock exchange contracted by more than 90% and this was followed by an economic recession.

What caused a beautiful and economic stable and growing constituency like Iceland to depression, shame and financial loss?

CAUSES OF BANKING CRISIS

There are two acknowledged causes of this crisis:

1. Overgrowth of banking organizations in relation to rest of the economy. The banks however had minimal exposure to the US sub-prime mortgage market. The real blunder was the exposure to foreign currencies as a way of financing and growing the national economy. When the US market suffered around September 2008, there was an international loss of investor confidence in credit markets worldwide. As a result, when these banks sought to refinance their international debt, no one was interested in renewing or refinancing these monster loans. The banks themselves did not have enough reserves in Euros, Swiss francs or dollars to pay these loans, nor did their central bank.

One bank defaulted on its loan and then the others defaulted. Then it was a downward spiral with the credit rating agencies downgrading Icelandic debt, followed with a currency and stock market crash. This was followed by a recession in which numerous Icelanders were fired as companies cut staff and closed down "en masse". Inflation increased to 18.6% in January 2009.

2. Activity by hedge funds and other international speculators further aided the freefall of the stock market and currency market as such organizations sought to exploit the weakness in the Icelandic banking and economic system.

LESSONS TO BE LEARNT FROM CRISIS

The Icelandic crisis was caused by overdependence on foreign investors and overleveraging in foreign currency obligations. No county, however big or small should rely so greatly on foreign capital. The international credit crisis of 2008–2009 destroyed any chance of Iceland to refinance its debts. In spite of having a good economic record and ample resources, once one bank defaulted, the mood became very somber and in time, all three banks collapsed and were taken over by the Government. But the problem could not be solved.

The large foreign loan portfolio of maturing loans still existed and the Icelandic government got a temporary reprieve and some financial stability when neighboring Norway and the International Monetary Fund provided bailout money.

The second lesson points to the urgent need to separate the powers of the central bank from that of the politicians. This is what happens in the US, where the Federal Reserve dictates independent monetary policy--- this is a better way to control financial systemic risk. In the case of Iceland, the former Prime Minister was Chief of the central bank and there was collusion in decision-making between the ruling political party and the central bank chief.

The third lesson from the Icelandic crisis is the wisdom that no country should ever borrow in a foreign currency unless it is absolutely necessary. Speculation in foreign currencies is a true death wish. In the case of the central bankers and politicians of Iceland, this lesson was learnt in a very cruel way. The hard lesson was that once a foreign currency rises in value against a targeted domestic currency, all the spoils of the economy are gone. As the kruner collapsed against the Euro, Swiss franc and the US dollar, and the Euro the country lost its ability to repay such loans. From an individual citizen's point of view, the Icelander who had borrowed in foreign currency simply lost the capacity to repay his loans since his earnings were in kruner, the domestic currency.

As a result of loss of purchasing power, directly attributed to overleveraging in foreign currencies, thousands of Icelanders lost their homes, cars and other possessions. This entire process of loss was a major individual and national financial disgrace and proved that no one in the country had resorted to appropriate financial planning exercises. It appeared that national and individual greed had clouded everyone's judgment in efficiently planning and executing an investment portfolio.

TIMELINE OF FINANCIAL CRISIS

Wall Street Journal has released a wonderful article (on January 29, 2009) on the timeline of the Icelandic crisis. Here it is reproduced for your attention and study.

Sept. 29, 2008 -- The government puts in $810 million for a 75% stake in one of Iceland's three big banks, Glitnir Bank. Ratings agencies cut Iceland's sovereign-debt ratings, and the cost of insuring the debt against default jumped.

Oct. 6, 2008 -- Prime Minister Geir Haarde says Iceland is at risk of "national bankruptcy." The parliament passes emergency legislation enabling the government to intervene extensively in Iceland's financial system.

Oct. 7, 2008 -- The government takes over two of Iceland's three largest banks, Landsbanki and Glitnir. Iceland gives its biggest bank, Kaupthing Bank, a loan of $703 million.

Oct. 8, 2008 -- British Prime Minister Gordon Brown says Britain will take legal action against Iceland to try to recover British deposits lost in Landsbanki's branch in the U.K.)

Oct. 9, 2008 -- Iceland takes over and nationalizes Kaupthing. With some 20 local governments in the U.K. also holding accounts worth well over $173 million in Icelandic banks, the British government uses powers under its terrorism laws to freeze Landsbanki's assets until the status of the deposits is resolved. Iceland's Prime Minister Geir H. Haarde criticizes British authorities at a press conference. The OMX Nordic Exchange Iceland halts trading on all equities, citing the "unusual market conditions."

Oct. 14, 2008 -- Upon the reopening of equities trading at Iceland's stock exchange, the market's key index plunges.

Oct. 15, 2008 -- Icelandic authorities register a complaint with NATO over Britain's invocation of anti-terrorism legislation to freeze assets of Icelandic banks in the U.K.

Oct. 20, 2008 -- New Kaupthing, Glitnir and Landsbanki banks are established to assume control over their respective domestic assets.

Oct. 24, 2008 -- Iceland reaches a deal for a $2 billion loan from the International Monetary Fund.

Oct. **28**,2008-- Iceland's central bank raises its key interest rate to 18%, from 12%.

Nov. **3, 2008** -- Norway's Minister for Foreign Affairs, Jonas Gahr Stoere, announces a five-year loan of $641 million to the Icelandic government.

Nov. **20, 2008** -- The IMF approves $2.1 billion loan for Iceland. Iceland becomes the first Western European nation to get an IMF loan since the U.K. in 1976.

Jan. **23, 2009** -- Mr. Haarde calls for elections in May -- two years early -- amid increasingly violent protests and the fracturing of its coalition.

Jan. **26 , 2009**-- Mr. Haarde announces that he and his cabinet will resign immediately.)

Jan. **27, 2009** -- Icelandic President Olafur Ragnar Grimsson asks the head of the leftist Social Democratic Alliance to lead talks to form a new minority coalition government.

MORAL OF STORY

The Icelandic collapse story is indeed a sad one. After the US investment and commercial banks had destroyed whatever investor confidence was left, there was a credit crisis. This credit crisis claimed the economic and banking life of a small but otherwise prosperous European country. The effects of this disastrous US credit crisis spread to a tiny country in Europe.

This cause-and-effect situation shows how networked the world is financially. In the vast financial center, with the US at the epicenter, a sneeze in the financial system in the US is likely to create a cold or fever in a smaller, comparatively weaker economy.

From an Icelandic investor point of view, it would assist such investor to understand the "financial bubbles and bursts" of yesteryears. A closer understanding of the role of banks in the economy would have caused an average intelligent citizen to refrain from taking property and car loans in foreign currencies. Lack of an understanding that there is no such thing as a free lunch caused all this havoc as the Icelandic local currency crashed and monthly car, house and loan payments doubled for some citizens, causing foreclosures, evictions and loss of hard-earned wealth.

Generally, from an international investor point of view, the Lesson comes out clearly that one should never put all your eggs in one basket, nor take on unnecessary currency risk. Returns may look attractive in currencies other than the US and Euro and may prompt you to make investments whether such investments are in the form of foreign or emerging market stocks or bonds. However one must truly understand that in the final analysis your loss or gain will be measured in US Dollars (assuming this is your reference currency for evaluating your portfolio).

Unless you have a ten to fifteen year time investment horizon and you have the capacity to stomach short-term currency losses and you do not need the money for any emergencies short-term, then as part of an overall investment strategy you may take some currency risk. Otherwise, stay far away from such investment exercises. The recent bankruptcy of the Icelandic citizen could be your story next, if you do not heed this advice.

CHAPTER 35

THE IMPACT OF THE FINANCIAL AND CREDIT CRISIS ON AUSTRALIA & ASIA

This section deals with the impact of the financial crisis on developing and developed nations of Australasia, a loose term to include Australia and all of Asia. Different nations are exposed to varying degrees of effect (as result of the current global financial and credit crisis). This crisis is essentially global in nature, with shockwaves emanating from the epicenter, the U.S. to numerous nations tied together through an intricate financial and trade network. We will now look at the local economic impact of this crisis in relationship to Australia and Asia.

THE INDIA SITUATION

India, as is well known is the "roaring giant" of Asia. It is the twelfth largest economy, when measured in absolute GNP terms and the fifth largest world economy when measured on a "purchasing-parity" basis. India also boasts the world's second fastest economic growth rate. With a stable working population and an incredibly large and well educated young workforce, India represents all the makings of a future economic superpower. However, India has not escaped the global banking and credit crisis.

INDIAN BANKING

The banking industry is well regulated and has a number of state and federal owned banks. Banking regulation is stringent. Owing to political reasons, the banks were not allowed a free hand as in the West. Credit was monitored strictly by government authorities. Also, most importantly, the country did not raise much international debt through bond offerings, which provided it with some insulation in this crisis. In terms of international investments by local Indian banks, these were regulated and controlled, and this saved the banking system from the crisis, unlike of happenings in the U.S. Investments by Indian banks in collaterized asset mortgages and sub- prime mortgages were reduced, so that the net banking industry had minimal losses.

The Reserve Bank of India, the premier government-run financial institution, comparable in role to the Federal Reserve in the US, reported that the combined mark-to-market losses of all Indian banks (as a result of collaterized debt obligations and credit-default swaps) amounted to around 450 million dollars as of July 2008. To provide an understanding of this, the total credit exposure to the subprime market was hardly two per cent of all banking assets nationwide. This limited exposure resulted in no banks failing in India, nor any banks receiving any bailout money from the Government.

However, it must be noted that no country, not even a giant like India, could escape unscathed from this crisis. Several problems existed as a result of the crisis. These are listed below:

1. One of the first things institutional investors did was to sell Indian equity assets to repatriate profits or losses home to meet with their commitment there. The sudden implosion of fund loss in domestic Indian rupees caused a great reduction in Indian stock market values.

2. With dollars leaving the country, the foreign exchange value of USD to Indian rupee was affected. The Indian rupee started depreciating vis-a-vis the USD, causing harm to several counterparties.

3. With shrinkage of liquidity worldwide and a higher risk sentiment, banks stopped lending as aggressively as they had in the past. This resulted in less loans being granted to small and medium-sized businesses and industry and less money available for domestic mortgage lending. All of these factors resulted in GDP growth slowing form a double digit figure to one around 7 per cent projected for 2009.

All in all, India was one of the few countries to do well in spite of this crisis. This is attributable to a strong economy primarily based on local domestic consumption and limited export contribution. It also has a lot to do with strict policing of the Indian banking system, including investments in international instruments---- which were one of the causes of this crisis.

CHINA AND THE GLOBAL CRISIS
China is the fastest growing economy in the world. China represents the best and brightest people in the world, when it comes to assimilation and application of international business knowledge. With their prudent lifestyle, the country has been able to accelerate domestic savings. Combined with an almost outstanding export record to the US, the Chinese have accumulated trillions of dollars and are destined to be the pre-eminent economic power in the world in the next ten to fifteen years.

FALLOUT FROM THE FINANCIAL AND CREDIT CRISIS
China has not been as fortunate as India in the fallout from this crisis. This is primarily due to two reasons:

1. China is too closely linked with the U.S. in terms of export trade. Export earnings constitute a big part of the Chinese economic miracle, and when the U.S. suffers economically, the Chinese exports to the U.S. drops and this effects everything there, resulting in mass factory closures(due to reduced export U.S. demand) to dramatic reduction in national surplus.

2. China invests its foreign currency reserves in US dollars---- this is done through the purchase of US Government bonds. In fact, China is one of the primary creditors and financiers of the US economic system. Due to perceived risks in the US and a faint perceived possibility of US government bankruptcy, there are great concerns in China now about the safety and value of their US hoarded reserves. With the US Government printing money in style to finance all the stimulus plans, there is a valid concern that this will lead to increased inflation in the US and a resultant depreciation in purchasing power of the US dollar. Top political leaders of China have urged the US leadership to honor their promise of not only repaying their Chinese debt, but also to protect the value of the US dollar by wise management and control of fiscal debt.

Here are some other startling figures of the exposure of China to the deceleration in the US economy in 2008 and early 2009. Keven Hamlin, in a Bloomberg news presentation on February 10, 2009 reported the following: "China's exports fell by the most in almost thirteen years as demand dried up in the US and Europe, worsening the outlook for jobs and industrial production in the world's third-biggest economy.

China's economic slide has already cost the jobs of 20 million migrant workers, adding pressure on the government to boos consumption and expand a 4 trillion Yuan (585 billion dollar) stimulus package. Government researchers have advocated weakening the Yuan against the dollar to support exports, a move that could add to trade tensions amid the worst financial crisis since World War 2."

However, China has the economic muscle and might to pull itself out of this crisis. With its massive stimulus package and a dedicated will of the government and common man, China along with India will be the first two countries in the world to get on their feet post this crisis.

THE JAPANESE SCENARIO

Japan is the world's second largest economy and home to the most productive people on earth. Japan has rebuilt itself from financial and industrial ruin after the attack on Hiroshima and Nagasaki by US forces. This nuclear attack decimated the two cities and caused them to unconditionally surrender to Allied Forces in World War 2. From this position of dejection, depression and humility, Japan has re-risen to assert its muscle and economic power and is a respected economic and world power.

JAPANESE ISSUES

Japan is an export economy and earns a lot of its income through exports of its products to the US. Since the US has gone into an economic tail dive, exports from Japan to the US have been hit big time. Sales of everything from Japanese cars to electronics have been affected negatively. Secondly, the yen has become so strong vis-a-vis the US dollar, that this has also affected the competitiveness of export markets. In addition, liquidity concerns have made it hard for small and medium-sized businesses to get funding capital ----- another factor in the economic slowdown.

Wall street Journal, an eminent US newspaper, reported the following story from Tokyo,

" Japan's land prices fell for the first time in three years in 2008, highlighting how the economic downturn is stifling demand for homes and offices. Land prices for residential real estate slipped 3.2% last year, while those for commercial properties dropped 4.7%, the Ministry of Land, Infrastructure, Transport and Tourism said Monday in its annual land price survey. Both fell after two years of rises. All of Japans 47 prefectures posted declines in residential and commercial land costs."

HISTORY OF JAPANESE FINANCIAL CRISIS

The global financial crisis first claimed a Japanese insurance company. Yamato Life insurance company----- this relatively small and unlisted issuer failed with 2.7 billion dollars in outstanding debt. Yamato got involved in high risk sub-prime investments.

These news were followed by a severe correction in the Japanese stock market and with threats of a recession. The global financial and credit crisis had hit home.

JAPANESE GOVERNMENT STIMULUS RESPONSE

To spur the economy, the government has set into place a multi-billion dollar fiscal stimulus package.

OVERALL EFFECT OF THE CRISIS

There has been a limited reaction in Japan compared to seismic effects in Europe and the U.S. This is due to the relatively small risk exposure to sub-prime and other collaterized mortgage risks by Japanese investors and financial institutions. The International Monetary fund reported that sub- prime losses at Japanese financial companies have totaled just eight billion dollars of a total of several trillion dollars worldwide.

However, there have been some losses in the following markets:

1. The stock market is down considerably, due to the worldwide lack of trust in equities and corporations with hidden debts.
2. The export market has taken a big hit as the U.S. simply imports less cars and electronic and other products, due to a dwindling economy.
3. As a result, economic expansion is limited and Japan is officially in recession as of the first quarter of 2009.

Other than the above losses noted, the Japanese market has held up relatively well. Only one insurer has collapsed since the beginning of the global financial and credit crisis and most importantly, no banks have failed. The government is still in control of economic events although manufacturing is limping along, with no adverse, substantive financial impact on the economy, banking or general business conditions.

THE AUSTRALIAN SITUATION

Australia has not been significantly hurt by the global financial crisis. This is due to less risk internationally in sub -prime securities. 4 of the top 11 banks in the world, in terms of ratings are Australian. Sub-prime assets as a percentage of all assets in Australian banks, amounted to only 1 percent of total risk exposure in early 2009.

ABC News Australia reported on March 29, 2009 the following; "Figures show that the financial wealth of Australians fell by almost 35 per cent--- the biggest annual fall on record. The Australia Bureau of Statistics show the average Australian lost 21000 dollars after wealth levels hit record heights just over a year earlier.

The net value of financial wealth held by the average Australian is just over 37500 dollars."

I need to congratulate the Australian for such a low level of stock and bond market investment. I believe that this fundamental character discrepancy has made them a brighter and more successful lot financially.

CHAPTER 36

THE MADOFF PONZI SCANDAL IN THE US

BACKGROUND

Bernard Madoff was a well known investment advisor in the US. He was former president of the NASDAQ and was a well regarded fund manager. That is, till his personal confession of fraud and resultant fallout from public grace. Madoff admitted to Judge Denny Chin, in a New York courtroom that he was involved in a giant Ponzi scheme of over 50 billion dollars. For those of you who do not know what a Ponzi scheme, it is an investment process where you take new money and pay back old money. New money refers to capital coming from new investors and old money is money paid to early subscribers. For example a fella like Madoff was known to promise astronomically higher guaranteed returns on a portfolio like, say 12 per cent. The promise of such a high return with no risk attached to a high profile respected fund manager, resulted in him attracting billions of dollars to his funds form right across the world. Suppose, in one year, this fund only realized a return of 2 percent instead of 12 per cent as promised--- Madoff would simply make up the 10 per cent difference from capital coming from new subscribers to his fund.

So, this massive investment exercise became a giant Ponzi scheme. New investors were financing underperformance in the portfolios of older investors, when the market did not do well. This was basically a deck of cards and had to come down sometime. The financial crisis undid this massive illegal empire since Madoff ran out of money to pay his older investors. Although no one knows what triggered his admission of fraud to the FBI, I would suspect that falling returns on his fund portfolios accompanied with demands from investors to return their money accompanied with a tremendous shortage of capital liquidity all triggered his admissions, which should have come years back but did not because he was in a fairly comfortable financial position as he was successfully robbing Paul to pay Peter.

The following is an admitted list of some very intelligent people he duped. A report by Morningstar and Reuters services on January 13/2009 provided an initial list of investors defrauded by various investment schemes by Madoff.

On the next page is a statement of criminal charges levied against Bernard Madoff.

David Voreacos in a path breaking report in Bloomberg reported on March 11/2009 the following news:

"March 11 (Bloomberg) -- Bernard Madoff was charged March 10 in federal court in Manhattan with 11 counts related to the largest Ponzi scheme in U.S. history. Prosecutors detailed the charges in a 25-page criminal information.

Below is a summary of each count:

Count 1, Securities Fraud: Bernard L. Madoff Investment Securities Inc. (BLMIS) was a broker-dealer with three types of business: market making; proprietary trading; and investment advisory services. Madoff Securities International Ltd. (MSIL) was a U.K. affiliate engaged in proprietary trading.

From the 1980s through Dec. 11, 2008, Madoff ran a "massive Ponzi scheme" as he used false pretenses to solicit billions of dollars of funds. On Dec. 1, 2008, BLMIS issued statements to 4,800 account holders showing they had total balances of $64.8 billion. The firm held "a small fraction" of that balance.

Madoff took money from individuals, charities, trusts, pension funds and hedge funds. He failed to invest funds as promised and converted them to his own use. He falsely promised to achieve high rates of return, including as much as 46 percent, with limited risk.

He falsely represented his "split strike conversion" investment strategy, saying he put money in a basket of stocks that would mimic price movements of the Standard & Poor's 100 Index, invest intermittently in government-issued securities, and buy and sell option contracts in stocks.

Madoff created a "broad infrastructure" at BLMIS to give the impression he ran "a legitimate investment advisory business in which client funds were actively traded as he had promised." He hired many back office employees who weren't qualified. He directed workers to generate false client account statements and trade confirmations that reflected fictitious returns and purportedly showed the firm bought and sold securities.

Madoff directed the transfer of $250 million from investment advisory clients' funds to his market making and proprietary trading businesses. Those transfers, through his London business, gave the false appearance that he was conducting transactions in Europe on behalf of investors.

Madoff repeatedly lied to the Securities and Exchange Commission in written submissions and sworn testimony. He caused the creation of false financial statements about the business.

Count 2, Investment Adviser Fraud: From at least the 1980s through Dec. 11, 2008, Madoff acted as an investment adviser for clients of BLMIS and employed devices and schemes to defraud clients and prospective clients.

Count 3, Mail Fraud: On Dec. 1, 2008, Madoff caused to be sent via the U.S. Postal Service a false and fraudulent account statement from BLMIS to a client in New York.

Count 4, Wire Fraud: On Aug. 5, 2008, as a part of a scheme to defraud, Madoff caused $2 million in investor funds to be wired from Bloomington, Minn., to New York.

Count 5, International Money Laundering to Promote Specified Unlawful Activity: From 2002 to December 2008, Madoff caused the transfer of funds from the BLMIS investor account in New York to MSIL accounts in London, and from those accounts to BLMIS accounts in New York. The money was derived from fraud in the sale of securities and theft from an employee benefit plan.

Count 6, International Money Laundering to Promote Specified Unlawful Activity: From 2006 to December 2008, Madoff caused the transfer of funds from BLMIS investor accounts in New York to MSIL accounts in London, then back to New York to give the false appearance that he was operating a legitimate investment advisory business. From 2002 to December 2008, he caused funds to be transferred from BLMIS accounts in New York to MSIL accounts in London, and from there to "purchase and maintain property and services for the personal use and benefit of Madoff, his family members and associates." The money was derived from fraud in the sale of securities and theft from an employee benefit plan.

Count 7, Money Laundering: On April 13, 2007, Madoff caused $54.5 million to be transferred from a BLMIS investor account in New York to a BLMIS account in London. The money was derived from fraud in the sale of securities and theft from an employee benefit plan.

Count 8, False Statements: On Jan. 7, 2008, Madoff caused the filing with the SEC of a Uniform Application for Investment Adviser Registration. The form falsely stated that BLMIS had custody of advisory clients' securities.

Count 9, Perjury: On May 19, 2006, Madoff made "numerous false and misleading statements" under oath to the SEC. He falsely testified that his firm executed stock and options trades on behalf of investment advisory clients; had custody of assets managed on behalf of those clients; and used the same trading strategy for all its investment advisory clients.

Count 10, False Filing With the SEC: On Dec. 20, 2007, Madoff caused the filing of a false and misleading certified BLMIS audit report.

Count 11, Theft From an Employee Benefit Plan: On Sept. 24, 2008, Madoff stole $10 million in pension fund assets sent to BLMIS by a master trust on behalf of about 35 labor union pension plans.

The criminal case is U.S. v. Madoff, 08-cr-00213, U.S. District Court for the Southern District of New York (Manhattan).

CURRENT DEVELOPMENTS

Madoff has pleaded guilty to most charges and is in jail, pending sentencing by the judge in June 2009. Several unresolved issues are:

1. Trying to find the money which was supposed to be in client accounts but have been found not to exist. Phony statements of investment were being made by his office to lure people into a false sense of security. Only about 1 billion dollars has been found as of April 1.2009 by the trustee in bankruptcy.

2. The involvement of any office staff and or advisors in supporting this Ponzi scheme. The jury on this is not out as of April 1,2009. It seems hard to believe that one man all on his own could organize, implement and manage such a huge 65 billion dollar scandal.

3. The money which is in Mrs. Madoff's account. Mrs. Madoff's legal position is that the money belongs to her and has nothing to do with her husband's illegal investment operations. Again this situation is not yet resolved.

BIGGER ISSUES

The really big issue is how, in such a powerful and technologically advanced country like the United States, one man could commit without detection, such a big fraud. This Ponzi scheme, as now known to all, was being conducted successfully, yet deceitfully for several years. Where were the government appointed financial watchdogs like the SEC? There were some complaints against Madoff earlier at the SEC but they were resolved without deeper investigation into Madoff's investment activities. Presumably, the SEC was sleeping in its watch. And how could Madoff type false statements indicating money was invested or assign arbitrary returns to it, without actually having money located where it was supposed to be? And no one in this whole wide world, including the smart investors from Asia and Europe detected this scandal early on?

The whole case is a mess. But it also indicates the unhealthy state of affairs in financial regulation both in the US and across the world as Madoff worked in numerous international and offshore jurisdictions. Unless there is a massive and urgent change in financial regulation there will be very little public and investor confidence in any investment schemes in the future.

And without public confidence, no one will buy anything and the banks will not lend. This will exacerbate the financial crisis and cause more hurt in every economy in the world. Strong international cooperation and tough domestic regulation is the only way to solve problems like the Madoff scandal and prevent their re-occurrence in the future.

CHAPTER 36

THE STANFORD SCANDAL

BACKGROUND

The Stanford Financial Group was a privately held international group of financial services companies, controlled by Allen Stanford, until it was seized by US authorities in early 2009. Headquartered in the Galleria 11 in Houston, Texas, it had 50 offices in several countries and claimed to manage around US 8.5 billion dollars for more than 30,000 clients in 136 countries on six continents. On February 17,2009 US Federal agents put the company under management of a receiver, because of charges of fraud. On February 27,2009 the US Securities and Exchange Commission amended its complaint to describe the alleged fraud as a " massive Ponzi scheme."
Allan Stanford traced his company to the insurance company founded in 1932 in Mexia,Texas by his grandfather, Lodis B. Stanford. Allen Stanford started his banking business in the 1980's in Montserrat---- he moved into banking by utilization of funds he had made in real estate in Houston in the 1980's.

Stanford Financial Company comprised several affiliate companies:

1. Stanford Capital Management, investment adviser, based in Houston, Texas.
2. Stanford Group Company, broker-dealer, based in Houston.
3. Stanford International Bank, which was started in 1986 in Montserrat where it was called Guardian International Bank. Stanford then relocated its operations to Antigua.
4. Stanford Trust Company, which is in the wealth management and administration business.
5. Bank of Antigua

CNN reported some of the charges brought against Stanford through a news article on March 11/2009. Here is part of the news article: "The U.S. Securities and Exchange Commission has charged Stanford, two of his top aides and three of his companies with operating a long running fraud involving high-yield certificates of deposit. He is also accused of misappropriating $1.6 billion in investor funds."

In a Bloomberg news release on February 19/2009, veteran reporter Alexis Leondis reported the following story, "The U.S. Securities and Exchange Commission said Feb. 17 that Stanford Group Co. Chairman R. Allen Stanford was running a "massive, ongoing fraud" while selling about $8 billion in certificates issued by the Antigua bank through his Houston-based firm.

229

Stanford International touted "improbable, if not impossible" returns earned on CD deposits, the SEC said in a civil complaint.

A Stanford International monthly report from December, which refers to more than 30,000 clients representing $8.5 billion in total assets, listed returns on 1 and 3-year CDs as 4.5 and 5.4 percent, respectively. E-mails sent to Bloomberg News yesterday by Stanford Group clients said the annual returns on 1, 3 and 5-year CDs ranged from 7 to 12 percent.

Rate Comparison

That compares with rates of 2.2 percent for a one-year CD and 2.7 percent for a 5-year CD, according to national overnight averages compiled by Bankrate.com. New York-based JPMorgan Chase & Co's 3-year CDs for retail investors pay 1.01 percent and New York-based Citigroup Inc.'s 3-year retail CDs offer an annual yield of 1.25 percent. "(end of news article).

News of this fraud had a ripple effect all across the world, including in Barbuda and Antigua and in Latin American and Mexico. Public depositors in his banks lined up to withdraw their savings from Stanford controlled banks and there was a panic put into motion.

RETALIATION BY EFFECTED COUNTRIES

It is reported that Venezuelan investors may have an exposure exceeding 3 billion dollars in various Stanford operations. Venezuela seized a bank in early 2009--- this local bank was owned and controlled by Stanford. In Panama, authorities have taken over a Stanford organization and similar actions have also occurred in Columbia and Ecuador.

A very serious problem exists in the banking system in the tiny nation of Antigua, a country which welcomed Stanford with open arms. Stanford was knighted here. He is the biggest employer here and also owns the largest newspaper here.

In a brilliant article on February 23/2009,at Bloomberg, reporter Thomas Black in Monterrey, Mexico had this story on actions taken by the government of Antigua and Barbuda. Here goes the story,

"R. Allen Stanford's Bank of Antigua has been seized, renamed and its shares divided among the island's government and five Caribbean lenders, the region's central bank president said today.

Antigua and Barbuda's government will be the largest shareholder, K. Dwight Venner, president of the Eastern Caribbean Central Bank, said in a recorded press conference in St. John's. The country of 75,000 will own 25 percent of Eastern Caribbean Amalgamated Financial Company Ltd., as the new lender is now called. The central bank is the monetary authority for eight island economies.

The five regional banks will each have a 15 percent stake, Venner said. The action effectively ends Stanford's ownership of the lender since 1990, according to Bank of Antigua's Web site.

"We were able to successfully avert a disaster and save the deposits and interests of the customers of the bank," said Antigua Finance Minister Errol Cort, according to the recording of the news conference.

The central bank seized Bank of Antigua after depositors lined up for hours last week to withdraw money. The U.S. Securities and Exchange Commission charged Stanford on Feb. 17 , 2009 with running an $8 billion fraud involving sales of certificates of deposit from Stanford International Bank Ltd., his offshore lender, which is also based in Antigua. That bank was seized and receivers appointed last week. Bank of Antigua wasn't named in the civil complaint.

A call to Brian Bertsch, a Stanford spokesman, reached a recording that referred all questions to the SEC.

$400 Million

Bank of Antigua had $400 million in deposits, about 80 percent from Antigua and Barbuda, Cort said. The central bank had the right to seize the institution under emergency powers granted it by a 1983 law, Venner said.

The five banks that together own a 75 percent stake in the bank are Antigua Commercial Bank Ltd.; Eastern Caribbean Financial Holdings Company Ltd. in St. Lucia; National Commercial Bank (SVG) Ltd. of St. Vincent and the Grenadines; National Bank of Dominica Ltd.; and St. Kitts-Nevis-Anguilla National Bank Ltd.

In a damaging article, calling for greater and proper regulation, two reporters, Jesse Westbrook and Ian Katz reported on February 18/2009 the following news. Here are the unedited news report,

"U.S. brokerage regulators fined R. Allen Stanford's firm more than a year ago for misleading investors while selling certificates of deposit, raising new questions about watchdogs already under scrutiny for missing Bernard Madoff's alleged $50 billion Ponzi scheme.

Stanford Group Co. was fined $10,000 by the Financial Industry Regulatory Authority in November 2007 for distributing marketing material that "failed to present fair and balanced treatment" of the risks associated with CDs.

The U.S. Securities and Exchange Commission yesterday filed a civil lawsuit calling the sales by the Houston-based firm a "massive, ongoing fraud."

"From what we know, the problem that led to the fine was a red flag," said Robert Hillman, a securities law professor at the University of California, Davis. "If you have a red flag of this nature, then you have to do something more than simply levy a fine and close the file."

The SEC accused Stanford of touting "improbable, if not impossible" returns for more than a decade on CDs issued by an affiliated bank in Antigua. The case follows congressional scrutiny of the SEC and Finra, which is funded by the brokerage industry, for missing Madoff's alleged scheme.

Finra spokeswoman Nancy Condon had no comment.

SEC Case

The SEC's case stems from an investigation opened in October 2006 after a routine inspection of Stanford Group, the New York Times reported today, citing Stephen Korotash, an associate enforcement director in the SEC's Fort Worth, Texas, office. The SEC "stood down" on its inquiry at the request of another federal agency that he declined to identify, the newspaper said. It resumed the investigation in December 2008.

He referred questions from Bloomberg News to the SEC's press office.

Agency spokesman John Nester said inquiries like the Stanford case involve a number of jurisdictional issues such as whether products being sold are securities and investigators' ability to access overseas records.

"We always cooperate with criminal authorities who have different techniques and tools at their disposal," he said. "And we are careful to make sure that civil investigations are conducted in a way so that they do not impede potential criminal actions."

'Reinvigorate' Enforcement

SEC Chairman Mary Schapiro last month said she would "reinvigorate" the agency's enforcement unit after it failed for more than a decade to detect that Madoff was paying off old investors with money raised from new ones. Schapiro was chief executive officer of Finra when the private regulator fined Stanford's firm in 2007.

Stanford Group had registered with the SEC as an investment adviser, making it subject to routine inspections. Finra had authority to examine Stanford because it was also registered as a brokerage firm.

Clients of Stanford Group were told their funds would be placed mainly in easily sellable financial instruments, monitored by more than 20 analysts and audited by Antiguan regulators, according to the SEC.

Instead, the "vast majority" of the portfolio was managed by Stanford himself and James Davis, the chief financial officer of the Antiguan subsidiary, the SEC said. A "substantial" portion of the portfolio may have been invested in assets such as private equity and real estate, according to the agency.

Whereabouts Unknown

The whereabouts of Stanford, 58, are unknown by U.S. regulators, according to Rose Romero, director of the SEC's Fort Worth office. Investigators are trying to account for the $8 billion in investor funds.

In its 2007 claim, Finra said Stanford Group failed to tell clients it had a potential conflict of interest because an affiliated bank based in Antigua was issuing the CDs. The same bank, Stanford International Bank Ltd., was named in the SEC's lawsuit.

Stanford Group Chief Compliance Officer Bernerd Young said in a letter to Finra that the company had revised its marketing material. He also said Finra and the SEC "conducted numerous examinations" of Stanford Group and its "solicitation" of Stanford International's CDs.

'Slap on Wrist'

"It goes to how deep" Finra looked, said Adam Pritchard, a former SEC lawyer who's now a professor at the University of Michigan Law School in Ann Arbor. "That $10,000 fine would be the archetypical slap on the wrist."

Probes of marketing material are often triggered by tips from consumers and competitors and are limited in scope, said Brian Rubin, a partner at Sutherland Asbill & Brennan LLP in Washington who was deputy chief counsel at NASD, a Finra predecessor. Examiners focus on the veracity of literature and don't broaden reviews unless they suspect further wrongdoing, he said.

"There's no reason that Finra would have dug deeper" unless there were Indications of misrepresentation related to returns or evidence of the fraud alleged by the SEC, Rubin said. "The fine is relatively low, which suggests that they were looking at a limited number of pieces" of literature.

Stanford Group clients have wrested at least $687,288 from the firm since 2003 in arbitration settlements related to transactions involving stocks, mutual funds and government securities, according to Finra records. Finra itself has fined Stanford Group at least $70,000. " (end of news article)

BIGGER ISSUES

Here we have the same big issues at fore: how can the US financial authorities regulate fraudulent business firms so poorly? Even when they knew there may be a potential problem a year back, they did nothing but slap a 10,000 US fine on Stanford's firm.

The other issue is how human greed gets the better of individuals and corporations. How could anyone invest in a Stanford CD without FDIC insurance? How could one ever place their money in a far way unregulated country like Antigua? There is only one motivating factor to this and that is human greed. Intelligent but greedy investors gave billions of dollars to Stanford, who in turn, invested the same money in private equity dealings and real estate, while making investors believing the money was safe and well invested. Public foolishness triggered by greed and reinforced by a billionaire's positive financial image caused this onslaught. And worse of all, no one knows how much money any investor will get back. Neither the government nor anyone except Stanford knows where this money is stashed away.

Poor government regulation, almost no international financial co-operation and strong public greed caused this collapse and loss in the Stanford financial empire. And worst of all, no one knows where Stanford is.

He is probably enjoying a beautiful cocktail with his girlfriend in some warm and inviting Caribbean beach while laughing at all the fools in the US regulatory body---- after all he is a confirmed citizen of Antigua, where he was knighted several years back. His name and reputation are destroyed in the US but his fortune is still with him. And the hard working investor who trusted him is left out in the cold. A little better regulation would have solved these great financial problems.

Financial regulation with international co-operation is the only solution to prevent such crises from reoccurring. The Madoff scandal and the Stanford Scandal are very similar cases, involving giant Ponzi schemes accompanied with laxity in financial regulation in the United States.

CHAPTER 38

INTERNATIONAL RETALIATORY MOVES TO CONTAIN CRISIS

This Chapter gives you a bird's eye view of the entire crisis since it erupted in 2007. The initial presentation involves a chronological account of all relevant events creating the global financial and credit crisis. We then explore international retaliatory moves to contain this crisis on a worldwide basis. Finally a special section is devoted to US Government initiatives in detail, in terms of how they reacted to control this crisis. This last section is particularly important given the fact that the US was the epicenter of the crisis--- any future world stabilization of financial and credit markets will be based on the success in the US in solving their domestic financial problems. The world is a vast network of relationships and unless stability is brought into the US, nothing will materially change worldwide.

A SHORT HISTORY OF THE CRISIS

The **global financial crisis of 2007-2009** emerged with the failure, merger, or <u>conservatorship</u> of several large United States-based financial firms and spread with the <u>insolvency</u> of additional companies, governments in Europe, recession, and declining stock market prices around the globe.

Development and Causation

The underlying causes leading to the crisis had been reported in business journals for many months before September 2008, with commentary about the financial stability of leading U.S. and European investment banks, insurance firms and mortgage banks consequent to the subprime mortgage crisis.[1][2][3][4]

Beginning with failures caused by misapplication of risk controls for bad debts, collateralization of debt insurance and fraud, large financial institutions in the United States and Europe faced a credit crisis and a slowdown in economic activity.[5][6] The impacts rapidly developed and spread into a global shock resulting in a number of European bank failures and declines in various stock indexes, and large reductions in the market value of equities[7] and commodities.[1] The credit crisis was exacerbated by Section 128 of the Emergency Economic Stabilization Act of 2008 which allowed the Federal Reserve to pay interest on excess reserve requirement balances held on deposit from banks, removing the incentive for banks to extend credit instead of placing cash on deposit with the Fed.[8][9][10][11][12][13][*dubious* - *discuss*] Moreover, the de-leveraging of financial institutions further accelerated the liquidity crisis, and a decrease in international trade.

241

World political leaders and national ministers of finance and central bank directors have coordinated their efforts[14] to reduce fears but the crisis is ongoing and continues to change, developing at the close of October, 2008 into a currency crisis with investors transferring vast capital resources into stronger currencies such as the yen, the dollar and the Swiss franc, leading many emergent economies to seek aid from the International Monetary Fund.[15][16]

The subprime mortgage crisis reached a critical stage during the first week of September 2008, characterized by severely contracted liquidity in the global credit markets[17] and insolvency threats to investment banks and other institutions.

Reserve balances from banks in the Federal Reserve System began increasing over required levels of about $10 billion at the beginning of September 2008, just after the Democratic and Republican national conventions, and just before the stock market crash and presidential debates. Beginning October 6, Section 128 of the Emergency Economic Stabilization Act of 2008 allowed the Federal Reserve System to pay interest on the excess balances, producing further pressure on international credit markets. Excess on reserve balances topped $870 billion by the end of the second week of January 2009. In comparison, the increase in reserve balances reached only $65 billion after September 11, 2001 before falling back to normal levels within a month.

September 2008 happenings

Government takeover of home mortgage lenders

The United States director of the Federal Housing Finance Agency (FHFA), James B. Lockhart III, on September 7, 2008 announced his decision to place two United States Government sponsored enterprises (GSEs), Fannie Mae (Federal National Mortgage Association) and Freddie Mac (Federal Home Loan Mortgage Corporation), into conservatorship run by FHFA.[18][19][20] United States Treasury Secretary Henry Paulson, at the same press conference stated that placing the two GSEs into conservatorship was a decision he fully supported, and said that he advised "that conservatorship was the only form in which I would commit taxpayer money to the GSEs." He further said that "I attribute the need for today's action primarily to the inherent conflict and flawed business model embedded in the GSE structure, and to the ongoing housing correction."[18] The same day, Federal Reserve Bank Chairman Ben Bernanke stated in support: "I strongly endorse both the decision by FHFA Director Lockhart to place Fannie Mae and Freddie Mac into conservatorship and the actions taken by Treasury Secretary Paulson to ensure the financial soundness of those two companies."[21]

MAJOR FINANCIAL FAILURE

The collapse of <u>Lehman Brothers</u> was a symbol of the global financial crisis. On Sunday, September 14, 2008 it was announced that <u>Lehman Brothers</u> would file for bankruptcy after the Federal Reserve Bank declined to participate in creating a financial support facility for Lehman Brothers. The significance of the Lehman Brothers bankruptcy is disputed with some assigning it a pivotal role in the unfolding of subsequent events. The principals involved, Ben Bernanke and Henry Paulson, dispute this view, citing a volume of toxic assets at Lehman which made a rescue impossible.[22][23] Immediately following the bankruptcy, <u>JPMorgan Chase</u> provided the broker dealer unit of <u>Lehman Brothers</u> with $138 billion to "settle securities transactions with customers of Lehman and its clearance parties" according to a statement made in a New York City Bankruptcy court filing.[24]

The same day, the sale of <u>Merrill Lynch</u> to <u>Bank of America</u> was announced.[25] The beginning of the week was marked by extreme instability in global stock markets, with dramatic drops in market values on Monday, September 15, 2008 and Wednesday, September 17, 2008. On September 16, 2008 the large insurer <u>American International Group</u> (AIG), a significant participant in the <u>credit default swaps</u> markets, suffered a <u>liquidity</u> crisis following the downgrade of its credit rating.

The Federal Reserve, at AIG's request, and after AIG has shown that it could not find lenders willing to save it from insolvency, created a credit facility for up to US$85 billion in exchange for a 79.9% equity interest, and the right to suspend dividends to previously issued common and preferred stock.[26]

Money market funds insurance and short sales prohibitions

On September 16, 2008 the Reserve Primary Fund, a large money market mutual fund, lowered its share price below $1 because of exposure to Lehman debt securities. This resulted in demands from investors to return their funds as the financial crisis mounted.[27] By the morning of September 18, 2008 money market sell orders from institutional investors totaled $0.5 trillion, out of a total market capitalization of $4 trillion, but a $105 billion liquidity injection from the Federal Reserve averted an immediate collapse.[28][29] On September 19, 2008 the U.S. Treasury offered temporary insurance (akin to FDIC insurance of bank accounts) to money market funds.[30] Toward the end of the week, short selling of financial stocks was suspended by the Financial Services Authority in the United Kingdom and by the Securities and Exchange Commission in the United States.[31] Similar measures were taken by authorities in other countries.[32] Some restoration of market confidence occurred with the publicity surrounding efforts of the Treasury and the Securities Exchange Commission[33][34]

245

Section 128

Speculation that the <u>Emergency Economic Stabilization Act of 2008</u> would accelerate the effective date of the Financial Services Regulatory Relief Act of 2006 from October 1, 2011 to October 1, 2008 may have precipitated this fall.[citation needed] By September 17, dramatic increases began in deposits with the Fed. [35] Section 128 was signed into law on October 3 effectively ending the commercial paper market.[citation needed]

US Troubled Asset Relief Program(TARP Program)

On September 19, 2008 a plan intended to ameliorate the difficulties caused by the <u>subprime mortgage crisis</u> was proposed by the Secretary of the Treasury, <u>Henry Paulson</u>. He proposed a <u>Troubled Assets Relief Program</u> (TARP), later incorporated into the <u>Emergency Economic Stabilization Act</u>, which would permit the United States government to purchase <u>illiquid</u> assets, informally termed *toxic assets*, from financial institutions.[36][37] The value of the securities is extremely difficult to determine.[38]

Consultations between the <u>Secretary of the Treasury</u>, the <u>Chairman of the Federal Reserve</u>, and the Chairman of the <u>U.S. Securities and Exchange Commission</u>, Congressional leaders and the <u>President of the United States</u> moved forward plans to advance a comprehensive solution to the problems created by illiquid mortgage-backed securities.

At the close of the week, the Secretary of the Treasury and President Bush announced a proposal for the federal government to buy up to US$700 billion of illiquid mortgage backed securities with the intent to increase the liquidity of the secondary mortgage markets and reduce potential losses encountered by financial institutions owning the securities. The draft proposal of the plan was received favorably by investors in the stock market. Details of the bailout remained to be acted upon by Congress.[39][40][41][42]

Week of September 21,2008

On Sunday, September 21, the two remaining investment banks, Goldman Sachs and Morgan Stanley, with the approval of the Federal Reserve, converted to bank holding companies, a status subject to more regulation, but with readier access to capital.[43] On September 21, Treasury Secretary Henry Paulson announced that the original proposal, which would have excluded foreign banks, had been widened to include foreign financial institutions with a presence in the US. The US administration was pressuring other countries to set up similar bailout plans.[44]

On Monday and Tuesday during the week of September 22, 2008 appearances were made by the Secretary of the Treasury and the Chairman of the Board of Governors of the Federal Reserve before Congressional committees and on Wednesday a prime-time presidential address was delivered by the President of the United States on television. Behind the scenes, negotiations were held refining the proposal which had grown to 42 pages from its original 3 and was reported to include both an oversight structure and limitations on executive salaries, with other provisions under consideration.

On September 25, 2008 agreement was reported by congressional leaders on the basics of the package;[45] however, general and vocal opposition to the proposal was voiced by the public.[46] On Thursday afternoon at a White House meeting attended by congressional leaders and the presidential candidates, John McCain and Barack Obama, it became clear that there was no congressional consensus, with Republican representatives and the ranking member of the Senate Banking Committee, Richard C. Shelby, strongly opposing the proposal.[47] The alternative advanced by conservative House Republicans was to create a system of mortgage insurance funded by fees on those holding mortgages; as the working week ended, negotiations continued on the plan, which had grown to 102 pages and included mortgage insurance as an option.[48][49][50]

On Thursday evening Washington Mutual, the nation's largest savings and loan, was seized by the Federal Deposit Insurance Corporation and most of its assets transferred to JPMorgan Chase.[51] Wachovia, one of the largest US banks, was reported to be in negotiations with Citigroup and other financial institutions.[52]

Week of September 28, 2008

Early Sunday morning an announcement was made by the United States Secretary of the Treasury and congressional leaders that agreement had been reached on all major issues: the total amount of $700 billion remained with provision for the option of creating a scheme of mortgage insurance.[53]

It was reported on Sunday, September 28, that a rescue plan had been crafted for the British mortgage lender Bradford & Bingley.[54] Grupo Santander, the largest bank in Spain, was slated to take over the offices and savings accounts while the mortgage and loans business would be nationalized.[55]

Fortis, a huge Benelux banking and finance company was partially nationalized on September 28, 2008, with Belgium, the Netherlands and Luxembourg investing a total of €11.2 billion (US$16.3 billion) in the bank. Belgium will purchase 49% of Fortis's Belgian division, with the Netherlands doing the same for the Dutch division.

Luxembourg has agreed to a loan convertible into a 49% share of Fortis's Luxembourg division.[56]

It was reported on Monday morning, September 29, 2008 that Wachovia, the 4th largest bank in the United States, would be acquired by Citigroup.[57][58]

On Monday the German finance minister announced a rescue of Hypo Real Estate, a Munich-based holding company comprising a number of real estate financing banks, but the deal collapsed on Saturday, October 4, 2008.

The same day the government of Iceland nationalized Glitnir, Iceland's third largest lender.[59][60]

Stocks fell dramatically Monday in Europe and the US despite infusion of funds into the market for short term credit.[61][62] In the US the Dow dropped 777 points (6.98%), the largest one-day point-drop in history (but only the 17th largest percentage drop).[63]

The U.S. bailout plan, now named the Emergency Economic Stabilization Act of 2008 and expanded to 110 pages was slated for consideration in the House of Representatives on Monday, September 29 as HR 3997 and in the Senate later in the week.[64][65] The plan failed after the vote being held open for 40 minutes in the House of Representatives, 205 for the plan, 228 against.[66][67] Meanwhile US stock markets suffered steep declines, the Dow losing 300 points in a matter of minutes, ending down 777.68, the Nasdaq losing 199.61, falling below the 2000 point mark, and the S.&P 500 off 8.77% for the day.[68] By the end of the day, the Dow suffered the largest drop in the history of the index.[69]

The S&P 500 Banking Index fell 14% on September 29 with drops in the stock value of a number of US banks generally considered sound, including Bank of New York Mellon, State Street and Northern Trust; three Ohio banks, National City, Fifth Third, and KeyBank were down dramatically.[70][71]

On Tuesday, September 30, 2008 stocks rebounded but credit markets remained tight with the London Interbank Offered Rate (overnight dollar Libor) rising 4.7% to 6.88%.[72] 9 billion USD was made available by the French, Belgian and Luxembourg governments to the French–Belgian bank Dexia.[73]

After Irish banks came under pressure on Monday, September 29, the Irish government undertook a two year "guarantee arrangement to safeguard all deposits (retail, commercial, institutional and inter-bank), covered bonds, senior debt and dated subordinated debt (lower tier II)" of 6 Irish banks: Allied Irish Banks, Bank of Ireland, Anglo Irish Bank, Irish Life and Permanent, Irish Nationwide and the EBS Building Society; the potential liability involved is about 400 billion dollars.[74]

Key risk indicators in September,2008

The TED spread - an indicator of credit risk - increased dramatically during September 2008.

Key risk indicators became highly volatile during September 2008, a factor leading the U.S. government to pass the Emergency Economic Stabilization Act of 2008. The "TED spread" is a measure of credit risk for inter-bank lending. It is the difference between: 1) the risk-free three-month U.S. treasury bill rate; and 2) the three-month London Interbank Offered Rate (LIBOR), which represents the rate at which banks typically lend to each other.

A higher spread indicates banks perceive each other as riskier counterparties. The t-bill is considered "risk-free" because the full faith and credit of the U.S. government is behind it; theoretically, the government could just print money so that the principal is fully repaid at maturity. The TED spread reached record levels in late September 2008. The diagram indicates that the Treasury yield movement was a more significant driver than the changes in LIBOR.

A three month t-bill yield so close to zero means that people are willing to forgo interest just to keep their money (principal) safe for three months - a very high level of risk aversion and indicative of tight lending conditions. Driving this change were investors shifting funds from money market funds (generally considered nearly risk free but paying a slightly higher rate of return than t-bills) and other investment types to t-bills.[75]

These issues are consistent with the September 2008 aspects of the underlined subprime mortgage crisis which prompted the Emergency Economic Stabilization Act of 2008 signed into law by the U.S. President on October 2, 2008. In addition, an increase in LIBOR means that financial instruments with variable interest terms are increasingly expensive. For example, car loans and credit card interest rates are often tied to LIBOR; some estimate as much as $150 trillion in loans and derivatives are tied to LIBOR.[76] Furthermore, the basis swap between one-month LIBOR and three-month LIBOR increased from 30 basis points in the beginning of September to a high of over 100 basis points. Financial institutions with liability exposure to 1 month LIBOR but funding from 3 month LIBOR faced increased funding costs. "Durvexity" spiked as markets rapidly deteriorated.] Overall, higher interest rates place additional downward pressure on consumption, increasing the risk of recession.

Reports of economic activity

On December 1, 2008   the National Bureau of Economic Research officially declared that the U.S. economy had entered recession in December 2007, a full year earlier.[77] The Labor Department said that the US lost 533,000 jobs in November 2008, the biggest monthly loss since 1974. This raised the unemployment rate from 6.5% to 6.7%.

On December 9, 2008, the Bank of Canada lowered its key interest rate by 0.75% to 1.5%, the lowest it had been since 1958; at the same time the Bank officially announced that Canada's economy was in recession.[78] This move came after the news that Canada lost 70,600 jobs in the month of November, the most since 1982.[79] The official Bank of Canada press release stated that "[the] outlook for the world economy has deteriorated significantly and the global recession will be broader and deeper than previously anticipated."[80]

On December 11, 2008, the FBI announces the arrest of Bernard Madoff in a Ponzi scheme which totals $50 billion by Madoff's own estimate, and which is soon found to affect banks, individuals, and charities in the U.S. and Europe. [81]

Events

After 5 positive days, on December 1 the S&P 500 fell 80 points to 816, down 9%. Financial stocks in the S&P 500 fell 17%. The Dow Jones Industrial Average closed at 8149 with a drop of 679 points 7.7% down. Oil fell below $50 a barrel in New York Trading.[82] The General Accounting Office released a report that claims that the Oversight of the Troubled Assets Relief Program requires additional actions to ensure "integrity, accountability, and transparency". (*Washington Post*) (bloomberg.com) (*Wall Street Journal*) (CNN Money)

On December 22, US industry leaders asked the Federal Reserve for assistance un-freezing the commercial real estate market, which has not securitized any loans in the last six months of 2008.[83]

Blue Monday 2009 Crash

On the evening of January 18, 2009, the Danish Parliament agreed to a financial package worth 100 billion Danish krone (17.6 billion USD).[84]. In response, markets panicked yet again. On January 22, the editorial board of *The Christian Science Monitor* wrote that the four largest U.S. banks "have lost half of their value since January 2."[85]

The two month period from January 1-February 27, 2009 represented the worst start to a year in the history of the S&P 500 with a drop in value of 18.62%. By March 2, 2009 the Dow Jones Industrial Average Index had dropped more than 50% from its summer 2008 peak.[86] The decline has been compared to that of the 1929 Great Depression, which was 53% between September 1929 and March 1931. [87]

On March 6, 2009 the Bank of England announced up to 150 billion pounds of quantitative easing, increasing the risk of inflation.[88] In March 2009, Blackstone Group CEO Stephen Schwarzman said that up to 45% of global wealth had been destroyed by the global financial crisis.[89]

By March 9, 2009, the Dow had fallen to 6440, a percentage decline exceeding the pace of the market's fall during the Great Depression and a level which the index had last seen in 1996. On March 10, 2009, a countertrend Bear Market Rally began, taking the Dow up to 7900 by March 26, 2009. Financial stocks were up more than 60% during this rally.

GLOBAL RESPONSES TO FINANCIAL & CREDIT CRISIS

Asia-Pacific Response

On September 15, 2008 China cut its interest rate for the first time since 2002. Indonesia reduced its overnight repo rate, at which commercial banks can borrow overnight funds from the central bank, by two percentage points to 10.25 percent. The Reserve Bank of Australia injected nearly $1.5 billion into the banking system, nearly three times as much as the market's estimated requirement.

The Reserve Bank of India added almost $1.32 billion, through a refinance operation, its biggest in at least a month.[90] On November 9, 2008 the 2008 Chinese economic stimulus plan is a RMB¥ 4 trillion ($586 billion) stimulus package announced by the central government of the People's Republic of China in its biggest move to stop the global financial crisis from hitting the world's third largest economy.

A statement on the government's website said the State Council had approved a plan to invest 4 trillion Yuan ($586 billion) in infrastructure and social welfare by the end of 2010. The stimulus package will be invested in key areas such as housing, rural infrastructure, transportation, health and education, environment, industry, disaster rebuilding, income-building, tax cuts, and finance.

China's export driven economy is starting to feel the impact of the economic slowdown in the United States and Europe, and the government has already cut key interest rates three times in less than two months in a bid to spur economic expansion. On the 28th of November, China Ministry of Finance and the State Administration of Taxation jointly announced a rise in export tax rebate rates on some labor-intensive goods. These additional tax rebates will take place on December 1, 2008.[91]

The stimulus package was welcomed by world leaders and analysts as larger than expected and a sign that by boosting its own economy, China is helping to stabilize the global economy. News of the announcement of the stimulus package sent markets up across the world. However, Marc Faber on January 16, 2009 said that China, according to him was in recession.

In Taiwan, the central bank on September 16, 2008 said it would cut its required reserve ratios for the first time in eight years. The central bank added $3.59 billion into the foreign-currency interbank market the same day.

257

Bank of Japan pumped $29.3 billion into the financial system on September 17, 2008 and the Reserve Bank of Australia added $3.45 billion the same day.[92]

United States Response

The Federal Reserve, Treasury, and Securities and Exchange Commission took several steps on September 19, 2008, to intervene in the crisis. To stop the potential run on money market mutual funds, the Treasury also announced on September 19 a new $50 billion program to insure the investments, similar to the Federal Deposit Insurance Corporation (FDIC) program.[75] Part of the announcements included temporary exceptions to section 23A and 23B (Regulation W), allowing financial groups to more easily share funds within their group.

The exceptions would expire on January 30, 2009, unless extended by the Federal Reserve Board.[93] The Securities and Exchange Commission announced termination of short-selling of 799 financial stocks, as well as action against naked short selling, as part of its reaction to the mortgage crisis.[94]

Market volatility within 401(k) and retirement plans in the United States

The Pension Protection Act of 2006 included a provision which changed the definition of Qualified Default Investments (QDI) for retirement plans from stable value investments, money market funds, and cash investments to investments which expose an individual to appropriate levels of stock and bond risk based on the years left to retirement. The Act required that Plan Sponsors move the assets of individuals who had never actively elected their investments and had their contributions in the default investment option. This meant that individuals who had defaulted into a cash fund with little fluctuation or growth would soon have their account balances moved to much more aggressive investments.

Starting in early 2008, most employer sponsored plans sent notices to their employees informing them that the Plan default investment was changing from a cash/stable option to something new, like a Retirement Date fund which had significant market exposure.

Most participants ignored these notices until September and October, when the market crash was on every news station and media outlet. It was then that participants called their 401(k) and retirement plan providers and discovered losses in excess of 30% in some cases.

Call centers for 401(k) providers experienced record call volume and wait times, as millions of inexperienced investors struggled to understand how their investments had been changed so fundamentally without their explicit consent, and reacted in a panic by liquidating everything with any stock or bond exposure, locking in huge losses in their accounts.

Due to the speculation and uncertainty in the market, discussion forums filled with questions about whether or not to liquidate assets[95] and financial gurus were swamped with questions about the right steps to take to protect what remained of their retirement accounts. During the third quarter of 2008, over $72 billion left mutual fund investments that invested in stocks or bonds and rushed into Stable Value investments in the month of October.[96] Against the advice of financial experts, and ignoring historical data illustrating that long-term balanced investing has produced positive returns in all types of markets, [97] investors with decades to retirement instead sold their holdings during one of the largest drops in stock market history.

During the week ending September 19, 2008, money market mutual funds had begun to experience significant withdrawals of funds by investors. This created a significant risk because money market funds are integral to the ongoing financing of corporations of all types.

Individual investors lend money to money market funds, which then provide the funds to corporations in exchange for corporate short-term securities called asset-backed commercial paper (ABCP). However, a potential bank run had begun on certain money market funds. If this situation had worsened, the ability of major corporations to secure needed short-term financing through ABCP issuance would have been significantly affected. To assist with liquidity throughout the system, the Treasury and Federal Reserve Bank announced that banks could obtain funds via the Federal Reserve's Discount Window using ABCP as collateral.[75][98]

FEDERAL RESERVE OF THE US LOWERS INTEREST RATES CHANGES (data after January 1, 2008)					
Date	Discount rate	Discount rate	Discount rate	Fed funds	Fed funds rate
		Primary	Secondary		
	rate change	new interest rate	new interest rate	rate change	new interest rate
Oct 8, 2008*	-.50%	1.75%	2.25%	-.50%	1.50%
Apr 30, 2008	-.25%	2.25%	2.75%	-.25%	2.00%
Mar 18, 2008	-.75%	2.50%	3.00%	-.75%	2.25%
Mar 16, 2008	-.25%	3.25%	3.75%		
Jan 30, 2008	-.50%	3.50%	4.00%	-.50%	3.00%
Jan 22, 2008	-.75%	4.00%	4.50%	-.75%	3.50%

– * Part of a coordinated global rate cut of 50 basis point by main central banks.[99]–

See more detailed US federal discount rate chart:[100]

Legislation

The Secretary of the United States Treasury, Henry Paulson and President George W. Bush proposed legislation for the government to purchase up to US$700 billion of "troubled mortgage-related assets" from financial firms in hopes of improving confidence in the mortgage-backed securities markets and the financial firms participating in it.[101] Discussion, hearings and meetings among legislative leaders and the administration later made clear that the proposal would undergo significant change before it could be approved by Congress.[102] On October 1, a revised compromise version was approved by the Senate with a 74-25 vote. The bill, HR1424 was passed by the House on October 3, 2008 and signed into law. The first half of the bailout money was primarily used to buy preferred stock in banks instead of troubled mortgage assets. [103]

Federal Reserve response

In an effort to increase available funds for commercial banks and lower the fed funds rate, on September 29, 2008 the U.S. Federal Reserve announced plans to double its Term Auction Facility to $300 billion.

Because there appeared to be a shortage of U.S. dollars in Europe at that time, the Federal Reserve also announced it would increase its swap facilities with foreign central banks from $290 billion to $620 billion.[104]

As of December 24, 2008, the Federal Reserve had used its independent authority to spend $1.2 trillion on purchasing various financial assets and making emergency loans to address the financial crisis, above and beyond the $700 billion authorized by Congress from the federal budget. This includes emergency loans to banks, credit card companies, and general businesses, temporary swaps of treasury bills for mortgage-backed securities, the sale of Bear Stearns, and the bailouts of American International Group (AIG), Fannie Mae and Freddie Mac, and Citigroup.[105]

European Union Response

The European Central Bank injected $99.8 billion in a one-day money-market auction. The Bank of England pumped in $36 billion. Altogether, central banks throughout the world added more than $200 billion from the beginning of the week to September 17.[92]

On September 29, 2008 the Belgian, Luxembourg and Dutch authorities partially nationalized Fortis. The German government bailed out Hypo Real Estate.

On 8 October 2008 the British Government announced a bank rescue package of around £500 billion[106] ($850 billion at the time). The plan comprises three parts. First, £200 billion will be made available to the banks in the Bank of England's Special Liquidity scheme.

Second, the Government will increase the banks' market capitalization, through the Bank Recapitalization Fund, with an initial £25 billion and another £25 billion to be provided if needed. Third, the Government will temporarily underwrite any eligible lending between British banks up to around £250 billion. In February 2009 Sir David Walker was appointed to lead a government inquiry into the corporate governance of banks.

In early December 2008, German Finance Minister Peer Steinbrück indicated that he does not believe in a "Great Rescue Plan" and indicated reluctance to spend more money addressing the crisis.[107] In March 2009, The European Union Presidency confirms that the EU is strongly resisting the US pressure to increase European budget deficits.[108]

Political effects and projections related to the economic crisis

Most political responses to the economic and financial crisis has been taken, as seen above, by individual nations. Some coordination took place at the European level, but the need to cooperate at the global level has led leaders to activate the G-20 major economies entity. A first summit dedicated to the crisis took place, at the Heads of state level in November 2008 (2008 G-20 Washington summit). The next one is planned for April 2nd 2009 in London.

At national levels, some localized social unrests and government premature changes attributed to the economic crisis have been noted. Also some medias and agencies have expressed fears that it would lead to general social and political instability.

Business Week in March 2009 stated that global political instability is rising fast due to the global financial crisis and is creating new challenges that need managing.[109] The Associated Press reported in March 2009 that: United States "Director of National Intelligence Dennis Blair has said the economic weakness could lead to political instability in many developing nations."[110] Even some developed countries are seeing political instability.[111] NPR reports that David Gordon, a former intelligence officer who now leads research at the Eurasia Group, said: "Many, if not most, of the big countries out there have room to accommodate economic downturns without having large-scale political instability if we're in a recession of normal length. If you're in a much longer-run downturn, then all bets are off."[112]

Forbes expresses concern saying "The recent wave of popular unrest was not confined to Eastern Europe. Ireland, Iceland, France, the U.K. and Greece also experienced street protests, but many Eastern European governments seem more vulnerable as they have limited policy options to address the crisis and little or no room for fiscal stimulus due to budgetary or financing constraints.

Deeply unpopular austerity measures, including slashed public wages, tax hikes and curbs on social spending will keep fanning public discontent in the Baltic states, Hungary and Romania. Dissatisfaction linked to the economic woes will be amplified in the countries where governments have been weakened by high-profile corruption and fraud scandals (Latvia, Lithuania, Hungary, Romania and Bulgaria)."[113]

In January 2009, the government leaders of Iceland were forced to call elections two years early after the people of Iceland staged mass protests and clashed with the police due to the government's handling of the economy.[111] Hundreds of thousands protested in France against President Sarkozy's economic policies.

Prompted by the financial crisis in Latvia, the opposition and trade unions there organized a rally against the cabinet of premier Ivars Godmanis. The rally gathered some 10-20 thousand people. In the evening the rally turned into a Riot.

The crowd moved to the building of the parliament and attempted to force their way into it, but were repelled by the state's police. In late February 2009, many Greeks took part in a massive general strike because of the economic situation and they shut down schools, airports, and many other services in Greece.

Police and protesters clashed in Lithuania where people protesting the economic conditions were shot by rubber bullets. In addition to various levels of unrest in Europe, Asian countries have also seen various degrees of protest.

Communists and others rallied in Moscow to protest the Russian government's economic plans. Protests have also occurred in China as demands from the west for exports have been dramatically reduced and unemployment has increased.

Beginning February 26, 2009 an Economic Intelligence Briefing was added to the daily intelligence briefings prepared for the President of the United States. This addition reflects the assessment of United States intelligence agencies that the global financial crisis presents a serious threat to international stability.[114]

References

1. ^ a b Evans-Pritchard, Ambrose (2007-07-25). "Dollar tumbles as huge credit crunch looms". Telegraph.co.uk (Telegraph Media Group Limited). http://www.telegraph.co.uk/money/main.jhtml?xml=/money/2007/07/25/cnusecon125.xml. Retrieved on 2008-10-15.

2. ^ *Torbat, Akbar E. (2008-10-13)*. "Global Financial Meltdown and the Demise of Neoliberalism". Global Research *(Center for Research on Globalization)*. http://www.globalresearch.ca/index.php?context=va&aid=10549. Retrieved on 2008-10-15. *"These happened in a matter of a few weeks in September, constituting the largest financial failure in the US since the great depression."*

3. ^ "Structural Cracks: Trouble ahead for global house prices". The Economist *(The Economist Newspaper Limited)*. *2008-05-22*. http://www.economist.com/finance/displaystory.cfm?story_id=11412394. Retrieved on 2008-10-15.

4. ^ "Tightrope artists: Managers of banks face a tricky balancing-act". The Economist *(The Economist Newspaper Limited)*. *2008-05-15*. http://www.economist.com/specialreports/displaystory.cfm?story_id=11325408. Retrieved on 2008-10-15.

5. ^ Bajaj, V. (November 20, 2008) "Stocks Are Hurt by Latest Fear: Declining Prices" *New York Times*

6. ^ *The Independent* (November 6, 2008) "Shipping: Holed beneath the waterline"

7. ^ *Norris, Floyd (2008-10-24)*. "United Panic". *The New York Times*. http://norris.blogs.nytimes.com/2008/10/24/united-panic. Retrieved on 2008-10-24.

269

8. ⋀ Federal Reserve Board of Governors (October 6, 2008) "Board announces that it will begin to pay interest on depository institutions required and excess reserve balance" *FRB press release*
9. ⋀ Crescenzi, T. (December 22, 2008) "Crescenzi: Banks Sitting on $1 Trillion Cash" *CNBC*
10. ⋀ Krell, E. (December 10, 2008) "What Is Wrong With TARP?" *Business Finance*
11. ⋀ Wilder, R. (December 10, 2008) "Why exactly does the Fed pay interest on reserves?" *RGE Monitor* (Roubini Global Economics, LLC)
12. ⋀ Lanman, S. (October 22, 2008) "Fed Raises Rate It Pays on Banks' Reserve Balances (Update2)" *Bloomberg*
13. ⋀ Federal Reserve Board of Governors (December 31, 2008) "Interest on Required Reserve Balances and Excess Balances" accessed January 5, 2008
14. ⋀ Central banks act to calm markets, *The Financial Times*, September 18, 2008
15. ⋀ *Landler, Mark (2008-10-23)*. "West Is in Talks on Credit to Aid Poorer Nations". *The New York Times*. http://www.nytimes.com/2008/10/24/business/worldbusiness/24emerge.html. Retrieved on 2008-10-24.
16. ⋀ *Fackler, Martin (2008-10-23)*. "Trouble Without Borders". *The New York Times*. http://www.nytimes.com/2008/10/24/business/worldbusiness/24won.html. Retrieved on 2008-10-24.
17. ⋀ Banks in Miser Mode

18. ^ *a b Paulson, Henry M., Jr.; (Press release statement) (2008-09-07).* "Statement by Secretary Henry M. Paulson, Jr. on Treasury and Federal Housing Finance Agency Action to Protect Financial Markets and Taxpayers". *United States Department of the Treasury.* http://www.treas.gov/press/releases/hp1129.htm. Retrieved on 2008-09-07.

19. ^ *Lockhart, James B., III (2008-09-07).* "Statement of FHFA Director James B. Lockhart". *Federal Housing Finance Agency.* http://www.ofheo.gov/newsroom.aspx?ID=456&q1=0&q2=0. Retrieved on 2008-09-07.

20. ^ "Fact Sheet: Questions and Answers on Conservatorship". *Federal Housing Finance Agency. 2008-09-07.* http://www.ofheo.gov/media/PDF/FHFACONSERVQA.pdf. Retrieved on 2008-09-07.

21. ^ *Bernanke, Ben S. (2008-09-007).* "Statement by Federal Reserve Board Chairman Ben S. Bernanke:". *Board of Governors of the Federal Reserve System.* http://www.federalreserve.gov/newsevents/press/other/20080907a.htm. Retrieved on 2008-09-10.

22. ^ *Grynbaum, Michael M. (2008-10-15).* "Bernanke Says Bailout Will Need Time to Work". *The New York Times.* http://www.nytimes.com/2008/10/16/business/economy/16bernanke.html. Retrieved on 2008-10-15.

271

23. ^ *Nocera, Joe; Edmund L. Andrews (2008-10-22).* "Struggling to Keep Up as the Crisis Raced On". *The New York Times.* http://www.nytimes.com/2008/10/23/business/ec onomy/23paulson.html. Retrieved on 2008-10-23.

24. ^ *Kary, Tiffany; Chris Scinta (2008-9-16).* "JPMorgan Gave Lehman $138 Billion After Bankruptcy". *Bloomberg.* http://www.bloomberg.com/apps/news?pid=2060 1087&sid=aX7mhYCHmVf8&refer=home. Retrieved on 2008-9-16.

25. ^ "Lehman Files for Bankruptcy; Merrill Is Sold" article by Andrew Ross Sorkin in *The New York Times September 14, 2008*

26. ^ See American International Group for details and citations.

27. ^ "Money Market Funds Enter a World of Risk" article by Tara Siegel Bernard in *The New York Times September 17, 2008*

28. ^ Gray, Michael. "Almost Armageddon: Markets Were 500 Trades from a Meltdown (September 21, 2008) New York Post

29. ^ House Representative Kanjorski about the $550 Billion "run on the banks" in two hours during September, 2008

30. ^ "Treasury Announces Guaranty Program for Money Market Funds" (September 19, 2008) Press Release. United States Department of the Treasury.

31. ^ "S.E.C. Issues Temporary Ban on Short-Selling" article by Vikas Bajaj and Jonathan D. Glater in *The New York Times* September 19, 2008

32. ^ "Australian short selling ban goes further than other bourses". *NBR. 2008-09-22.* http://www.nbr.co.nz/article/australian-short-selling-ban-goes-further-other-bourses-35494. Retrieved on 2008-09-22.

33. ^ "Stocks Surge as U.S. Acts to Shore Up Money Funds and Limits Short Selling" article by Graham Bowley in *The New York Times* September 19, 2008

34. ^ "Congressional Leaders Were Stunned by Warnings" article by David M. Herszenhorn in *The New York Times* September 19, 2008

35. ^ http://research.stlouisfed.org/fred2/data/WRESBAL.txt

36. ^ "Vast Bailout by U.S. Proposed in Bid to Stem Financial Crisis" article by Edmund L. Andrews in *The New York Times* September 18, 2008

37. ^ "Paulson Argues for Need to Buy Mortgages" article by David Stout in *The New York Times* September 19, 2008

38. ^ "Plan's Mystery: What's All This Stuff Worth?" article by Vikas Bajaj in *The New York Times* September 24, 2008

39. ^ "Bush Officials Urge Swift Action on Rescue Powers}" article by Edmund L. Andrews in *The New York Times* September 19, 2008

40. ^ Draft Proposal for Bailout Plan (September 21, 2008). *New York Times*

41. ^ "Rescue Plan Seeks $700 Billion to Buy Bad Mortgages" article by The Associated Press in *The New York Times* September 20, 2008

42. ^ "$700 Billion Is Sought for Wall Street in Vast Bailout" article by David M. Herszenhorn in *The New York Times* September 20, 2008

43. ^ "Shift for Goldman and Morgan Marks the End of an Era" article by Andrew Ross Sorkin and Vikas Bajaj in *The New York Times* September 21, 2008

44. ^ *Schwartz, Nelson D.; Carter Dougherty (2008-09-22).* "Foreign Banks Hope Bailout Will Be Global ". The New York Times. http://www.nytimes.com/2008/09/22/business/2 2global.html?hp.

45. ^ "Lawmakers Agree on Outline of Bailout" article by David M. Herszenhorn in *The New York Times* September 25, 2008

46. ^ "Lawmakers' Constituents Make Their Bailout Views Loud and Clear" article by Sheryl Gay Stolberg in *The New York Times* September 24, 2008

47. ^ "Talks Implode During Day of Chaos; Fate of Bailout Plan Remains Unresolved" article by David M. Herszenhorn, Carl Hulse, and Sheryl Gay Stolberg in *The New York Times* September 25, 2008

48. ^ "Conservatives Viewed Bailout Plan as Last Straw" article by Carl Hulse in *The New York Times* September 26, 2008

49. ^ "Politics Take Hold of Bailout Proposal" article by David M. Herszenhorn in *The New York Times September 26, 2008*

50. ^ "House Republicans Support a Plan That Would Insure Troubled Mortgages" article by Edmund L. Andrews in *The New York Times* September 26, 2008

51. ^ "Government Seizes WaMu and Sells Some Assets" article by Eric Dash and Andrew Ross Sorkin in *The New York Times*

52. ^ "Wachovia, Looking for Help, Turns to Citigroup" article by Ben White and Eric Dash in *The New York Times September 26, 2008*

53. ^ "Breakthrough Reached in Negotiations on Bailout" article by David M. Herszenhorn and Carl Hulse in *The New York Times* September 27, 2008

54. ^ "Britain Close to Takeover of Another Lender" article by Landon Thomas, Jr. in *The New York Times* September 28, 2008

55. ^ The Times. "Taxpayers must risk billions for Bradford & Bingley" article by Philip Webster, Patrick Hosking and Tim Reid in *The Times* September 29, 2008

56. ^ *van der Starre, Martijn; Meera Louis (2008-09-29).* "Fortis Gets EU11.2 Billion Rescue From Governments". *Bloomberg.* http://www.bloomberg.com/apps/news?pid=2060 1087&sid=ahlKDjeO0Lik&refer=home. Retrieved on 2008-09-29.

57. ^ *Sorkin, Andrew Ross (2008-09-30).* "Citigroup to Buy Wachovia Banking Operations". *The New York Times blog Dealbook.* http://dealbook.blogs.nytimes.com/2008/09/29/c itigroup-nears-a-deal-for-wachovia/index.html. Retrieved on 2008-09-29.

58. ^ *Sorkin, Andrew Ross; Eric Dash (2008-09-28).* "Citigroup and Wells Fargo Said to Be Bidding for Wachovia". *The New York Times.* http://www.nytimes.com/2008/09/29/business/2 9bank.html. Retrieved on 2008-09-29.

59. ^ Glitnir, *About Glitnir, News: 29.09.2008, The government of Iceland acquires 75 percent share in Glitnir Bank*

60. ^ Prime Minister's Office, *News and Articles: The Government of Iceland provides Glitnir with new equity (9/29/08)*

61. ^ *Hunter, Michael; Neil Dennis (2008-09-29).* "Heavy stock losses after Fed action". *The Financial Times.* http://www.ft.com/cms/s/0/d925b966- 8dec-11dd-8089-0000779fd18c.html. Retrieved on 2008-09-29.

62. ^ *Politi, James; Krishna Guha, Daniel Dombey and Harvey Morris (2008-09-29).* "Central banks pump cash into system". *The Financial Times.* http://www.ft.com/cms/s/0/f9525dd4-8d24-11dd-83d5-0000779fd18c.html. Retrieved on 2008-09-29.

63. ^ "U.S. stocks slide, Dow plunges 777 points, as bailout fails". MarketWatch. *2008-09-29.* http://www.marketwatch.com/news/story/us-stocks-slide-dow-plunges/story.aspx?guid={7F45BE2A-0486-494E-B87C-76D9F2688338}. Retrieved on 2008-09-29.

64. ^ Information from C-Span September 29, 2008

65. ^ *Hulse, Carl; David M. Herszenhorn (2008-09-28).* "Bailout Plan in Hand, House Braces for Tough Vote". *The New York Times.* http://www.nytimes.com/2008/09/29/business/29bailout.html. Retrieved on 2008-09-29.

66. ^ C-Span 2 PM 9/30/08

67. ^ *Hulse, Carl; David M. Herszenhorn (2008-09-29).* "House Rejects Bailout Package, 228-205, But New Vote Is Planned; Stocks Plunge". *The New York Times.* http://www.nytimes.com/2008/09/30/business/30bailout.html. Retrieved on 2008-09-29.

68. ^ *Grynbaum, Michael M. (2008-09-29).* "For Stocks, Worst Single-Day Drop in Two Decades". *The New York Times.* http://www.nytimes.com/2008/09/30/business/30markets.html. Retrieved on 2008-09-29.

69. ∧ *Twin, Alexandra (2008-09-29)*. "Stocks crushed".
CNN Money.
http://money.cnn.com/2008/09/29/markets/mark
ets_newyork/index.htm?postversion=2008092916.
Retrieved on 2008-09-29.

70. ∧ *Smith, Aaron (2008-09-29)*. "Wondering which
bank is next: Analysts brace for more bank failures
after Wachovia sells out banking assets to Citi;
bank stocks plunge after House rejects bailout
bill.". *CNN Money*.
http://money.cnn.com/2008/09/29/news/compan
ies/bank_failures/index.htm. Retrieved on 2008-
09-29.

71. ∧ *Dash, Eric (2008-09-29)*. "With Wachovia Sale,
the Banking Crisis Trickles Up". *The New York
Times*.
http://www.nytimes.com/2008/09/30/business/3
0citi.html. Retrieved on 2008-09-29.

72. ∧ *Guha, Krishna; Harvey Morris and James Politi in
Washington and Paul J Davies (2008-09-30)*.
"Banking's crisis of confidence deepens". *The
Financial Times*.
http://www.ft.com/cms/s/0/17ce4468-8f22-
11dd-946c-0000779fd18c.html. Retrieved on
2008-09-30.

73. ^ *Daneshkhu, Scheherazade; Ben Hall (2008-09-30).* "Dexia receives €6.4bn capital injection". *The Financial Times.* http://www.ft.com/cms/s/0/116457fe-8ebc-11dd-946c-0000779fd18c.html. Retrieved on 2008-09-30.

74. ^ "Government statement (of the Government of Ireland)". *The Irish Times. 2008-10-01.* http://www.irishtimes.com/newspaper/ireland/2008/1001/1222724598521.html. Retrieved on 2008-10-01.

75. ^ *a b c* Gullapalli, Diya and Anand, Shefali. "Bailout of Money Funds Seems to Stanch Outflow", The Wall Street Journal, September 20, 2008.

76. ^ Markewatch Article – LIBOR Jumps to Record

77. ^ *Grynbaum, Michael M.; David Jolly (2008-12-01).* "It's Official: Recession Started One Year Ago". *The New York Times.* http://www.nytimes.com/2008/12/02/business/02markets.html. Retrieved on 2008-12-01.

78. ^ [1][*dead link*]

79. ^ *Grant, Tavia (2008-12-09).* "Canadian job cuts looming". *Globe and Mail.* http://business.theglobeandmail.com/servlet/story/RTGAM.20081209.wmanpower1208/BNStory/Business/home. Retrieved on 2009-01-12.

279

80. ^ *Bank of Canada (2008-12-09). Bank of Canada lowers overnight rate 2008*. Press release. http://www.bankofcanada.ca/en/fixed-dates/2008/rate_091208.html. Retrieved on 2009-01-12.

81. ^ Continually updated list of banks, individuals, and charities which claim losses due to Madoff at *The New York Times* Retrieved January 24, 2009

82. ^ *Grynbaum, Michael M. (2008-12-01).* "Cheer Fades as Stocks Plunge 9%". *The New York Times.* http://www.nytimes.com/2008/12/02/business/02markets.html. Retrieved on 2008-12-01.

83. ^ Commercial Properties Seek Federal Bailout

84. ^ "Denmark agrees on 13.4-bln-euro line of credit to banks: govt". *France 24. 2009.* http://www.france24.com/en/20090118-denmark-agrees-134-bln-euro-line-credit-banks-govt-0. Retrieved on 2009-01-19.

85. ^ "Obama's First Crisis: Dud Banks", *The Christian Science Monitor* (January 22, 2009)

86. ^ Dow Down 50% Since Peak, Major Indices Approach New Lows, 27 Feb 2009, CNBC.com

87. ^ Steep Market Drops Highlight Despair Over Rescue Efforts

88. ^ BoE cuts rate to 0.5%, embraces 'quantitative easing'. Financial Post.

89. ^ 45 percent of world's wealth destroyed: Blackstone CEO. Reuters. March 10, 2009.

90. ^ "Asian central banks spend billions to prevent crash". *International Herald Tribune. 2008-09-16.* http://www.iht.com/articles/2008/09/16/business /cbanks.php. Retrieved on 2008-09-21.

91. ^ "Chinese pharmaceutical exporters to benefit from latest tax rebates increases". *Asia Manufacturing Pharma. 2008-12-01.* http://www.asia-manufacturing.com/news-232-chinesepharmaceutical-exporters-taxrebates-increases.html. Retrieved on 2008-12-01.

92. ^ *a b* "Germany Rescues Hypo Real Estate ". *Deutsche Welle. 2008-10-06.* http://www.dw-world.de/dw/article/0,2144,3692522,00.html.

93. ^ (Press Release) FRB: Board Approves Two Interim Final Rules, Federal Reserve Bank, September 19, 2008.

94. ^ Boak, Joshua (*Chicago Tribune*). "SEC temporarily suspends short selling", San Jose Mercury News, September 19, 2008.

95. ^ [2]. Tickerforum.com

96. ^ http://www.washingtonpost.com/wp-dyn/content/article/2008/12/25/AR20081225007 59.html

97. ^ http://www.washingtonpost.com/wp-dyn/content/article/2008/10/11/AR20081011001 77_2.html?sid=ST2008101102372&s_pos=

98. ^ Bull, Alister. "Fed says to make loans to aid money market funds", Reuters, September 19, 2008.

99. ∧ "BBC NEWS | Business | Central banks cut interest rates". *News.bbc.co.uk. Page last updated at 22:28 GMT, Wednesday, October 8, 2008 23:28 UK.* http://news.bbc.co.uk/2/hi/business/7658958.stm. Retrieved on 2008-10-19.

100.   ∧ "Historical Changes of the Target Federal Funds and Discount Rates - Federal Reserve Bank of New York". *Newyorkfed.org.* http://www.newyorkfed.org/markets/statistics/dly rates/fedrate.html. Retrieved on 2008-10-19.

101.   ∧ "Administration Is Seeking $700 Billion for Wall Street". *New York Times. 2008-09-20.* http://www.nytimes.com/2008/09/21/business/2 1cong.html?bl&ex=1222228800&en=007cf9e8faaa f52a&ei=5087%0A. Retrieved on 2008-09-25.

102.   ∧ House of Representatives Roll Call vote results. Library of Congress THOMAS website. Retrieved on September 29, 2008.

103.   ∧ "Common (Stock) Sense about Risk-Shifting and Bank Bailouts". *SSRN.com. December 29, 2009.* http://papers.ssrn.com/sol3/papers.cfm?abstract_i d=1321666. Retrieved on January 21, 2009.

104.   ∧ "Fed Pumps Huge Wads of Cash Into System- page 2 of 2 - TheStreet.com". *Thestreet.com.* http://www.thestreet.com/story/10439813/2/fed-pumps-huge-wads-of-cash-into-system.html. Retrieved on 2008-10-19.

105.   ∧ "Fed's spending is risky business".
Marketplace. 2008-12-22.
http://marketplace.publicradio.org/display/web/2
008/12/22/pm_shadow_bailout/. Retrieved on
2009-01-12.

106.   ∧ ""Gordon Brown should say 'sorry'"".
Telegraph.co.uk. 2009-03-09.
http://www.telegraph.co.uk/news/newstopics/polit
ics/gordon-brown/4961897/Gordon-Brown-
should-say-sorry-over-economy-minister-
says.html. Retrieved on 2009-03-09.

107.   ∧ ""It Doesn't Exist!"". *Newsweek.com.*
2008-12-06.
http://www.newsweek.com/id/172613. Retrieved
on 2008-12-15.

108.   ∧ EU resists deficits

109.   ∧ Business Week article "Economic Woes
Raising Global Political Risk" by Jack Ewing
published March 10, 2009

110.   ∧ The Associated Press article "Experts:
Financial crisis threatens US security" by STEPHEN
MANNING published March 11, 2009

111.   ∧ *a b* BBC

112.   ∧ NPR article "Economic Crisis Poses Threat
To Global Stability" by Tom Gjelten

A SPECIAL NOTE ON US GOVERNMENT INITIATIVES

Several positive moves happened in the U.S. Given the depth and breadth of the financial crisis, there was great panic in the US. American investors heard stories of friends and acquaintances who had so much trust in the banking system that they invested more than 100,000 dollars(the then FDIC limit on insurance on customer deposits) in a particular bank, only to find that any excess investment over 100,000 dollars was frozen and exhibited no chance of repayment. Stories were floating around the US media that if a client had, say, 250,000 dollars in a US bank that the additional 150000 dollars(over the 100000 dollars insured) was frozen and negotiations would ensue in terms of how much of that excess over 100000 dollars would be paid out to clients. Some banks were reported to say that maybe 50% of uninsured deposits would be paid out in due course of time. All of this talk and bad media gossip created a fundamental lack of trust and confidence in the US banking system.

To avoid multiple bank runs and to restore a sense of financial and banking stability the FDIC temporarily increased its insurance on individual deposits in banks from 100,000 dollars to 250,000 dollars.

This temporary increase in insurance was for a one year period, which would expire on December 31,2009 with a possibility for further continuation review.

This was a brilliant move on part of the FDIC short-term, to increase public confidence in the banking system.

284

However, long-term this created major financing problems because the FDIC in early 2009 realized they had inadequate reserves to fund any future bank failures and sent a bill to participating FDIC banks worth several billion dollars to bolster the fund to meet with any anticipated and unanticipated bank failures and the losses there from.

THE EMERGENCY ECONOMIC STABILIZATION ACT OF 2008

When the effects of the crisis were felt severely in the third quarter of 2008, emergency measures were instituted by the US Congress. The Emergency Economic Stabilization Act of 2008, commonly referred to as the " bailout" of the US financial system, was a law enacted in response to the global financial crisis starting in 2007. This Act authorized the United States Secretary of the Treasury to spend up to 700 billion dollars to purchase distressed assets, especially mortgage backed securities, and make capital injections into banks. The Act was proposed by Treasury Secretary Henry Paulson during the global financial crisis .
However, after much debate, Congress only approved the first tranche of funds to be used to buy preferred securities of banks and not as direct injections involving purchase of toxic mortgage assets. This, to me, is one of the biggest mistakes made by the US administration.
I suspect, this had a lot to do with President Bush's authority to veto any passed bill by both Houses and the Republican response to inject capital into banks without requiring any assurances to either them lending more money or purchase of mortgage toxic assets.

This laxity in investment and free money to the banks with no implicit or explicit requirements to lend resulted in billions of dollars just being added to their balance sheets. There was, most unfortunately, no improvement in either commercial lending or any other kind of lending after infusion and allotment of this public money into banks. Even the interbank lending market dried up. One bank could not trust another bank to lend money for a few days, since there was fear that the other bank would go under. This flawed bill created nothing. Instead in resulted in a full blown credit crisis. Enough said about free enterprise and the misplaced trust of Congress in greedy, unconscionable bankers.

INITIATIVES BY THE OBAMA ADMINISTRATION

President Obama stands out as one individual who has the honesty, character and integrity to make a positive change in America. Over and over again, the American people have endorsed his guts, character and vision.

The second tranche of the bailout money was under his control and he brought an entirely different financial vision to the country. He viewed solving the problems on several fronts and not just in bailing out banks.

He believed that banks needed to be bailed out because they were simply too big to fail and any consequent failure could disrupt the entire financial system and pose a systemic risk. And this is something no one wanted.

However, President Obama was not only interested in short-term results by solving the banking and credit crisis.

He was also interested in reducing US dependence on foreign oil, and also to develop and create new energy generation systems. He also believed that good education was a predominant indicator of US citizen successes in the international market place and strived to improve education systems in the US. Also he saw quite rightly that the US health care system was bleeding the people and proposed a wide ranging number of reforms to change the health care system and its delivery.

NEW STIMULUS PLAN

President Obama rightfully saw that the TARP bill would not be able to make the significant and deep changes in the US system. The country needed to upgrade its worker sills, control global warming, reduce dependence on foreign oil and revamp the entire health delivery system. All of these systems working in coordination would create a sustained push towards American superiority and winning in a highly competitive market place. In this sense, the President has a world vision and not a short-term vision like his predecessor, George Bush.

DETAILS OF NEW STIMULUS PLAN

In a brilliant exposition on its website, SFPartnership LLC, Chartered Accountants, International Tax Services Group, summarizes the new Obama Stimulus plan and its impact on Canadians.

The information is very valuable in understanding the range of initiatives announced by President Obama. Here is their web news release,

"On February 13, 2009, the United States Congress passed a $787 billion economic stimulus bill, which is being touted as the most sweeping economic package in decades. President Obama signed the bill into law February 17, 2009.

The following are highlights of some of the key provisions of the new law, officially titled "The American Recovery and Reinvestment Tax Act of 2009", that would affect individuals who reside in Canada and file a U. S. individual income tax return:

Making Work Pay Credit

Each US citizen and resident alien is entitled to a refundable tax credit for each of 2009 and 2010. The credit is the lesser of:

6.2 percent of a taxpayer's earned income, and

 $400 ($800 in the case of a joint return)

The credit is phased out at a rate of two percent of the eligible individual's modified adjusted gross income above US$75,000 ($150,000 in the case of a joint return). For these purposes, an eligible individual's modified adjusted gross income is the eligible individual's adjusted gross income increased by exclusions for:

- · Foreign earned income

- · Foreign housing

- · Income from U.S. possessions, and

- · Income from Puerto Rico

Thus, while nonresident aliens would not qualify for the credit, citizens, resident aliens ("green card" holders) living in Canada and non-citizen individuals required to file as resident individuals because they meet the substantial presence test would qualify for the credit

Child tax credit

Under present law, taxpayers who have one or more qualifying child may be entitled to a child tax credit of $1,000 per qualifying child through the tax year 2010 and $500 thereafter. The credit can be claimed by individuals who have one or more qualified children. The child must be a citizen or resident of the United States.

The credit is allowable against the regular tax and the alternative minimum tax (AMT) liability of the taxpayer. To the extent that that the child tax credit exceeds the liability, the taxpayer is eligible for a refundable credit (known as the "additional child tax credit") equal to the lesser of the unclaimed portion of the nonrefundable credit amount or 15% of the taxpayer's earned income in excess of a threshold dollar amount (the "earned income formula"). The threshold dollar amount is $12,550 for the year 2009, and is indexed for inflation.

The bill increases the additional child tax credit by reducing the threshold amount in the earned income formula to $3,000 for taxable years beginning in 2009 and 2010.

American Opportunity Tax Credit

Under current law, individual taxpayers may a claim a *nonrefundable* credit, the Hope scholarship credit, for qualified tuition and related expenses paid for the first two years of an eligible student's post secondary education in a degree or vocational training program. For 2008 and 2009, the credit amount per eligible student is 100% of the first $1,200 and 50% of the next $1,200 of qualified expenses.

The eligible student must be the taxpayer, the taxpayer's spouse, or a dependent.

The bill modifies the credit and renames it the American Opportunity Tax Credit for 2009 and 2010. The modified credit rate is 100 percent of the first $2,000 and 25% of the next $2,000 of qualified tuition and related expenses per eligible student. The modified credit is available with respect to the first four years of an eligible student's post-secondary education. The modified credit would be phased out for taxpayers with modified adjusted gross income between $160,000 and $180,000 for joint filers.

Under the new law, forty per cent of a taxpayer's otherwise allowable credit is refundable (subject to certain limitations).

Alternative Minimum Tax ("AMT")

The bill increases the individual AMT exemption amount from $45,000 to $70,950 for joint filers for the year 2009. For tax year 2009, the bill also allows a taxpayer to offset the entire regular tax liability and AMT liability by the nonrefundable personal tax credits

Other Provisions

The above is a summary of the key provisions of the bill potentially affecting many U.S. taxpayers residing in Canada.

It is to be noted that there are other personal income tax related provisions in the bill that may affect a relatively small percentage of such taxpayers:

Increase of the amount of the refundable First Time Home Buyer credit for qualified purchase of homes in the United States to $8,000 and removal of the obligation for repayment of the credit for homes purchased after January 1, 2009

Increase in the earned income tax credit for working families with three or more children.

Allowance of a deduction for state and local sales and excise taxes paid on purchase of new cars, trucks and other vehicles.

Credit for purchase of certain electric-powered vehicles.

The bill also has many tax incentives for businesses that may affect individual taxpayers who own and operate businesses. Some of the key incentives in this category are:

Extension of the 50% first year bonus depreciation deduction to eligible business property placed in service in 2009.

Extension of the $250,000 Section 179 expensing limit to eligible business property placed in service in 2009.

Extension of the carry back period of NOL generated in 2008 to five years.

The **American Recovery and Reinvestment Act of 2009** (Pub.L. 111-5, PDF, H.R. 1, S. 1) is a spending bill enacted by the 111th United States Congress and signed into law by President Barack Obama on February 17, 2009. The Act of Congress was based largely on proposals made by President Obama and is intended to provide a stimulus to the U.S. economy in the wake of the economic downturn. The Act includes federal tax cuts, expansion of unemployment benefits and other social welfare provisions, and domestic spending in education, health care, and infrastructure, including the energy sector. The Act also includes numerous non-economic recovery related items that were either part of longer-term plans (e.q. a study of the effectiveness of medical treatments) or desired by Congress (*e.g.* a limitation on executive compensation in federally aided banks added by Senator Dodd and Rep. Frank). The government action is much larger than the Economic Stimulus Act of 2008, which consisted primarily of tax rebate checks.

The bill was first approved by the House of Representatives, and then by the Senate. Congressional negotiators announced on February 11 that they had completed the Conference Report of the bill.[1] The Conference Report with final handwritten provisions was made available to the public on February 13.[2]

293

On that day, the Conference Report was voted on and passed as Roll Call Vote 70 by the House, 246–183.

The vote was largely along party lines with all 246 Yea votes given by Democrats and the Nay vote split between 176 Republicans and 7 Democrats.[3] No Republicans in the House voted for the bill. Later that day, the Senate passed the bill, 60–38, with all Democrats and Independents voting for the bill along with three Republicans.[3] The remaining 38 Republican senators voted against the bill.[4][5] The bill was signed into law on February 17 by President Obama at an economic forum he was hosting in Denver, Colorado.

The **American Recovery and Reinvestment Act of 2009** (Pub.L. 111–5, PDF, H.R. 1, S. 1) is a spending bill enacted by the 111th United States Congress and signed into law by President Barack Obama on February 17, 2009. The Act of Congress was based largely on proposals made by President Obama and is intended to provide a stimulus to the U.S. economy in the wake of the economic downturn. The Act includes federal tax cuts, expansion of unemployment benefits and other social welfare provisions, and domestic spending in education, health care, and infrastructure, including the energy sector. The Act also includes numerous non-economic recovery related items that were either part of longer-term plans (e.g. a study of the effectiveness of medical treatments) or desired by Congress (*e.g.* a limitation on executive compensation in federally aided banks added by Senator

Dodd and Rep. Frank). The government action is much larger than the Economic Stimulus Act of 2008, which consisted primarily of tax rebate checks.

The bill was first approved by the House of Representatives, and then by the Senate. Congressional negotiators announced on February 11 that they had completed the Conference Report of the bill.[1] The Conference Report with final handwritten provisions was made available to the public on February 13.[2] On that day, the Conference Report was voted on and passed as Roll Call Vote 70 by the House, 246–183.

The vote was largely along party lines with all 246 Yea votes given by Democrats and the Nay vote split between 176 Republicans and 7 Democrats.[3] No Republicans in the House voted for the bill. Later that day, the Senate passed the bill, 60–38, with all Democrats and Independents voting for the bill along with three Republicans.[3] The remaining 38 Republican senators voted against the bill.[4][5] The bill was signed into law on February 17 by President Obama at an economic forum he was hosting in Denver, Colorado.[6]

Legislative history

House of Representatives

The House version of the bill, H.R. 1, was introduced on January 25, 2009. It was sponsored by Democrat David

Obey, the House Appropriations Committee chairman, and was co-sponsored by nine other Democrats. On January 23, Speaker of the House Nancy Pelosi said that the bill was on track to be presented to President Obama for him to sign into law before February 16, 2009.[7] Although 206 amendments were scheduled for floor votes, they were combined into only 11, which enabled quicker passage of the bill.[8]

On January 28, 2009, the House passed the bill by a 244–188 vote.[9] All but 11 Democrats voted for the bill, and 177 Republicans voted against it (one Republican, Ginny Brown-Waite, did not vote).[10]

Senate

The Senate version of the bill, S. 1, was introduced on January 6, 2009, and later substituted as an amendment to the House bill, S.Amdt. 570. It was sponsored by Harry Reid, the Majority Leader, co-sponsored by 16 other Democrats and Joe Lieberman, an independent who caucuses with the Democrats.

The Senate then began consideration of the bill starting with the $275 billion tax provisions in the week of February 2, 2009.[11] A significant difference between the House version and the Senate version was the inclusion of a one-year extension of revisions to the alternative minimum tax which added $70 billion to the bill's total.

296

Republicans proposed several amendments to the bill directed at increasing the share of tax cuts and downsizing spending as well as decreasing the overall price.[12] President Obama and Senate Democrats hinted that they would be willing to compromise on Republican suggestions to increase infrastructure spending and to double the housing tax credit proposed from $7,500 to $15,000 and expand its application to all home buyers, not just first-time buyers.[13]

Other considered amendments included the Freedom Act of 2009, an amendment proposed by Senate Finance Committee members Maria Cantwell (D) and Orrin Hatch (R) to include tax incentives for plug-in electric vehicles[14] and an amendment proposed by Jim DeMint (R) to remove language from the bill that would prohibit funds which would be "used for sectarian instruction, religious worship, or a school or department of divinity; or in which a substantial portion of the functions of the facilities are subsumed in a religious mission".[15]

The Senate called a special Saturday debate session for February 7 at the urging of President Obama. The Senate voted, 61–36 (with 2 not voting) on February 9 to end debate on the bill and advance it to the Senate floor to vote on the bill itself.[16] On February 10, the Senate voted 61–37 (with one 1 not voting)[17] All the Democrats voted in favor, but only three Republicans voted in favor (Susan Collins, Olympia Snowe, and Arlen Specter).[18] At one point, the Senate bill stood at $838 billion.[19]

Comparison of the House, Senate and Conference versions

Senate Republicans forced a near unprecedented level of changes (near $150 billion) in the House bill which had more closely followed the Obama plan. The biggest losers were States[20] (severely restricted Stabilization Fund) and the low income workers (reduced tax credit) with major gains for the elderly (largely left out of the Obama & House plans) and high income tax-payers.

A comparison of the $827 billion economic recovery plan drafted by Senate Democrats with a $820 billion version passed by the House and the final $787 billion conference version shows huge shifts within these similar totals.

Additional debt costs would add about $350 billion or more over 10 years. Many provisions will expire in two years.[21]

The main funding differences between the Senate bill and the House bill are: More funds for health care in the Senate ($153.3 vs $140 billion), for green energy programs ($74 vs. $39.4 billion), for home buyers tax credit ($35.5 vs. $2.6 billion), new payments to the elderly and a one year increase in AMT limits. The House has more funds appropriated for education ($143 vs. $119.1 billion), infrastructure ($90.4 vs. $62 billion) and for aid to low income workers and the unemployed ($71.5 vs. $66.5 billion).[22]

Conference report

On February 12, 2009, House Majority Leader <u>Steny Hoyer</u> scheduled the vote on the bill for the next day, before wording on the bill's content had been completed and despite House Democrats having previously promised to allow a 48-hour public review period before any vote. The bill was not completed and posted on a House website until 10:45 PM on February 12.[23]

The next day, the House passed a revised version of the bill by a vote of 246-183,[24] with no Republicans voting in favor and 7 Democrats voting against.[25]

The Senate vote was the same as for the earlier version.

Provisions of the Act

Composition of the Act:

Tax Relief – includes $15 B for Infrastructure and Science, $61 B for Protecting the Vulnerable, $25 B for Education and Training and $22 B for Energy, so total funds are $126 B for Infrastructure and Science, $142 B for Protecting the Vulnerable, $78 B for Education and Training, and $65 B for Energy.
State and Local Fiscal Relief – Prevents state and local cuts to health and education programs and state and local tax increases.

The Act specifies that 37% of the package is to be devoted to tax cuts equaling $288 billion and $144 billion or 18% is allocated to state and local fiscal relief (more than 90% of the state aid is going to Medicaid and education). 45% or $357 billion is allocated to federal social programs and federal spending programs.

The following are details to the different parts of the final bill[26][27] [28][29]:

Tax cuts

Total: $288 billion

Tax relief for individuals

Total: $237 billion

- $116 billion: New payroll tax credit of $400 per worker and $800 per couple in 2009 and 2010. Phase-out begins at $75,000 for individuals and $150,000 for joint filers. [30]
- $70 billion: Alternative minimum tax: a one year increase in AMT floor to $70,950 for joint filers for 2009.[30]
- $15 billion: Expansion of child tax credit: A $1,000 credit to more families (even those that do not make enough money to pay income taxes).

- $14 billion: Expanded college credit to provide a $2,500 expanded tax credit for college tuition and related expenses for 2009 and 2010. The credit is phased out for couples making more than $160,000.
- $6.6 billion: Homebuyer credit: $8,000 refundable credit for all homes bought between 1/1/2009 and 12/1/2009 and repayment provision repealed for homes purchased in 2009 and held more than three years. This only applies to first-time homebuyers.[31]
- $4.7 billion: Excluding from taxation the first $2,400 a person receives in unemployment compensation benefits in 2009.
- $4.7 billion: Expanded earned income tax credit to increase the earned income tax credit — which provides money to low income workers — for families with at least three children.
- $4.3 billion: Home energy credit to provide an expanded credit to homeowners who make their homes more energy-efficient in 2009 and 2010. Homeowners could recoup 30 percent of the cost up to $1,500 of numerous projects, such as installing energy-efficient windows, doors, furnaces and air conditioners.
- $1.7 billion: for deduction of sales tax from car purchases, not interest payments phased out for incomes above $250,000.

Tax relief for companies

Total: $51 billion

- $15 billion: Allowing companies to use current losses to offset profits made in the previous five years, instead of two, making them eligible for tax refunds.
- $13 billion: to extend tax credits for renewable energy production (until 2014).
- $11 billion: Government contractors: Repeal a law that takes effect in 2012, requiring government agencies to withhold three percent of payments to contractors to help ensure they pay their tax bills. Repealing the law would cost $11 billion over 10 years, in part because the government could not earn interest by holding the money throughout the year.
- $7 billion: Repeal bank credit: Repeal a Treasury provision that allowed firms that buy money-losing banks to use more of the losses as tax credits to offset the profits of the merged banks for tax purposes. The change would increase taxes on the merged banks by $7 billion over 10 years.
- $5 billion: Bonus depreciation which extends a provision allowing businesses buying equipment such as computers to speed up its depreciation through 2009.

Healthcare

More than 11% of the total bill is allocated to help states with Medicaid.

Total: $147.7 billion

- $86.6 billion for Medicaid
- $24.7 billion to provide a 65 percent subsidy of health care insurance premiums for the unemployed under the COBRA program
- $19 billion for health information technology
- $10 billion for health research and construction of National Institutes of Health facilities
- $1.3 billion for medical care for service members and their families (military)
- $1 billion for prevention and wellness
- $1 billion for the Veterans Health Administration
- $2 billion for Community Health Centers
- $1.1 billion to research the effectiveness of certain healthcare treatments
- $500 million to train healthcare personnel
- $500 million for healthcare services on Indian reservations

Education

Total: $90.9 billion

- $44.5 billion in aid to local school districts to prevent layoffs and cutbacks, with flexibility to use the funds for school modernization and repair (State Equalization Fund)
- $15.6 billion to increase Pell Grants from $4,731 to $5,350
- $13 billion for low-income public schoolchildren
- $12.2 billion for IDEA special education
- $2.1 billion for Head Start
- $2 billion for childcare services
- $650 million for educational technology
- $300 million for increased teacher salaries
- $250 million for states to analyze student performance
- $200 million to support working college students
- $70 million for the education of homeless children

Environment

Total: $7.2 billion

- $4 billion for wastewater infrastructure
- $2 billion for drinking water infrastructure
- $600 million for hazardous waste cleanup at Superfund sites

- $300 million for reductions in emissions from diesel engines
- $200 million for cleanup of <u>Leaking Underground Storage Tanks</u>
- $100 million for cleaning former industrial and commercial sites (<u>Brownfields</u>)

Aid to low income workers, unemployed and retirees (including job training)

Payments to Social Security recipients and people on Supplemental Security Income were parts of the final bill.

Total: $82.5 billion

.$40 billion to provide extended unemployment benefits through Dec. 31, and increase them by $25 a week

- $19.9 billion for the <u>Food Stamp Program</u>
- $14.2 billion to give one-time $250 payments to Social Security recipients, people on Supplemental Security Income, and veterans receiving disability and pensions.
- $3.95 billion for job training
- $3 billion in temporary welfare payments
- $500 million for vocational training for the disabled
- $400 million for employment services
- $120 million for subsidized community service jobs for older Americans

- $150 million to help refill <u>food banks</u>
- $100 million for meals programs for seniors, such as <u>Meals on Wheels</u>
- $100 million for <u>free school lunch programs</u>

Infrastructure Investment

Total: $80.9 billion

Core investments (roads, bridges, railways, sewers, other transportation)

Highway construction is the biggest single line infrastructure item in the final bill

Total: $51.2 billion

- $27.5 billion for <u>highway</u> and <u>bridge</u> <u>construction</u> projects
- $8 billion for intercity passenger rail projects and rail congestion grants, with priority for <u>high-speed rail</u>
- $6.9 billion for new equipment for public transportation projects (<u>Federal Transit Administration</u>)
- $6 billion for wastewater and drinking water infrastructure (<u>Environmental Protection Agency</u>)
- $1.3 billion for <u>Amtrak</u>
- $100 million to help <u>public transit agencies</u>

- $750 million for the construction of new public rail transportation systems and other fixed guideway systems.
- $750 million for the maintenance of existing public transportation systems.

Investment into government facilities and vehicle fleets

Total: $29.5 billion

- $4.6 billion for the <u>Army Corps of Engineers</u> for environmental restoration, flood protection, hydropower, and navigation infrastructure projects
- $4.5 billion to the U.S. <u>General Services Administration</u> (GSA) for energy efficiency and renewable energy.
- $4.2 billion to repair and modernize Defense Department facilities.
- $4 billion toward the establishment of an <u>Office of Federal High-Performance Green Buildings</u> within the GSA.
- $4 billion for the <u>Clean Water State Revolving Fund</u> (wastewater treatment infrastructure improvements)
- $2 billion for the Drinking Water State Revolving Fund (drinking water infrastructure improvements)
- $4 billion for public housing improvements and energy efficiency (<u>Department of Housing and Urban Development</u> (HUD).

- $2 billion for the Drinking Water State Revolving Fund (drinking water infrastructure improvements)
- $890 million to improve housing for service members
- $300 million to acquire <u>electric vehicles</u> for the <u>federal vehicle fleet</u>
- $250 million to improve <u>Job Corps</u> training facilities.
- $240 million for new <u>child development</u> centers.
- $150 million for the construction of state extended-care facilities.
- $100 million to improve facilities of the <u>National Guard</u>.
- $240 million for the maintenance of <u>United States Coast Guard</u> facilities.

Supplemental investments

Total: $15 billion

- $7.2 billion for complete <u>broadband</u> and <u>wireless Internet</u> access
- $1.5 billion for competitive grants to state and local governments for transportation investments
- $1.38 billion for rural drinking water and waste disposal projects
- $1 billion to the <u>Bureau of Reclamation</u> for drinking water projects for rural or drought-likely areas
- $750 million to the <u>National Park Service</u>
- $650 million to the <u>Forest Service</u>

- $515 million for wildfire prevention projects
- $500 million for Bureau of Indian Affairs infrastructure projects
- $340 million to the Natural Resources Conservation Service for watershed infrastructure projects
- $320 million to the Bureau of Land Management
- $280 million for National Wildlife Refuges
- $280 million for the National Fish Hatchery System
- $220 million to the International Boundary and Water Commission to repair flood control systems along the Rio Grande
- $220 million for other public lands management agencies
- $500 million to update the computer center at the Social Security Administration
- $290 million to upgrade IT platforms at the State Department
- $50 million for IT improvements at the Farm Service Agency

Energy

Loans and investments into green energy technology is a significant part of the final bill

Total: $61.3 billion

- $11 billion funding for an electric smart grid
- $6.3 billion for state and local governments to make investments in energy efficiency
- $6 billion for renewable energy and electric transmission technologies loan guarantees
- $6 billion for the cleanup of radioactive waste (mostly nuclear power plant sites)
- $5 billion for weatherizing modest-income homes
- $4.5 billion for the Office of Electricity and Energy Reliability to modernize the nation's electrical grid and smart grid.
- $4.5 billion for state and local governments to increase energy efficiency in federal buildings
- $3.4 billion for carbon capture experiments
- $3.25 billion for the Western Area Power Administration for power transmission system upgrades.
- $2.5 billion for energy efficiency research
- $2 billion for manufacturing of advanced car battery (traction) systems and components.
- $3.2 billion toward Energy Efficiency and Conservation Block Grants

- $500 million for training of <u>green-collar workers</u> (by the <u>Department of Labor</u>)
- $400 million for <u>electric vehicle</u> technologies
- $300 million for <u>federal vehicle fleets</u>, to cover the cost of acquiring <u>electric vehicles</u>, including <u>plug-in hybrid vehicles</u>.
- $300 million to buy energy efficient appliances
- $300 million for reducing <u>diesel fuel</u> emissions
- $300 million for state and local governments to purchase energy efficient vehicles
- $250 million to increase energy efficiency in low-income housing
- $600 million to clean up <u>hazardous waste</u> that threaten health and the environment
- $200 million to cleanup petroleum leaks from <u>underground storage tanks</u>
- $100 million to evaluate and cleanup <u>brownfield land</u>
- $400 million for the <u>Geothermal Technologies Program</u>

Housing

Total: $12.7 billion

- $4 billion to the <u>Department of Housing and Urban Development</u> (HUD) for repairing and modernizing public housing, including increasing the energy efficiency of units.
- $2.25 billion in tax credits for financing low-income housing construction
- $2 billion for <u>Section 8 housing</u> rental assistance
- $2 billion to help communities purchase and repair foreclosed housing
- $1.5 billion for rental assistance and housing relocation
- $510 million for the rehabilitation of Native American housing
- $200 million for helping rural Americans buy homes
- $130 million for rural community facilities
- $100 million to help remove <u>lead paint</u> from public housing

Scientific research

NASA is among the research centers receiving additional funds under the Act

Total: $8.9 billion

- $3 billion to the National Science Foundation
- $2 billion to the United States Department of Energy
- $1.3 billion for university research facilities
- $1 billion to NASA
- $600 million to the National Oceanic and Atmospheric Administration (NOAA)
- $580 million to the National Institute of Standards and Technology
- $230 million for NOAA operations, research and facilities
- $140 million to the United States Geological Survey

Other

Total: $18.1 billion

- $8.8 billion: State Block Grants: in aid to states to defray budget cuts.
- $4 billion for state and local law enforcement agencies
- $1.1 billion for improving airport security
- $1 billion in preparation for the 2010 census

- $720 million for improving security at the border and ports of entry
- $750 million for DTV conversion coupons and DTV transition education
- $210 million to build and upgrade fire stations
- $150 million for the security of transit systems
- $250 million for the security of ports
- $26 million to improve security systems at the Department of Agriculture headquarters
- $150 million for an increase of claims processing military staff
- $150 million for VA general operating expenses
- $50 million for the National Endowment for the Arts to support artists
- $50 million for the National Cemetery Administration

Assessments by economists

Economists such as Martin Feldstein, Daron Acemoglu, National Economic Council director Larry Summers, and Nobel Memorial Prize in Economic Sciences winners Joseph Stiglitz[32] and Paul Krugman[33] favor large economic stimulus to counter the economic downturn. Some economists, such as Stiglitz and Krugman, favor a much larger measure. While in favor of a stimulus package, Feldstein expressed concern over the act as written, saying it needs revision to address consumer spending and unemployment more directly.[34]

Other economists, including John Lott,[35] Robert Barro and Nobel Prize-winners Robert Lucas, Jr.,[36] Vernon L. Smith, Edward C. Prescott and James M. Buchanan have been more critical of the government spending, saying that the package will increase unemployment and place more debt on future generations.[37]

REFERENCES

1. ∧ New York Times *Deal Struck on $789 Billion Stimulus.* New York Times. February 11, 2009.
2. ∧ *"COMMITTEE ON RULES – Conference Report to Accompany H.R. 1 – The American Recovery and Reinvestment Act of 2009".* *Rules.house.gov.* http://www.rules.house.gov/bills_details.aspx?New sID=4149. Retrieved on February 18, 2009.
3. ∧ *a b* *"US Congress passes stimulus plan".* *BBC.* *February 14, 2009.* http://news.bbc.co.uk/2/hi/business/7889897.st m. Retrieved on February 17, 2009.
4. ∧ *"Dems power stimulus bill through Congress".* *Associated Press. February 14, 2009.* http://www.msnbc.msn.com/id/29179041/.
5. ∧ *"U.S. Senate: Legislation & Records Home > Votes > Roll Call Vote".* *Senate.gov.* http://www.senate.gov/legislative/LIS/roll_call_list s/roll_call_vote_cfm.cfm?congress=111&session=1 &vote=00064#position. Retrieved on 2009-02-18.

6. ∧ *"Stimulus: Now for the hard part".* CNN.com. *February 17, 2009.* http://money.cnn.com/2009/02/17/news/econom y/obama_stimulus_meas_success/index.htm?postv ersion=2009021713.

7. ∧ *"Obama seeks congressional consensus on stimulus plan".* Newsday. *January 24, 2009.* http://www.newsday.com/services/newspaper/prin tedition/saturday/news/ny-bzecon246010682jan24,0,7242108.story.

8. ∧ cqpolitics.com

9. ∧ *"House Passes Stimulus Plan Despite G.O.P. Opposition".* New York Times. *January 29, 2009.* http://www.nytimes.com/2009/01/29/us/politics/ 29obama.html?hp.

10. ∧ House Vote On Passage: H.R. 1: American Recovery and Reinvestment Act of 2009

11. ∧ NewsDay.com

12. ∧ See, for example: S.Amdt. 106, S.Amdt. 107, S.Amdt. 108, and S.Amdt. 109

13. ∧ *Sheryl Gay Stolberg (February 2, 2009). "Obama Predicts Support From G.O.P. for Stimulus Proposal".* New York Times. http://www.nytimes.com/2009/02/02/us/politics/ 02obama.html?ref=business.

14. ∧ cantwell.senate.gov

15. ∧ HR1. SEC. 9302. HIGHER EDUCATION MODERNIZATION, RENOVATION, AND REPAIR. The amendment was ultimately rejected by a vote of 54–43: S.Amdt. 189. Vote on Amendment

16. ^ Roll call vote 59
17. ^ Senator Judd Gregg (R) did not vote because, at the time, he was a nominee of the Democratic president to become Secretary of Commerce. Gregg also did not participate in the cloture vote.
18. ^ Roll call vote 60
19. ^ *David Espo. "Stimulus bill survives Senate test". Associated Press* via *Atlanta Journal-Constitution.* http://www.ajc.com/services/content/printedition/ 2009/02/10/stimulus0210.html.
20. ^ JSOnline.com
21. ^ "Stimulus bill far from perfect, Obama says" MSNBC
22. ^ Stimulus bill survives Senate test, via AJC.com
23. ^ Even After the Deal, Tinkering Goes On, The New York Times, February 12, 2009
24. ^ The Senate passed the bill with 60 votes later that night. FINAL, via Clerk.House.gov
25. ^ House passes Obama's economic stimulus bill, via Breitbart.com
26. ^ *"SUMMARY: AMERICAN RECOVERY AND REINVESTMENT". Committee on Appropriations. 2009-02-13.* http://appropriations.house.gov/pdf/PressSummar y02-13-09.pdf. Retrieved on 2009-02-17.
27. ^ recovery.gov ^ http://www.wmtw.com/money/18706385/detail.ht ml

28. ^ Note that there are deviations in how some sources allocate spending and tax incentives and loans to different categories
29. ^ *a b* House Conference report 111-? Final partially handwritten report released by Nancy Pelosi's Office 2/13/09
30. ^ ARRA of 2009 Questions & Answers
31. ^ Stiglitz: Stimulus Must Be Big, Provide Relief To States, morningstar.com
32. ^ Stimulus Gone Bad, NYTimes.com
33. ^ Boston Herald, January 30, 2009
34. ^ *"Obama's Stimulus Package Will Increase Unemployment - Opinion". FOXNews.com. 2009-02-03.* http://www.foxnews.com/story/0,2933,487425,00.html. Retrieved on 2009-02-18.
35. ^ Bernanke Is the Best Stimulus Right Now, wsj.com
36. ^ Investor's Business Daily
37. ^ Economists say stimulus won't work, St. Louis Post-Dispatch, January 29, 2009.
38. ^ Cato Institute petition against Obama 2009 stimulus plan
39. ^ http://online.wsj.com/article/SB123671107124286261.html Obama, Geithner Get Low Grades From Economists
40. ^ Official CBO report to the Senate budget committee

41. ^ CBO-Budgetary Impact of ARRA letter by Douglas W. Elmendorf, director of the CBO, February 11, 2009

In an article by reporters Mark Pittman and Bob Ivry, entitled " Financial Rescue Approaches GDP as US pledges $ 12.8 trillion," by reporters Mark Pittman and Bob Ivry (as reported in Bloomberg) on March 31/2009, the impact of trillions of dollars of Debt is discussed. All this debt represents honest efforts by successive US administrations to control and Stabilize the US financial and credit crisis. The vast amounts of debt incurred as a result of this process are staggering. The article is very interesting and revealing and is reproduced in its original format in Bloomberg News.

Here is an excerpt of the article:

"The U.S. government and the Federal Reserve have spent, lent or guaranteed $12.8 trillion, an amount that approaches the value of everything produced in the country last year, to stem the longest recession since the 1930s. New pledges from the Fed, the Treasury Department and the Federal Deposit Insurance Corp. include $1 trillion for the Public-Private Investment Program, designed to help investors buy distressed loans and other assets from U.S. banks. The money works out to $42,105 for every man, woman and child in the U.S. and 14 times the $899.8 billion of currency in circulation.

The nation's gross domestic product was $14.2 trillion in 2008.

President Barack Obama and Treasury Secretary

Timothy Geithner met with the chief executives of the nation's 12 biggest banks on March 27 at the White Houseto enlist their support to thaw a 20-month freeze in bank lending. "The president and Treasury Secretary Geithner have said they will do what it takes," Goldman Sachs Group Inc. Chief Executive Officer Lloyd Blankfein said after the meeting. "If it is enough, that will be great. If it is not enough, they will have to do more." Commitments include a $500 billion line of credit to the FDIC from the government's coffers that will enable the agency to guarantee as much as $2 trillion worth of debt for participants in the Term Asset-Backed Lending Facility and the Public-Private Investment Program.

FDIC Chairman Sheila Bair warned that the insurance fund to protect customer deposits at U.S. banks could dry up because of bank failures.

'Within an Eyelash'

The combined commitment has increased by 73 percent since November, when Bloomberg first estimated the funding, loans and guarantees at $7.4 trillion.

"The comparison to GDP serves the useful purpose of underscoring   how extraordinary the efforts have been to stabilize the credit markets," said Dana Johnson, chief economist for Comerica Bank in Dallas. "Everything the Fed, the FDIC and the Treasury do doesn't always work out right but back in October we came within an eyelash of having a truly horrible collapse of our financial system, said Johnson, a former Fed senior economist.

"They used their creativity to help the worst-case scenario from unfolding and I'm awfully glad they did it."

The following table details how the Fed and the government have committed the money on behalf of American taxpayers over the past 20 months, according to data compiled by Bloomberg.

```
=====================================
======================
           --- Amounts (Billions)---
                Limit          Current
=====================================
======================
Total              $12,798.14      $4,169.71
-----------------------------------------------
----------
```

	Limit	Current
Federal Reserve Total	$7,765.64	$1,678.71
Primary Credit Discount	$110.74	$61.31
Secondary Credit	$0.19	$1.00
Primary dealer and others	$147.00	$20.18
ABCP Liquidity	$152.11	$6.85
AIG Credit	$60.00	$43.19
Net Portfolio CP Funding	$1,800.00	$241.31
Maiden Lane (Bear Stearns)	$29.50	$28.82
Maiden Lane II (AIG)	$22.50	$18.54
Maiden Lane III (AIG)	$30.00	$24.04
Term Securities Lending	$250.00	$88.55
Term Auction Facility	$900.00	$468.59
Securities lending overnight	$10.00	$4.41
Term Asset-Backed Loan Facility	$900.00	$4.71
Currency Swaps/Other Assets	$606.00	$377.87
MMIFF	$540.00	$0.00
GSE Debt Purchases	$600.00	$50.39
GSE Mortgage-Backed Securities	$1,000.00	$236.16
Citigroup Bailout Fed Portion	$220.40	$0.00
Bank of America Bailout	$87.20	$0.00
Commitment to Buy Treasuries	$300.00	$7.50

```
------------------------------------------- -------
----------
```

FDIC Total	$2,038.50	$357.50
Public-Private Investment*	$500.00	0.00
FDIC Liquidity Guarantees	$1,400.00	$316.50
GE	$126.00	$41.00
Citigroup Bailout FDIC	$10.00	$0.00
Bank of America Bailout FDIC	$2.50	$0.00

```
-----------------------------------------------
----------
```

Treasury Total		$2,694.00
$1,833.50		
TARP	$700.00	$599.50
Tax Break for Banks	$29.00	$29.00
Stimulus Package (Bush)	$168.00	$168.00
Stimulus II (Obama)	$787.00	$787.00
Treasury Exchange Stabilization		$50.00
$50.00		
Student Loan Purchases		$60.00
$0.00		
Support for Fannie/Freddie		$400.00
$200.00		
Line of Credit for FDIC*		$500.00
$0.00		

```
-----------------------------------------------
----------
```

HUD Total	$300.00	$300.00
Hope for Homeowners FHA	$300.00	$300.00

```
-----------------------------------------------
----------
```

323

The FDIC's commitment to guarantee lending under the Legacy Loan Program and the Legacy Asset Program includes a $500
billion line of credit from the U.S. Treasury.

CONCLUSION

The great financial and credit crisis is like no other since the Great Depression. Governments and more important, people, have become economically destabilized worldwide as a result of greedy, callous and irresponsible/ fraudulent behavior of predominantly American commercial and investment banks. The crisis has spread like an uncontrollable cancer all over the world. In the words of Ben Bernanke and several other commentators, the financial system came close to a complete meltdown in the third and fourth quarter of 2008.

With great difficulty and not very well co-ordinated financial intervention, the financial system was saved and the world was prevented from going into an economic tailspin resulting in a depression.

The US, the perpetrator of this crisis responded aggressively in trying to control this crisis. Under the positive guidance and leadership of President Obama, all stops were pulled out to control the problem.

However, in spite of trillions and trillions of dollars spent, the problem is still not solved completely as of early April 2009. I believe, that with time there will be returning stability to the stock markets, credit markets and most important public confidence. And without public confidence and trust, nothing will change.

This is what President Obama is trying to attempt to change and I pray he is successful, because he is the most powerful and influential leader in the world with the capacity to reverse all the damage not only in the United States but the world at large.

THIS PAGE LEFT INTENTIONALLY BLANK

PART 3

-WHAT WENT WRONG & HOW TO FIX
THE PROBLEM PERMANENTLY

CHAPTER 39

THE WORLD FINANCIAL SYSTEM EXPLAINED

BACKGROUND

The world financial system is an intricate network of "money" relationships between people of different countries. Since people of the world have chosen or been forced to adopt certain political frameworks of governance, the world financial system now reflects, in addition to the traditional "money relationships" an additional influence represented by the development and conflicts in relationships between different political entities around the world.

Each political entity exists to further the interest of its members or citizens and is tainted by whatever political view they possess as a whole. Therefore, the world financial system is nothing but a push-and-pull structure with each country pushing the other to sell its goods and services--- the net result of which is to build national wealth and hopefully, provide a better life to its citizens.

We must therefore understand the global financial system as one not only covering money relationships stemming from the actual trade and service relationships between independent nations but also the financial methods of doing business and most importantly, the attitude and confidence which stands behind such relationships. Trust is a great differentiatior in financial relationships.

Imagine a million dollars of merchandise moving from China to the United States. The Chinese exporter, on the strength of a letter of a credit has trusted the movement of his merchandise to far away shores in the US. That letter of credit is guaranteed by a US bank, which indicates that if the buyer examines and accepts the merchandise shipped that funds will be credited to the exporter's account. Now imagine a situation, not dissimilar to what the world faced in the Spring of 2009 where US banks are "technically insolvent" with several in partial nationalization mode. Surveying these developments in Spring 2009, if the exporter failed to trust the US bank as a trustworthy financier, then this resulted in a lost sale. The lost sale does not only involve a loss to the exporter but to his home country. The new business could have had a marked effect to the livelihood of the exporter's nation through mechanisms of wealth distribution. This would not happen now if there existed distrust in the relationship. In this instance, the world financial system breakdown of trust has severely inhibited trade between nations. In reality, the financial, trade and political system all work together in the modern economy.

One cannot, therefore, view the global financial system in isolation but as an integral part of commerce and politics.

FINANCIAL ARCHITECTURE

An understanding and appreciation of architecture involved in GFS (Global financial System) design will aid in an appreciation of the current crisis. The GFS is a financial system consisting of institutions and regulations that act on the international level. The main players in this arena are the International Monetary Fund and Bank for International Settlements, national agencies and finance ministries including central banks of independent nations and global banks, global private equity groups and hedge funds. Imagine the financial architecture being comprised of any player who is moving money around the world or making financial decisions which affect the currency value of any nation. Shifts in currency values effect trade patterns and ultimately impact on trade surpluses or deficits.

The financial architecture unfortunately, only delineates the players but not their influence. For reasons unknown to me, most commodities and products are denominated in US dollars. The actual architecture is comprised of a non-level playing field--- on one side are the rich and economically/political powerful nations like the U.S., the European Union, Japan and China and on the other table are the emerging nations like India, Korea and others. The fundamental relationships among the rich and emerging nations are flawed.

The rich countries dictate policy to the world and make such policies appear rational and palatable. With the current crisis, this balance of power in relationships will undergo a fundamental modification. Since the U.S. is no longer the economic power it was, new nations will challenge this domination and hopefully, new systems and links will be developed in the financial architecture---links which will help restore a more fair and democratic way of doing business.

Now let us not forget the thread of intermediation. These are the financial intermediaries who represent buyers and sellers in different part of the world. Most notable among these are the global banks and global insurance companies as well as hedge funds and private equity groups. The current financial crisis has put to question the role of these global banks and insurance companies. Once perceived as being very strong, their entire financial solvency and value is now in question. Also, hedge funds and private equity groups have been seen as distorting market mechanisms due to their unbridled greed and speculation in international financial markets and there is talk of regulation them more closely----- this will assist in prevention of financial crises in the future.

So, to close this section on financial architecture, imagine all independent nations with their manufacturing and export power dealing with other nations through intermediaries of banks, insurance companies, institutional investors, hedge funds, private equity groups. You now get to understand the vast world trade, financial and political system with each nation using capital markets and banks and insurance companies to enable money transfer and secure financial risk transactions.

This is the financial architecture which underpins our global financial system.

INTERNATIONAL INSTITUTIONS WHICH CONTROL THE GFS

The following international institutions have a major role to play in the international financial system:

1. The International Monetary Fund, also known as the IMF keeps account of international balance of payments accounts of member states/nations. The IMF acts as a lender of last resort for member nations in financial distress, e.g. when there is a currency crisis or when there is national debt default on international obligations.

2. The Bank of International Settlements, which monitors world economies and world financial systems.

3. The World Bank provides funding to international projects; it also takes credit risk or offers favorable terms to development projects in developing nations.

4. The World Trade Organization settles trade disputes and negotiates international trade agreements in its various rounds of talks.
5. The G20 is a group of the top 20 industrialized countries in the world which comprise more than 75% of the world economic production. The G20 is more a consultative organization rather than a controlling entity. The G20 may be viewed more as a consultative venue for discussions between nations in areas like the current global financial crisis.

GOVERNMENT INSTITUTIONS WHO PLAY A ROLE IN THE GFS

Individual nations act in the world stage in GFS. Each nation passes laws and regulations for financial markets and set the tax burden for private players e.g. banks, funds and exchanges. Governments also influence the economy through discretionary spending. They are closely connected to central banks which issue government debt, set interest rates and deposit requirements and intervene in the foreign exchange market. All these activities delineate the rise or fall of a national economic power and influence trade and finances between different countries.

PRIVATE PLAYERS IN THE GFS

Players acting in the stock-, bond-, foreign exchange-, derivatives- and commodities -markets and investment banking are:

1. Commercial banks
2. Pension funds
3. Hedge funds
4. Private Equity funds.

THE WASHINGTON CONSENSUS

This consensus was drafted and acted on in the United States initially but its impact is now felt worldwide in the Global Financial System. The consensus refers to a ruling ideology on which is based economic, political and banking systems. This liberal view holds that the exchange of currencies should be determined not by state institutions but instead individual players at a market level. Such view has been labeled as the Washington consensus. However, this view is now expanded to affect the philosophical view behind the global financial system. We now have a situation called," Market fundamentalism," which basically calls for a "laissez-faire "(leave things alone) attitude. This view was recently applied by the US administration to commercial and investment banks, where they allowed them to do whatever they wanted hoping that it would be for the benefit of all.

Only after October 2008 when the crisis intensified, did the authorities decided not to use this view and exerted strict and stringent controls on banks, eliminating some and nationalizing others.

Dani Rodrik, Professor of International Political Economy at Harvard University has the following comments on the Washington consensus, "While the lessons drawn by proponents and skeptics differ, it is fair to say that nobody really believes in the Washington consensus anymore. The question now is not whether the Washington consensus is dead or alive; it is what will replace it."

WORLD TRADE v GLOBAL FINANCIAL SERVICES

Recently I heard a presentation from an important representative of the World Trade organization. In this speech, he mentioned there was a starking difference between regulation of trade and regulation of global financial services. This imbalance in my mind, has contributed to the current crisis. Investment and commercial banks skip regulatory oversight both in their domestic and international markets. Financial services due to their speed and increasing complexity escape most regulations. The moral of this lesson is that unless stringent regulation is applied to global financial services as it is to world trade, the situation will not improve appreciably and we will have to live with this crisis for many years.

There is also an intimate relationship between world trade and world finance. Numerous exporting enterprises from the developing world need financing to consummate their deals and with the global financial crisis there has been a severe deterioration in the amount of capital available from banks and other funding sources for export trade financing. Reuters reported that Mr. Lamy, Director General of the WTO as quoting in early 2009, " The basic message is that trade finance is the most secure, the safest, the least toxic asset which you can trade in banking and insurance." In spite of this advice trade financing is deteriorating at a very rapid rate. Affordable access to trade financing is a shock absorber to developing nations to cushion the shock coming from the global financial crisis.

THE FINANCIAL STABILITY FORUM

According to the website of the Financial Stability Forum, they describe their activities and purpose as follows: "The Financial Stability Forum (FSF) brings together senior representatives of national financial authorities (e.g. central banks, supervisory authorities and treasury departments), international financial institutions, international regulatory and supervisory groupings, committees of central bank experts and the European Central Bank. The FSF is serviced by a small secretariat housed at the Bank of International Settlements in Basel, Switzerland.

In closing this chapter an understanding of the financial architecture surrounding the global financial system--- hopefully this understanding will assist you in appreciating the current crisis better. Read on to see how the financial architecture created the current crisis and what the challenges are in solving this incredible global problem.

CHAPTER 40

COMPREHENSIVE UNDERSTANDING OF THE GLOBAL FINANCIAL CRISIS

BACKGROUND

As we all know, the problems compounding and developing the great global financial crisis had its roots in 2007. A growing sub-prime crisis caused by irresponsible lending by commercial banks in the U.S., compounded with fraud by numerous mortgage origination agents and brokers and accompanied with massive multibillion dollar securitization by investment banks caused a bubble in the property market in the US. Initially the problem was restricted to the sub-prime market but it later mysteriously transformed itself into new markets.

TRANSFORMATION OF PROBLEM TO BANKING CRISIS

As numerous US households could not pay their mortgages, particularly the subprime candidates, banks faced an incredible funding crisis. This was due to two reasons primarily:
Firstly, there were huge default rates in their mortgage loan portfolio accompanied with dwindling real estate values.

Secondly, there was the participation in the shadow banking market, where banks like Citibank held off-balance sheets to generate immense profits. The compositions of such off-balance sheet items were the very subprime mortgage assets, which were securitized. So the banks compounded the problems by not only having their own mortgage and poor credit issues but by also taking over other institutions' problems through the medium of securitized mortgages.

TRANSFORMATION OF BANKING CRISIS TO STOCK MARKET CRASH & CREDIT CRISIS

October 2008 was a particularly brutal period for stock markets around the world. With questions of solvency of banks and more importantly, uncertainty surrounding composition of subprime mortgage portfolio created conditions which made evaluation of value impossible. This resulted in world stock markets declining big time as investors lost the power to judge the risk worthiness of any asset. With banks not trusting each other and liquidity been affected worldwide, the banking crisis converted to a full blown credit crisis.

TRANSFORMATION TO REAL ECONOMY CRISIS

With dwindling individual wealth as a result of decimated stock and real estate portfolios, the average American investor basically had his job as the last bastion of financial security.

But when the fallout of the crisis transformed from a purely financial event to something which spilled out to the real economy, causing contractions in gross domestic product, the investor was alarmed and panicked. As the U.S. lost over 4 million jobs from January 1/08 to April 09, the funding source for Americans was gone. So less cars got purchased, no new homes were acquired, businesses closed doors due to lack of appropriate bank financing and the roller ball of anxiety, fear and panic imploded.

The problem had now gone full circle, form a simpler subprime housing problem to a banking crisis to a stock market crash, then spilling over to the entire economy. The U.S. government responded aggressively by investing over 12 trillion dollars into various bailout and stimulus packages. However, the problem was still very much alive as of April 1, 2009.

GLOBALIZATION OF FINANCIAL MARKETS

Globalization created a further problem. Since international capital moved freely across borders with very little control or regulation, the world responded to the movements of big money barons. These barons included the whims and fancies of the US government, the European establishment and Japanese capital bosses along with the huge multilateral agencies like the IMF and World Bank. No less influential were the large pension and hedge funds and the culprit US and European commercial and investment banks.

Since most financial markets are linked, disturbances at the epicenter affect everyone. This happens in many different ways. Since the US investment banks sold investments in US subprime mortgages though the securitization process, the collapse of this market resulted in the losses amounting to billions of dollars by the large European and Swiss banks, who had foolishly and trustingly invested client capital in these exotic products, hoping as always to make a lot of profit. The fallout from such investments was felt in money centers in Singapore, Kuwait, Dubai and numerous locales.

Secondly, as international investors got frightened and hid in the safety of Swiss francs and US dollars, the US dollar reversed its earlier decline and advanced in the last half of 2008 and first quarter of 2009 against other world currencies.

Thirdly, with the liquidity crisis created by the US, international funding evaporated. So gone were the infrastructure projects for the poorer people in Asia and also investments in their stock, bond and currency markets.

Fourthly, as US and other international players sold emerging market positions to pay the obligations at home and have a less overall risky portfolio, local stock markets in emerging nations like Russia, Brazil, India and China got decimated.

Globalization of financial markets with no adequate regulation of capital and currency markets created unnecessarily havoc in Asia due to no fault of their own.

The insecurity and instability had been transported from the US epicenter to all peripheral centers of the global financial network.

ISSUES

All these events and occurrences from 2007 to the first quarter of 2009 points out to fundamental flaws in the world financial architecture. Some of the questions which need to be addressed are:
1. Why did things go so wrong?
2. What caused the crisis?
3. How do we improve our financial architecture so that such crises do not reoccur in the future?
4. What do we need to do in terms of domestic and international financial regulation to better manage the problem now?
5. How long will it take to have a certain sense of normalcy and confidence in the capital markets?
6. How do we change the Washington consensus?
7. What role does the US have in the new global financial order?
8. What obstacles are in the way of international co-operation in global financial affairs?

These and other questions will be addressed in this part of the book.

CHAPTER 41

COMPREHENSIVE UNDERSTANDING OF THE GLOBAL CREDIT CRISIS

The credit crisis was the second major leg of this financial crisis. Firstly, there was the US subprime crisis and at some point this problem converted into a complete and utter lack of confidence in the US money market and US banking industry. A point was reached when no one trusted anyone. The interbank lending market froze up, the commercial paper market dried up and small and medium-sized businesses could not obtain financing for their normal operations. Welcome to a full blown credit crisis, US style. This credit crisis now metamorphosed into a worldwide credit bubble. Such a crisis now created the next evolutionary stage of the financial crisis---- a spillover into the natural and real economy of the US and later into the real economies of the world. The major contribution of the credit crisis was derived from billions of dollars of banks' exposures to a synthetic financial product, called credit derivatives. By banks taking wrong bets on these products, they lost billions. Some investment banks like Bear Stearns and Lehman Brothers lost everything due to these wrong bets, while the largest insurer in the world AIG ,got burnt with another credit derivative product called a credit default swap. To start, let us look at definitions of what a credit derivative is.

In finance, a **credit derivative** is a derivative whose value derives from the credit risk on an underlying bond, loan or other financial asset. In this way, the credit risk is on an entity other than the counterparties to the transaction itself.[1] This entity is known as the *reference entity* and may be a corporate, a sovereign or any other form of legal entity which has incurred debt.[2] Credit derivatives are bilateral contracts between a buyer and seller under which the seller sells protection against the credit risk of the reference entity.[2]

The parties will select which credit events apply to a transaction and these usually consist of one or more of the following:

bankruptcy (the risk that the reference entity will become bankrupt) failure to pay (the risk that the reference entity will default on one of its obligations such as a bond or loan)

obligation default (the risk that the reference entity will default on any of its obligations)

obligation acceleration (the risk that an obligation of the reference entity will be accelerated e.g. a bond will be declared immediately due and payable following a default)

repudiation/moratorium (the risk that the reference entity or a government will declare a moratorium over the reference entity's obligations)

- restructuring (the risk that obligations of the reference entity will be restructured).

Where credit protection is bought and sold between bilateral counterparties this is known as an unfunded credit derivative. If the credit derivative is entered into by a financial institution or a special purpose vehicle (SPV) and payments under the credit derivative are funded using securitization techniques, such that a debt obligation is issued by the financial institution or SPV to support these obligations, this is known as a funded credit derivative.

This synthetic securitization process has become increasingly popular over the last decade, with the simple versions of these structures being known as synthetic CDOs; credit linked notes; single tranche CDOs, to name a few. In funded credit derivatives, transactions are often rated by rating agencies, which allows investors to take different slices of credit risk according to their risk appetite.

Market size and participants

Credit default products are the most commonly traded credit derivative product[3] and include unfunded products such as credit default swaps and funded products such as collateralized debt obligations (see further discussion below).

The ISDA[4] reported in April 2007 that total notional amount on outstanding credit derivatives was $35.1 trillion with a gross market value of $948 billion (ISDA's Website). As reported in The Times on September 15th, 2008, the "Worldwide credit derivatives market is valued at $62 trillion". [5] Although the credit derivatives market is a global one, London has a market share of about 40%, with the rest of Europe having about 10%.[3] The main market participants are banks, hedge funds, insurance companies, pension funds, and other corporates.[3]

Types

Credit derivatives are fundamentally divided into two categories: funded credit derivatives and unfunded credit derivatives. An **unfunded credit derivative** is a bilateral contract between two counterparties, where each party is responsible for making its payments under the contract (i.e. payments of premiums and any cash or physical settlement amount) itself without recourse to other assets. A **funded credit derivative** involves the protection seller (the party that assumes the credit risk) making an initial payment that is used to settle any potential credit events. The advantage of this to the protection buyer is that it is not exposed to the credit risk of the protection seller[6].

Unfunded credit derivative products include the following products:

- Credit default swap (CDS)
- Total return swap
- Constant maturity credit default swap (CMCDS)
- First to Default Credit Default Swap
- Portfolio Credit Default Swap
- Secured Loan Credit Default Swap
- Credit Default Swap on Asset Backed Securities
- Credit default swaption
- Recovery lock transaction
- Credit Spread Option
- CDS index products

Funded credit derivative products include the following products:

- Credit linked note (CLN)
- Synthetic Collateralized Debt Obligation (CDO)
- Constant Proportion Debt Obligation (CPDO)
- Synthetic Constant Proportion Portfolio Insurance (Synthetic CPPI)

Key unfunded credit derivative products

Credit default swap

The credit default swap or CDS has become the cornerstone product of the credit derivatives market. This product represents over thirty percent of the credit derivatives market[3]. A credit default swap, in its simplest form (the unfunded single name credit default swap) is a bilateral contract between a *protection buyer* and a *protection seller*. The credit default swap will reference the creditworthiness of a third party called a reference entity: this will usually be a corporate or sovereign. The credit default swap will relate to the specified debt obligations of the reference entity: perhaps its bonds and loans, which fulfill certain pre-agreed characteristics. The protection buyer will pay a periodic fee to the protection seller in return for a *contingent payment* by the seller upon a *credit event* affecting the obligations of the *reference entity* specified in the transaction.

The relevant credit events specified in a transaction will usually be selected from amongst the following: the bankruptcy of the reference entity; its failure to pay in relation to a covered obligation; it defaulting on an obligation or that obligation being accelerated; it agreeing to restructure a covered obligation or a repudiation or moratorium being declared over any covered obligation.

If any of these events occur and the protection buyer serves a credit event notice on the protection seller detailing the credit event as well as (usually) providing some publicly available information validating this claim, then the transaction will settle.

This means that, in the case of a physically settled transaction, the protection buyer can deliver an amount of the reference entity's defaulted obligations to the protection seller, in return for their full face value (notwithstanding that they are now worth far less). In the case of a cash settled transaction, a relevant obligation of the reference entity will be valued and the protection seller will pay the protection buyer the full face value of the reference obligation less its current value (i.e. compensating the protection buyer for the decline in the obligation's creditworthiness).

Credit default swaps have unique characteristics that distinguish them from insurance products and financial guaranties. The protection buyer does not need to own an underlying obligation of the reference entity. The protection buyer does not need to suffer a loss. Since the reference entity is not a party to agreement between the protection buyer and seller, the seller of protection has no inherent recourse to the reference entity in the event of default and no right to sue the reference entity for recovery.

However, if the transaction were to be physically settled the seller of protection could derive a right to take action against the reference entity on the basis of the loan or securities acquired during the settlement process.

The product has many variations, including where there is a basket or portfolio of reference entities, although fundamentally, the principles remain the same. A powerful recent variation has been gathering market share of late: credit default swaps which relate to asset-backed securities[7].

Total return swap

A total return swap (also known as *Total Rate of Return Swap*) is a contract between two counterparties whereby they swap periodic payments for the period of the contract. Typically, one party receives the total return (interest payments plus any capital gains or losses for the payment period) from a specified reference asset, while the other receives a specified fixed or floating cash flow that is not related to the creditworthiness of the reference asset, as with a vanilla Interest rate swap. The payments are based upon the same notional amount. The reference asset may be any asset, index or basket of assets.

The TRS is simply a mechanism that allows one party to derive the economic benefit of owning an asset without use of the balance sheet, and which allows the other to effectively "buy protection" against loss in value due to ownership of a credit asset.

The essential difference between a *total return swap* and a *credit default swap* is that the credit default swap provides protection against specific credit events. The total return swap protects against the loss of value irrespective of cause, whether default, widening of credit spreads or anything else i.e. it isolates both credit risk and market risk.

Key funded credit derivative products

Credit linked notes

A credit linked note is a note whose cash flow depends upon an event, which may be a default, change in credit spread, or rating change. The definition of the relevant credit events must be negotiated by the parties to the note. A CLN in effect combines a credit-default swap with a regular note (with coupon, maturity, redemption). Given its note like features, a CLN is an on-balance-sheet asset, in contrast to a CDS.

Typically, an investment fund manager will purchase such a note to hedge against possible down grades, or loan defaults. Numerous different types of credit linked notes (CLNs) have been structured and placed in the past few years. Here we are going to provide an overview rather than a detailed account of these instruments.

The most basic CLN consists of a bond, issued by a well-rated borrower, packaged with a credit default swap on a less creditworthy risk. For example, a bank may sell some of its exposure to a particular emerging country by issuing a bond linked to that country's default or convertibility risk. From the bank's point of view, this achieves the purpose of reducing its exposure to that risk, as it will not need to reimburse all or part of the note if a credit event occurs.

However, from the point of view of investors, the risk profile is different from that of the bonds issued by the country. If the bank runs into difficulty, their investments will suffer even if the country is still performing well.

The credit rating is improved by using a proportion of government bonds, which means the CLN investor receives an enhanced coupon. Through the use of a credit default swap, the bank receives some recompense if the reference credit defaults.

There are several different types of securitized product, which have a credit dimension. CLN is a generic name related to any bond whose value is linked to the performance of a reference asset, or assets. This link may be through the use of a credit derivative, but does not have to be.

- Credit–linked notes **CLN**: Credit–linked note is a generic name related to any bond whose value is linked to the performance of a reference asset, or assets. This link may be through the use of a credit derivative, but does not have to be.
- Collateralized debt obligation **CDO**: Generic term for a bond issued against a mixed pool of assets – There also exists CDO–squared (CDO^2) where the underlying assets are CDO tranches.
- Collateralized bond obligations **CBO**: Bond issued against a pool of bond assets or other securities. It is referred to in a generic sense as a **CDO**

- Collateralized loan obligations **CLO**: Bond issued against a pool of bank loan. It is referred to in a generic sense as a **CDO**

CDO refers either to the pool of assets used to support the CLNs or, confusingly, to the **CLN**s themselves.

Collateralized debt obligations (CDO)

Collateralized debt obligations or CDOs are a form of credit derivative offering exposure to a large number of companies in a single instrument. This exposure is sold in slices of varying risk or *subordination* – each slice is known as a tranche.

In a cash flow CDO, the underlying credit risks are bonds or loans held by the issuer. Alternatively in a synthetic CDO, the exposure to each underlying company is a credit default swap.

A synthetic CDO is also referred to as CSO. Other more complicated CDOs have been developed where each underlying credit risk is itself a CDO tranche. These CDOs are commonly known as CDOs-squared.

Risks

Risks involving credit derivatives are a concern among regulators of financial markets. The US Federal Reserve issued several statements in the Fall of 2005 about these risks, and highlighted the growing backlog of confirmations for credit derivatives trades. These backlogs pose risks to the market (both in theory and in all likelihood), and they exacerbate other risks in the financial system.

One challenge in regulating these and other derivatives is that the people who know most about them also typically have a vested incentive in encouraging their growth and lack of regulation. (The incentive may be indirect, e.g., academics have not only consulting incentives, but also incentives in keeping open doors for research.)

CREDIT DERIVATIVES AND THE GLOBAL BANKING CRISIS

We should start by talking about the biggest banking culprit of all, the venerable Citibank of the United States. This bank pioneered Structured Investment Vehicles, another well known credit derivative product. To avoid detection and effective regulation by US financial authorities, these SIV's were put into an off-balance sheet item. An off- balance sheet item is items of asset and liability not shown in a typical "public" financial statement of a bank.

By shifting the SIV's into a secret investment vehicle out of reach of US authorities, Citibank was able to set up a shadow banking system. Inside this shadow banking system resided billions of dollars of bets--- "what if situations" in which the bank would either gain or loss if certain events occurred in the future. Numerous other US banks participated in this shady investment process. The shadow banking system had so many assets and liabilities that it eclipsed regular bank balance sheets.

One of the toxic items in the off-balance sheet was bets on sub-prime mortgages. When banks were pricing the risk of defaults on subprime mortgages their mathematical risk models failed to see two things:

Firstly, the model ignored the probability of massive defaults by borrowers and more importantly, secondly, the model completely ignored the collapse of real estate prices in the US.

These two aberrations caused billions of dollars of loss and fundamentally depleted most of their capital, although till today, the banks have not admitted to the scope of the financial losses.

The second major disaster using credit derivatives were by AIG Company, the largest insurer in the world. They lost billions of dollars by mispricing the risk on several products. They did this by guaranteeing credit default swaps at their London financial unit. AIG received a hefty premium for insuring these risks. When these risks translated into reality they had to pay billions in claims and as a result went belly up. AIG received three bailouts from the US Government and is now controlled and owned majority wise by US taxpayers. With bank capital being eroded as a result of disastrous bets on the credit derivative market, the next stage in the banking cycle was to hold on to reserves as long as possible and avoid taking more risks in the market. As banks restricted lending, consumers, businesses and corporations went bankrupt as a result of non-availability of capital for their individual or business needs.

The capital markets froze so that businesses could not borrow additional capital in the marketplace. Use of credit derivatives led to a disastrous conclusion, resulting in limited bank lending leading to a liquidity crisis. Welcome the US and world credit crisis.

Notes and references

1. ^ *Das, Satyajit (2005).* Credit Derivatives: CDOs and Structured Credit Products, 3rd Edition. *Wiley.* ISBN 978-0-470-82159-6.

2. ^ *a b "PLC Finance Practice Note: Credit Derivatives by Edmund Parker".* http://www.mayerbrown.com/london/article.asp?id=4234&nid=1575.

3. ^ *a b c d "British Banker Association Credit Derivatives Report" (PDF).* http://www.bba.org.uk/content/1/c4/76/71/Credit_derivative_report_2006_exec_summary.pdf.

4. ^ *"ISDA".* http://www.isda.org.

5. ^ http://business.timesonline.co.uk/tol/business/industry_sectors/banking_and_finance/article4761839.ece

6. ^ *Dominic O'Kane. "Credit Derivatives Explained" (PDF). Lehman Brothers, posted at Simon Fraser University.* http://www.sfu.ca/~sp6048/Reading/LEH%20O'Kane%20Credit%20Derivatives%20Explained%200301.pdf. Retrieved on 2008-07-02.

7. ^ *"Documenting credit default swaps on asset backed securities, Edmund Parker and Jamila Piracci, Mayer Brown".* http://www.mayerbrown.com/london/article.asp?id=3517&nid=1575

CHAPTER 42

THE ROLE AND RESPONSIBILITY OF
FEDERAL RESERVE, FANNIE MAE & FREDDIE MAC
IN AMPLIFYING THE CRISIS

BACKGROUND

Owning a home has always been an American dream. With home prices being way high compared to average national income in America, a mechanism was required to put people into homes. This was done by way of loaning a significant percentage of the home value through the mechanism of a mortgage. Several banks stepped into this vacuum by providing loans to ordinary Americans to finance their home. However, prior to the Great Depression, the banks pretty well controlled the shots and opportunities for refinancing were few and far between.

From a political perspective, too, it was a wise move to encourage home ownership in the U.S. Americans had learnt from the period of the Great Depression that thousands of homes had been lost due to no help to homeowners, from the government or any other financing source. Right after the Great Depression, the FDIC was formed to guarantee individual savings in banks. Prior to the Great Depression home loan amortization periods were in a range of five to ten years.

On maturity of the loan, the bank had the right to call or extend the loan at its wish and fancy. As a result of all the homes lost due to non-renewal of loans during the Great Depression, the amortization periods on mortgages were shifted to fixed rates of 20 to 25 years. This created more dependability in mortgage payments for an average home buyer. It also assured a homeowner that as long as he was willing to make payments on his mortgage that the bank could not refuse to extend his loan. During the Great Depression most mortgages were for 5 to 10 year periods and if the loan was not renewed at the whim and fancy of the lender, then on maturity, the lenders/banks just took the house away.

THE CREATION OF FANNIE MAE AND FREDDIE MAC

These two government chartered enterprises were put into place to encourage sponsorship of home mortgages---- they provided funding to average Americans directly or indirectly as they bought homes. But the big mistake made by several US administrations was to allow these institutions to stay in private hands. They had an implicit guarantee from the government and this started massive speculation in these markets. The bosses at Freddie Mac and Fannie Mae had nothing to lose.

They could take on as many investment risks as they wanted and knew they would probably be bailed out financially by the Government if they made wrong investment decisions and incurred losses, as a result of such poor decisions.

This type of behavior was followed by a period of time when there was severe accounting mistakes made to hide losses. Finally, the government was forced to put them into conservatorship in 2009. In the meantime, the American taxpayer had to shoulder all the losses out of generations of poor executive and investment decision-making ability at these enterprises.

THE ROLE OF THE FEDERAL RESERVE IN AMPLIFYING THE CRISIS

Alan Greenspan, a onetime President of the US Federal Reserve, made some very serious mistakes in monetary policy. His loose policies with very low interest rates encouraged a generation of gambling and massive stock and real estate speculation. With interest rates so low and the cost of borrowing on a real basis (after adjustment for inflation) negative, hordes of gamblers, speculators and fraudsters got into the stock and real estate markets. This caused a massive bubble, which burst finally in both stock and real estate markets. These negative occurrences added to the financial crisis. Had Greenspan gradually raised interest rates instead of keeping it artificially low, we may have been able to either avoid or reduce the effects of this crisis.

The philosophy of growth at any cost without a long-term perspective (on the impact of such monetary policies) on the entire economy, twenty, thirty or even fifty years down caused this financial damage.

Unfortunately the short-term view of things has always got the US into trouble, whether it is emphasizing short-term profits in US corporations or Greenspan's view to bolster the economy short-term at the expense of Americans long-term future.

CHAPTER 43

INDICATORS OF THE BROADER CRISIS

When one views the global financial crisis, one needs to look at several causative factors and contributing circumstances. Circumstances refer to environmental trends, which affect the solution to this crisis long-term. Several current environmental influences are particularly disturbing, as it deals with the US situation. Since the US is the epicenter of this crisis, ongoing stability in the financial markets in the US is crucial to worldwide economic stability.

Looking at environmental trends the following areas are of crucial importance to long term world economic stability. These trends in the US may be defined as the following:

1. The ongoing health and Medicare crisis in the U.S.
2. The global warming crisis and America's role in same.
3. The US dependence on foreign oil.
4. The notorious overspending by the US government and Americans on both a fiscal, trade and personal basis, resulting in negative surpluses and huge international balance of payments.

THE ONGOING US HEALTH AND MEDICARE CRISIS

The problem

The bigger picture is that the U.S. cannot continue to build up negative trade balances and fiscal deficits. This mode of living and spending is not sustainable. If it is allowed to continue, there will not only be further debasement of the US dollar but greater worldwide economic instability as the dollar loses international value and U.S. inflation starts with massive government spending. One of the major contributory factors to the budget and fiscal deficit is the billions of dollars being sucked out of the US economy and budget to finance ongoing expenses related to medical needs of its citizens. The entire system of health delivery, nursing and hospital expenses and doctor's fees are out of whack. Here we live In a situation where the doctors, hospitals and large drug companies have formed a cartel to control the price of medical care. Even more disturbing is the fact that medical delivery costs are escalating beyond reason and eating up a greater proportion of the national budget.

The solution

The solution calls for an immediate revamping and major overhaul of the entire medical delivery system in the U.S. President Obama has already initiated discussions in this regard but has opened up the field for all interested players to come up with practical and reasonable ways to achieve the following two objectives:

1. To make health insurance available to everyone, with the possibility of setting up a public-sponsored health insurance outfit, to compete with current private market players.
2. To bring overall costs down of medical insurance.

So far, the private industry including insurance companies, medical associations, the drug companies and hospitals have come up with no practical solution. All they have done as of April 1, 2009 is to protest against the idea of setting up a public health insurance fund. Their resistance is well understood, because any move to reduce overall health insurance costs will reduce their revenue stream and profitability and this is something they do not want. This cartel of conspirators has milked the American people and U.S. government for decades and are not interested in any scheme to reduce their net profits.

However, moving forward a complete health care reform may be the only practical solution and it must be done immediately. To understand the problem in perspective, as of early 2009 almost twenty per cent of Americans were not insured health-wise--- a situation which is not sustainable long-term. Numerous stories have circulated in the press where Americans have lost their homes and life savings just because they could not pay their medical and operation bills.

This barbaric state of affairs must end immediately. People have a right to access medical services and why a great county like the U.S. cannot organize its medical affairs remains a mystery. Any future action must involve doing all the following:

1. Removing pre-existing conditions in health insurance policies, both group and private.
2. Reducing overall cost of procuring policies
3. Reducing, by negotiation, all caps on medical surgery and other extensive medical procedures.
4. Setting caps on physicians expenses for consultation and surgery.
3. Setting caps on hospital expenses, standardized across the board.   Only a tough, well negotiated plan to bring down costs and provide universal access will resort public confidence and give a sense of trust, fairness and honesty in the medical delivery business.   The global warming crisis and America's role in same.

THE GLOBAL WARMING CRISIS

The problem

Global warming represents one of the biggest environmental hazards of the twenty- first century. We are burning our way out of existence. The amount of greenhouse gases being produced are phenomenal and the situation is quickly getting out of control.

One of the great environmental polluters is the United States, followed by Europe, India and China. There needs to be leadership on part of the U.S. to come to the table with workable international emission standards as defined by the Kyoto Protocol. The US has always fought against the imposition of universally agreed emission standards---- this position has now changed with the arrival of President Obama, who has a most practical and pragmatic point of view. In short, the problem is that the U.S. must commit to better and cleaner environmental standards and work hard to coordinate this effort with their trading partners.

The solution

The solution lies in examining all the energy needs of Americans and to cut and reduce emissions such as greenhouse gases. To start with, we need cars which have more advanced catalytic converters. Going even more ahead, we need to reduce the reliance of Americans on cars with the development of proper road and transportation infrastructure.

Take a modern nation like Singapore, from which the US could learn a lot. An advanced rail and bus system makes owning a car almost unnecessary in Singapore. Why could we not have a system of mass urban transportation like Singapore? Americans would save on gas consumption and the overall economy would function better with individuals being transported to and from work in fuel efficient mass public transportation vehicles.

US DEPENDENCE ON FOREIGN OIL

The problem

The US imports far too much foreign oil. With such great volatility in oil prices, the nation can ill-afford to operate in an environment where their energy needs are dictated by foreign powers. Also oil-based products in the manufacturing sector, hurts the environment by creating and sustaining high greenhouse effects.

The solution

The US needs to find, develop and streamline new energy generation systems. Nuclear and wind energy are two practical alternatives. Although the start-up costs for such ventures are prohibitive, these energy systems are going to be more worthwhile long-term for the U.S.

In addition there has to be an initiative to produce and distribute electric or hybrid cars in the U.S. to hold down dependence on foreign oil.

These cars would pollute the skies less thus contributing to holding down greenhouses and controlling the global warning problem.

THE NOTORIOUS OVERSPENDING BY US GOVERNMENT AND AMERICANS

Problem

The world has lived far too long in the shadow of the U.S. These conditions are slowly coming to an end. To protect the nation from an ever dwindling lifestyle there needs to be an awareness on how notorious overspending by the US government and Americans on both a fiscal, trade and personal basis, results in negative surpluses and huge international balance of payments. We are going down a one way road of wealth decimation and we need to return to a more simpler way of living.

Solution

Although no one can tell anyone what to buy in the U.S., the Government needs to lead by example by spending national assets frugally. In order to do so, the budgets must be a balanced and the financial authorities must try to reduce the national debt to zero as soon as possible. This can be done by reducing billions of dollars of subsidies and wasteful expenditures at the Federal level.

President Obama has the right idea as he is on path to reduce substantially the federal deficit and has vowed to examine each and every item of expense to conserve the national wealth.

In closing, attention and action on all wasteful expenses in the US economy combined with an awareness of our needs to help others through positive governance, reduced environmental emission standards will help America continue to be a paradise in the future---- a dream which has been shattered through this financial and credit crisis. But rebuilding is within the realm of the strong and resolute American spirit and we must explore all avenues to grow and build this mighty nation.

CHAPTER 44

PRACTICAL SOLUTIONS TO THE GREAT FINANCIAL & CREDIT CRISIS

The challenges in front of us are numerous--- but they are not insurmountable. What is required is a clear and unbiased awareness of the strengths and weaknesses of the global financial system and an immediate action plan to get rid of the weak parts, which caused this great financial and credit crisis.

My humble suggestions to fix this problem, now and permanently in the future, involve implementation and ongoing monitoring of several areas impacting on the crisis.

Here is my recommended list of action steps required:

1. More regulation of financial markets and all its intermediaries, including insurance companies, commercial and investment banks, stockbrokers, financial advisors and all other relevant players.

2. Immediate revamping of the Federal Reserve with special emphasis on granting them additional responsibilities as systemic risk controller in the U.S.

3. A fundamental change in philosophical orientation to booms and busts, such change being enforced by financial authorities and the Federal Reserve.

4. Executive compensation caps to become a permanent feature in the banking, securities and financial intermediary industry. Caps to be permanent and to become non-negotiable.
5. Immediate temporary or permanent nationalization of the top 20 commercial banks in the U.S.
6. Immediate termination of the shadow banking system. No off-balance sheet entities allowed anywhere.
7. More effective and efficient risk modeling. Institutions are forced to share their risk modeling systems with regulators to ensure appropriate reserve allocation for named and unnamed risks.
8. Immediate licensing of all real estate mortgage brokers. Jail terms for all selling mortgages without appropriate licensing.
9. An immediate cessation of 30:1 leverage ratios in US financial institutions.
10. A greater auditing and intensive supervision role of financial institutions by all applicable governmental watchdogs, including the Federal Reserve, the FDIC, etc.
11. All SIV's (Shadow investment vehicles) to be disclosed as on balance sheet items immediately with applicability primarily to commercial and investment banks and hedge funds.
12. An immediate performance report every quarter by every hedge fund registered in or outside the US.

13. Immediate establishment of an independent government regulatory agency to monitor the credit assessment systems of all major rating agencies.

14. Establishment of a several thousand government audit team to assess, evaluate and monitor all high risk investments made by financial institutions, including investments in SIV's, other securitization products and all other exotic financial instruments, with particular attention to derivative products.

15. Continual and ongoing monthly stress testing of all financial institutions particularly the largest 20 commercial and investment banks, the top 10 life and health and retirement insurers, the top 10 property and casualty insurers.

16. Immediate re-opening of the credit granting process by financial institutions. This should be easy if nationalization is achieved, since the government can decide what needs to be done to open the credit tap.

17. Assessment, evaluation and maintenance of objectives arrived at with respect to the credit granting process, divided by individual institutions in terms of percentage of target achieved.

18. Continual federal backing of commercial paper issuers, to extend to A and AA credit rated issuers in addition to the AAA issuers approved as of April 1, 2009.

19. FBI investigation of all criminal activity relating to executives in the financial services industry and immediate prosecution with jail terms for all offenders.
20. Total disclosure to required government watchdog of all positions entered into with respect to credit default swap transactions with immediate ongoing assessment, evaluation of proper risk methodologies used in terms of risk transference and its impact on systemic risk.
21. Immediate and permanent regulation of all hedge funds, both domestic and international.
22. Greater transparency and financial reporting of all credit derivative positions engaged to by all financial institutions. In short, more transparency, greater visibility of all risk items and financial and legal accountability by all offending bankers, securities and credit derivative traders.
23. Reformation of international financial institutions like the IMF and World Bank as international lenders of last resort.
24. Promotion of global trade and international capital flows.

ITEM 1: MORE REGULATION OF FINANCIAL MARKETS AND ALL ITS INTERMEDIARIES INCLUDING INSURANCE COMPANIES, COMMERCIAL AND INVESTMENT BANKS, STOCKBROKERS, FINANCIAL ADVISORS AND ALL OTHER RELEVANT PLAYERS.

Lack of financial regulation of hedge funds, including poor oversight of risk-taking mechanisms by private and investment banks in the US and a poor investigative process by SEC put the entire financial system at risk, resulting in the global system coming close to a meltdown in the third quarter of 2008. In terms of regulation, not only is there a need for US regulation but coordinated international financial regulation is required, particularly with respect of large global players like hedge funds, institutional funds and sovereign government funds as they move billions of dollars in and out of currency, stock and bond markets every day, causing disruption at every point.

ITEM 2; IMMEDIATE REVAMPING OF THE FEDERAL RESERVE WITH SPECIAL EMPHASIS ON ADDITIONAL RESPONSIBILITIES AS SYSTEMIC RISK CONTROLLER IN THE US.

The Federal Reserve has not played an optimal role in controlling this crisis. Through this power to influence national interest rates, it went overboard under Alan Greenspan in letting interest rates stay low for far too long, encouraging an atmosphere of speculation and fraud. With real rates of interest negative(after adjusting for inflation) there were numerous opportunities for investors to take untold risks; all of such risks compounded into a bubble which burst in the stock, real estate and liquidity markets from 2007 to 2009.

The Federal Reserve of the US needs more authority to deal with non-financial institutions like AIG--- this power must include the legal ability to close or reorganize such institutions as and when such is required for systemic stability.

Also, it might be a wise point to put a several thousand audit team inside the SEC to monitor risk-taking mechanisms. This process must be supported by efficient mathematical modeling, which supports the audit process and assists in presentation of early monitors of major systemic risk occurrence.

ITEM 3: A FUNDAMENTAL CHANGE IN PHILOSOPHICAL ORIENTATION TO BOOMS AND BUSTS, SUCH CHANGE BEING ENFORCED BY FINANCIAL AUTHORITIES AND THE FEDERAL RESERVE

There needs to be a government sponsored public education program targeted at investors and the general public that acceptable financial performance has an added dimension of ethical contribution---- this includes the obligation of corporations and speculators alike to contribute to the betterment of their communities and that just short-term profit (quarterly profits booked) is not the judge of a good corporation. The same attitude needs to be translated into the mindsets of Federal Reserve Authorities.

Never again, and I mean never again, should one man's vision (yours truly, Alan Greenspan) influence the shape and future of such a critical economy like the United States. Leaving interest rates low for such a long period, created speculative conditions which lead to a bubble.

This financial bubble could have been avoided if interest rates were gradually increased instead of having the narrow minded mentality of profit and any cost---this was very apparent in the boom years when corporations and individuals were very profitable(during the heydays of the Greenspan area). In short, Greenspan compromised the long term stability of the financial system in favor of short- term profits.

ITEM 4: EXECUTIVE COMPENSATION CAPS TO BECOME A PERMANENT FEATURE IN THE BANKING, SECURITIES AND FINANCIAL INTERMEDIARY INDUSTRY. CAPS TO BE PERMANENT AND TO BECOME NON-NEGOTIABLE.

The current global financial crisis has shown how Chief Executive officers and their senior management cronies milked the system even when their companies were bleeding financially. Several notable cases come to mind here; more recently was a press release naming Vikram Pandit (CEO of Citigroup) earning 14 million dollars as approximate total compensation in 2008. Another notable waste of resources was indicated in a news article which pointed out to John Thain, CEO of Merrill Lynch spending more than one million dollars in refurbishing his office.

He also was very unethical in authorizing the payment of millions of dollars in bonuses to his senior executives prior to the merger with Bank of America. Here was a company (Merrill Lynch) steep in losses, which had to be saved by a government bailout.

In the midst of such trying financial times and billion dollar losses, this Chief Executive felt fit to grant million dollars in bonuses to his senior executives. Another example which comes to mind is the well publicized case involving the AIG Insurance Company, which after suffering billions of dollars in losses in 2008, approved a payment of more than 150 million dollars as retention bonuses to certain executives. The era of high compensation is gone in the United States and indeed in the whole world. A simple message to all greedy bankers is: "Get out and stay out of the banking and money management system. We do not need you."

Executive compensation caps are a must at every global financial institution. Such caps should be permanent and non negotiable. Only then will there be a semblance of public confidence in banking and investment/insurance executives, who get paid millions of dollars, in good times and bad.

ITEM 5: IMMEDIATE TEMPORARY / PERMANENT NATIONALIZATION OF THE TOP 20 COMMERCIAL BANKS IN THE US.

One of the gravest mistakes being made by the US administration and the Treasury Secretary, Timothy Geithner is to allow banks to run under their original management. In addition the last President George Bush made a further mistake of providing around 350 billion dollars of TARP money to banks and other financial institutions with no collateral conditions for quantum of lending levels to be achieved.

In short, banks got a blank check to do what they wished with taxpayer money. This has changed somewhat under the Obama administration but there is still a lack of long-term financial vision for the banks. There is only one way to solve this problem quickly and this is to nationalize the banks, fire the CEO and board of directors, wipe out all existing debt and zero out the shareholders and start again.

Force the lending process through the auspices of experts in the files appointed by the government. Cut off and close down unprofitable businesses and regroup the business to do what it must do first, which is lend money to consumers and to small and medium sized business. As of April 1, 2009 in spite of all the sincere and serious efforts of the Obama administration and billions of dollars of bailout money, credit markets are seized, lending is down to a trickle and none of the objectives of the bailout money have been achieved.

380

To solve this difficult problem requires urgent, active and decisive action. The nationalized banks can be sold later, when conditions improve and the government will definitely get a good return on its investment. In the meantime, there is no one else except the government that can pull it off and most unfortunately the government does not want to get into management of the banking business, even temporarily. This misplaced philosophical orientation is going to cause more misery to the American people as it will take years to restore banking to the level of normalcy seen in the past. This is another unbelievable philosophical and business blunder.

ITEM 6; IMMEDIATE TERMINATION OF THE SHADOW BANKING SYSTEM. NO OFF-BALANCE SHEET ENTITIES ALLOWED ANYWHERE

There needs to be a complete and immediate end to the entire shadow banking system. Such a parallel banking system has caused the assumption of major risks outside the balance sheets of financial institutions. Such risks were not calculated scientifically and were mostly unhedged in nature. When the sub-prime market collapsed, this situation called for counterparty payment worth billions of dollars, depleting bank capital and causing several major investment bank failures.

All off-balance sheet entities must be immediately and completed transferred as balance sheet items and all losses or gains properly recorded.

The accounting standards board of the US must make this a permanent change in accounting reporting rules for all corporations in the US.

ITEM 7: MORE EFFECTIVE AND EFFICIENT RISK MODELING. INSTITUTIONS ARE FORCED TO SHARE THEIR RISK MODELING SYSTEMS WITH REGULATORS TO ENSURE APPROPRIATE RESERVE ALLOCATION FOR NAMED AND UNNAMED RISKS

Risk modeling systems of the large financial institutions need to be monitored constantly.
For example, the risk modeling system in big banks ignored two important variables: firstly, that real estate values would plummet in the US and secondly, that there would be mass defaults in the subprime mortgage business.

Lack of incorporation of these two important variable resulted in improper risks been taken by such institutions and contributed to billions of dollars in losses, which again created the financial mess in this crisis. The responsibility for preventing systemic risk should be provided to the Federal Reserve with direct participation by such authority into every financial institutions risk modeling portfolio. This would prevent crisis like the one we have now from re-occurring again.

ITEM 8: IMMEDIATE LICENSING OF ALL REAL ESTATE MORTGAGE BROKERS. JAIL TERMS FOR ALL SELLING MORTGAGES WITHOUT APPROPRIATE LICENSING

All mortgage brokers and mortgage origination agents need to be appropriately licensed and regulated. The last subprime crisis in the US saw the presence of several unlicensed, unregulated individuals posing as mortgage brokers. In some cases, financial institutions were reported to paying as much as ten thousand dollars per incoming client. The temptations of money and the lack of government regulation led to numerous fraudulent cases where honest, hardworking citizens were conned into taking mortgages they could not afford to pay, given their assets, liability and income situation.
The resulting collapse of the subprime market started the great financial and credit crisis.

ITEM 9: AN IMMEDIATE CESSATION OF 30:1 LEVERAGE RATIOS IN US FINANCIAL INSTITUTIONS

The traditional banking model for investment and commercial banks was a 30:1 leverage in the US. This model was prevalent prior to the onset of the financial and credit crisis. For example, every million dollars of capital inside a bank resulted in a loan of 30 million dollars. With improper risk controls and unhedged investment portfolios, it did not take a long time to see how a downturn in market conditions could decimate bank's balance sheets.

The days of rampant risk taking are gone forever. And so are the days of high leverage of customer's deposits. Regulation must be put into place immediately to limit leverage use to probably not more than 10:1 with proper reportable risk controls to the government.

ITEM 10: A GREATER AUDITING AND INTENSIVE SUPERVISION ROLE OF FINANCIAL INSTITUTIONS BY ALL APPLICABLE GOVERNMENTAL WATCHDOGS INCLUDING THE FEDERAL RESERVE, THE FDIC, ETC.

Auditing standards must be revamped immediately. Quarterly detailed onsite visits to financial institutions under the direction of the Federal Reserve or another competent authority must be mandatory. In such visits, all items must be put on the table.

There should be a thorough study of all risk portfolios, risk monitoring mechanisms and portfolio compositions. Any risks to systemic equilibrium should be immediately reported to the government authorities and remedial action enforced.

ITEM 11: ALL SIV'S TO BE DISCLOSED AS ON BALANCE SHEET ITEMS IMMEDIATELY WITH APPLICABILITY PRIMARILY TO COMMERCIAL ANDINVESTMENT BANKS AND HEDGE FUNDS

Structured investment vehicles must always find their way to appear as an on balance sheet item. SIV's brought the banking system to its knees by inflicting great losses.

But this ruling must apply not only to financial institutions but also to private equity funds, hedge funds and institutional funds, including pension funds. The investing public has a right to know about the riskiness of their investments and only full disclosure and complete transparency will restore permanent investor confidence--- a component so critical in the ordering function of capital and financial markets worldwide.

ITEM 12: AN IMMEDIATE PERFORMANCE REPORT EVERY QUARTER BY EVERY HEDGE FUND REGISTERED IN OR OUTSIDE THE US.

All hedge funds, private equity funds and other applicable mutual funds must provide a performance report every quarter.

In such report must be disclosed the balance sheet of the fund, the liability and risk position and the method of performance calculation. This report must go to every investor and every major credit rating agency and a government watchdog like the SEC. Any large risky positions contributive to systemic risk must be immediately sold to restore some balance to the global financial system. Again, the days for very wealthy investors to take massive risks through the mechanism of hedge funds are over. Such hedge funds and their investment behavior pose great financial risks to the entire US and world global financial system.

ITEM 13: IMMEDIATE ESTABLISHMENT OF AN INDEPENDENT GOVERNMENT REGULATORY AGENCY TO MONITOR THE CREDIT ASSESSMENT SYSTEMS OF ALL MAJOR RATING AGENCIES

The credit reporting agencies in the US were part of the problem in the current financial crisis. This was due to their hand in rating paper wrongfully. How could you expect an unbiased reporting system when the rating companies were paid by the same issuers who needed a good rating for their various structured and non-structured vehicles? No one in the United States, including the SEC paid any heed or attention to this obvious conflict of interest. Based on these ratings, investors and institutions worldwide invested in numerous securities which were inherently more risky than the rating would indicate.

This misplaced trust resulted in disastrous investment actions leading to billions of dollars of losses in European, Australian and Asian banks.

What is required is an "internal affairs" department for the rating agencies except that this internal affairs department is the government team, who monitor the methodology of risk allocation to various issues in the capital markets. This system will catch poorly researched or inaccurately reported credit ratings and give investors worldwide a level playing field in terms of ascertaining the riskiness of various investments.

ITEM 14 : ESTABLISHMENT OF A SPECIAL CELL COMPRISING SEVERAL THOUSAND GOVERNMENT AUDIT TEAM TO ASSESS, EVALUATE AND MONITOR ALL HIGH RISK INVESTMENTS MADE BY FINANCIAL INSTITUTIONS, INCLUDING INVESTMENTS IN SIV'S, OTHER SECURITIZATION PRODICTS AND ALL OTHER EXOTIC FINANCIAL INSTRUMENTS, WITH PARTICULAR ATTENTION TO DERIVATIVE PRODUCTS

There needs to be consideration, at the highest levels of the US government, to establishing rules, procedures and resources to assess, evaluate and monitor systemic risk at all financial institutions, both domestic and multinational. The current financial and credit crisis showed the absence of interest or muscle power in rectifying any anomalies or poor investment moves by large financial institutions. This entire situation needs to be reversed immediately.

And if the financial institution resists, fire the top brass, wipe out the current shareholders and start fresh. Let what can survive profitably stay and let everything else go. Above all, do not allow anyone, anywhere, to take the monumental risks in search of greed and unbridled profits. This had brought the financial system down now---- but should not bring the system down ever again. This can be achieved by close monitoring and supervision by government authorities.

ITEM 15 : CONTINUAL AND ONGOING MONTHLY STRESS TESTING OF ALL FINANCIAL INSTITUTIONS PARTICULARLY THE LARGEST 20 COMMERCIAL AND INVESTMENT BANKS, THE TOP 10 LIFE AND HEALTH AND RETIREMENT INSURERS, THE TOP 10 PROPERTY AND CASUALTY INSURERS

The stress testing, which is underway in major banks, as of April 2009 must continue ad infinitum. Particular attention should be paid to the portfolios of the top 10-20 commercial and investment banks and life and non-life insurers. Stress testing should include the capacity of the institution to weather very adverse economic and market conditions and must be employed to determine the potential solvency or insolvency of such institutions under such conditions. Immediate action must be taken to rectify any potential difficulties, including the possibility of shutting down or selling an non- complying financial institution or insurer.

ITEM 16: IMMEDIATE RE-OPENING OF THE CREDIT GRANTING PROCESS BY FINANCIAL INSTITUTIONS. THIS SHOULD BE EASY IF NATIONALIZATION IS ACHIEVED, SINCE THE GOBVERNMENT CAN DECIDE WHAT NEEDS TO BE DONE TO OPEN THE CREDIT TAP.

Opening up the credit tap is the most important priority in the US today. It is the only way to effectively create conditions of financial normalcy. As of April 1, 2009 the credit markets are still frozen and banks still do not trust each other in the interbank lending market.

Nor do banks easily grant credit to individuals, students and small and medium- sized businesses. This credit tightening situation is not sustainable in the future. This is such an important element in solving the financial crisis that I have separated this out as a major issue.

The success of what any government or financial authority does must be measured by its ability to restore lending again and doing so as quickly as possible. In this matter, the US authorities should learn from Gordon Brown, the pre-eminent leader of the UK government, who has extracted and enforced promises from the banks to lend in exchange for receipt of UK government bailout funds. Those banks who failed this process were immediately taken over with their entire board of senior management pitched out. Strong and decisive action to restore lending is the only way to move out of this crisis fast.

ITEM 17:   ASSESSMENT, EVALUATION AND MAINTENANCE OF OBJECTIVES ARRIVED AT WITH RESPECT TO THE CREDIT GRANTING   PROCESS,   DIVIDED   BY   INDIVIDUAL INSTITUTIONS IN TERMS OF PERCENTAGE OF TARGET ACHIEVED

As a continuation of Item 16, the government must set up objectives in terms of minimum lending required by banks and monitor it constantly and intensively. All banks not following these rules must be punished. This is not a time for bickering or hesitation in lending money.

Banks serve an essential function in their economy and they need to fulfill their needed role. Sacrifice of bank independence in favor of the public interest is called for in this crisis. Banks not following these new rules should be punished or closed down as an extreme action for continual, non-compliance.

ITEM 18: CONTINUAL FEDERAL BACKING OF COMMERCIAL PAPER ISSUERS, TO EXTEND TO A AND AA CREDIT RATED ISSUERS IN ADDITION TO THE AAA ISSUERS APPROVED AS OF APRIL 1,2009

Commercial paper is the mechanism used by big and small firms alike to raise money in the capital markets. With the development of this financial crisis, investors stopped putting money into purchase of commercial paper, causing a funding crisis for such businesses. The US government stepped in to guarantee purchases of all AAA corporate paper.

Given the deterioration in numerous credit markets due to the economic downturn, the government needs to go further to guarantee A and AA corporate paper, too. This will provide much needed financing to companies which have weakened credit-wise in this economic downturn. In time, the Government should provide guarantees to weaker credit-rated business organizations, too.

ITEM 19: FBI INVESTIGATION OF ALL CRIMINAL ACTIVITY RELATING TO EXECUTIVES IN THE FINANCIAL SERVICES INDUSTRY AND IMMEDIATE PROSECUTION WITH JAIL TERMS FOR ALL OFFENDERS

It is a shame that very few executives who contributed to this crisis have gone to jail. Several months back it was mentioned that the FBI was going to conduct investigations and then determine if anyone should be charged. The culprits are all out and in the open--- they are moving freely with all their ill-gotten gains. One perpetrator, Allan Stanford, has skipped the country and no one knows where he is. When is the US going to get serious as a country to make public examples of these corporate thieves? Why should they be allowed to get away with fraudulent activity? Just because they are rich? Or well connected? It is a pitiful and most shameful state of affairs.

ITEM 20: PROMOTION OF GLOBAL TRADE AND INTERNATIONAL CAPITAL FLOWS IN AN ATMOSPHERE DEVOID OF NATIONAL PROTECTIONISM.

Global trade and international capital flows must be encouraged. There is always a tendency for a country to shut off its trade and capital borders, while they "unconsciously" blame other countries and foreign entities for their problems. Only free and open trade and capital flows can increase world GDP.

Therefore, in all instances protectionism policies must be avoided by national governments as everyone co-operatively tries to solve this problem.

A spirit of co-operation and reconciliation has already started and I am heartened to see that the world is finally working together to solve a universal problem--- how to have a good economy and provide food, water, housing and other resources to national citizens while co-operating with other countries who are trying to achieve the same objectives. In the absence of hate and violence and implementation of such initiatives lies our hope and future salvation.

I would like to close this chapter by releasing the communiqué of the G20 conference in London on April 2, 2009. This spirit of friendship, inter-commitment and mutual collaboration is what we need as a world to solve this incredibly difficult global problem.

JOINT COMMUNIQUE G-20
MEETING
Leaders' Statement
April 2, 2009, London

1. We, the Leaders of the Group
of Twenty, met in London on 2
April 2009.

2. We face the greatest challenge
to the world economy in modern
times; a crisis which has
deepened since we last met,
which affects the lives of women,
men, and children in every
country, and which all countries
must join together to resolve. A
global crisis requires a global
solution.

3. We start from the belief that prosperity is indivisible; that growth, to be sustained, has to be shared; and that our global plan for recovery must have at its heart the needs and jobs of hard-working families, not just in developed countries but in emerging markets and the poorest countries of the world too; and must reflect the interests, not just of today's population, but of future generations too. We believe that the only sure foundation for sustainable globalization and rising prosperity for all is an open world economy based on market principles, effective regulation, and strong global institutions.

4. We have today therefore pledged to do whatever is necessary to:

• restore confidence, growth, and jobs;
• repair the financial system to restore lending;

- strengthen financial regulation to rebuild trust;
- fund and reform our international financial institutions to overcome this crisis and prevent future ones;
- promote global trade and investment and reject protectionism, to underpin prosperity; and
- build an inclusive, green, and sustainable recovery.

By acting together to fulfill these pledges we will bring the world economy out of recession and prevent a crisis like this from recurring in the future.

5.The agreements we have reached today, to treble resources available to the IMF to $750 billion, to support a new SDR allocation of $250 billion, to support at least $100 billion of additional lending by the MDBs, to ensure $250 billion of support for trade finance, and to use the additional resources from agreed IMF gold sales for concessional finance for the poorest countries, constitute an additional $1.1 trillion programme of support to restore credit, growth and jobs in the world economy. Together with the measures we have each taken nationally, this constitutes a global plan for recovery on an unprecedented scale.

Restoring growth and jobs

6. We are undertaking an unprecedented and concerted fiscal expansion, which will save or create millions of jobs which would otherwise have been destroyed, and that will, by the end of next year, amount to $5 trillion, raise output by 4 per cent, and accelerate the transition to a green economy. We are committed to deliver the scale of sustained fiscal effort necessary to restore growth.

7. Our central banks have also taken exceptional action. Interest rates have been cut aggressively in most countries, and our central banks have pledged to maintain expansionary policies for as long as needed and to use the full range of monetary policy instruments, including unconventional instruments, consistent with price stability.

8. Our actions to restore growth cannot be effective until we restore domestic lending and international capital flows. We have provided significant and comprehensive support to our banking systems to provide liquidity, recapitalize financial institutions, and address decisively the problem of impaired assets. We are committed to take all necessary actions to restore the normal flow of credit through the financial system and ensure the soundness of systemically important institutions, implementing our policies in line with the agreed G20 framework for restoring lending and repairing the financial sector.

9. Taken together, these actions will constitute the largest fiscal and monetary stimulus and the most comprehensive support programme for the financial sector in modern times.

Acting together strengthens the impact and the exceptional policy actions announced so far must be implemented without delay. Today, we have further agreed over $1 trillion of additional resources for the world economy through our international financial institutions and trade finance.

10. Last month the IMF estimated that world growth in real terms would resume and rise to over 2 percent by the end of 2010. We are confident that the actions we have agreed today, and our unshakeable commitment to work together to restore growth and jobs, while preserving long-term fiscal sustainability, will accelerate the return to trend growth. We commit today to taking whatever action is necessary to secure that outcome, and we call on the IMF to assess regularly the actions taken and the global actions required.

11. We are resolved to ensure long-term fiscal sustainability and price stability and will put in place credible exit strategies from the measures that need to be taken now to support the financial sector and restore global demand. We are convinced that by implementing our agreed policies we will limit the longer-term costs to our economies, thereby reducing the scale of the fiscal consolidation necessary over the longer term.

12. We will conduct all our economic policies cooperatively and responsibly with regard to the impact on other countries and will refrain from competitive devaluation of our currencies and promote a stable and well-functioning international monetary system.

We will support, now and in the future, to candid, even-handed, and independent IMF surveillance of our economies and financial sectors, of the impact of our policies on others, and of risks facing the global economy.

Strengthening financial supervision and regulation

1. Major failures in the financial sector and in financial regulation and supervision were fundamental causes of the crisis. Confidence will not be restored until we rebuild trust in our financial system.
   2. We will take action to build a stronger, more globally consistent, supervisory and regulatory framework for the future financial sector, which will support sustainable global growth and serve the needs of business and citizens.

3. We each agree to ensure our domestic regulatory systems are strong. But we also agree to establish the much greater consistency and systematic cooperation between countries, and the framework of internationally agreed high standards that a global financial system requires. Strengthened regulation and supervision must promote propriety, integrity and transparency; guard against risk across the financial system; dampen rather than amplify the financial and economic cycle; reduce reliance on inappropriately risky sources of financing; and discourage excessive risk-taking. Regulators and supervisors must protect consumers and investors, support market discipline, avoid adverse impacts on other countries, reduce the scope for regulatory arbitrage, support competition and dynamism, and keep pace with innovation in the marketplace.

4. To this end we are implementing the Action Plan agreed at our last meeting, as set out in the attached progress report. We have today also issued a Declaration, Strengthening the Financial System. In particular we agree:

•to establish a new Financial Stability Board (FSB) with a strengthened mandate, as a successor to the Financial Stability Forum (FSF), including all G20 countries, FSF members, Spain, and the European Commission;

•that the FSB should collaborate with the IMF to provide early warning of macroeconomic and financial risks and the actions needed to address them;

• to reshape our regulatory systems so that our authorities are able to identify and take account of macro-prudential risks;

· to extend regulation and oversight to all systemically important financial institutions, instruments and markets. This will include, for the first time, systemically important hedge funds;

· to endorse and implement the FSF's tough new principles on pay and compensation and to support sustainable compensation schemes and the corporate social responsibility of all firms;

· to take action, once recovery is assured, to improve the quality, quantity, and international consistency of capital in the banking system. In future, regulation must prevent excessive leverage and require buffers of resources to be built up in good times;

•to take action against non-cooperative jurisdictions, including tax havens. We stand ready to deploy sanctions to protect our public finances and financial systems. The era of banking secrecy is over. We note that the OECD has today published a list of countries assessed by the Global Forum against the international standard for exchange of tax information;

•to call on the accounting standard setters to work urgently with supervisors and regulators to improve standards on valuation and provisioning and achieve a single set of high-quality global accounting standards; and

•to extend regulatory oversight and registration to Credit Rating Agencies to ensure they meet the international code of good practice, particularly to prevent unacceptable conflicts of interest.

16. We instruct our Finance Ministers to complete the implementation of these decisions in line with the timetable set out in the Action Plan. We have asked the FSB and the IMF to monitor progress, working with the Financial Action Taskforce and other relevant bodies, and to provide a report to the next meeting of our Finance Ministers in Scotland in November.

Strengthening our global financial institutions

17. Emerging markets and developing countries, which have been the engine of recent world growth, are also now facing challenges which are adding to the current downturn in the global economy. It is imperative for global confidence and economic recovery that capital continues to flow to them.

This will require a substantial strengthening of the international financial institutions, particularly the IMF. We have therefore agreed today to make available an additional $850 billion of resources through the global financial institutions to support growth in emerging market and developing countries by helping to finance counter-cyclical spending, bank recapitalization, infrastructure, trade finance, balance of payments support, debt rollover, and social support.

To this end:

· we have agreed to increase the resources available to the IMF through immediate financing from members of $250 billion, subsequently incorporated into an expanded and more flexible New Arrangements to Borrow, increased by up to $500 billion, and to consider market borrowing if necessary; and

· we support a substantial
increase in lending of at least
$100 billion by the Multilateral
Development Banks (MDBs),
including to low income
countries, and ensure that all
MDBs, including have the
appropriate capital.

18. It is essential that these
resources can be used effectively
and flexibly to support growth.
We welcome in this respect the
progress made by the IMF with its
new Flexible Credit Line (FCL) and
its reformed lending and
conditionality framework which
will enable the IMF to ensure that
its facilities address effectively
the underlying causes of
countries' balance of payments
financing needs, particularly the
withdrawal of external capital
flows to the banking and
corporate sectors. We support
Mexico's decision to seek an FCL
arrangement.

19. We have agreed to support a general SDR allocation which will inject $250 billion into the world economy and increase global liquidity, and urgent ratification of the Fourth Amendment.

20. In order for our financial institutions to help manage the crisis and prevent future crises we must strengthen their longer term relevance, effectiveness and legitimacy. So alongside the significant increase in resources agreed today we are determined to reform and modernize the international financial institutions to ensure they can assist members and shareholders effectively in the new challenges they face. We will reform their mandates, scope and governance to reflect changes in the world economy and the new challenges of globalization, and that emerging and developing economies, including the poorest, must have greater voice and representation.

This must be accompanied by action to increase the credibility and accountability of the institutions through better strategic oversight and decision making. To this end:

• we commit to implementing the package of IMF quota and voice reforms agreed in April 2008 and call on the IMF to complete the next review of quotas by January 2011;

• we agree that, alongside this, consideration should be given to greater involvement of the Fund's Governors in providing strategic direction to the IMF and increasing its accountability;

• we commit to implementing the World Bank reforms agreed in October 2008. We look forward to further recommendations, at the next meetings, on voice and representation reforms on an accelerated timescale, to be agreed by the 2010 Spring Meetings;

• we agree that the heads and senior leadership of the international financial institutions should be appointed through an open, transparent, and merit-based selection process; and

• building on the current reviews of the IMF and World Bank we asked the Chairman, working with the G20 Finance Ministers, to consult widely in an inclusive process and report back to the next meeting with proposals for further reforms to improve the responsiveness and adaptability of the IFIs.

21. In addition to reforming our international financial institutions for the new challenges of globalization we agreed on the desirability of a new global consensus on the key values and principles that will promote sustainable economic activity. We support discussion on such a charter for sustainable economic activity with a view to further discussion at our next meeting.

We take note of the work started in other fora in this regard and look forward to further discussion of this charter for sustainable economic activity.

Resisting protectionism and promoting global trade and investment

22. World trade growth has underpinned rising prosperity for half a century. But it is now falling for the first time in 25 years. Falling demand is exacerbated by growing protectionist pressures and a withdrawal of trade credit. Reinvigorating world trade and investment is essential for restoring global growth. We will not repeat the historic mistakes of protectionism of previous eras.

To this end:

• we reaffirm the commitment made in Washington: to refrain from raising new barriers to investment or to trade in goods and services, imposing new export restrictions, or implementing World Trade Organization (WTO) inconsistent measures to stimulate exports. In addition we will rectify promptly any such measures. We extend this pledge to the end of 2010;

• we will minimize any negative impact on trade and investment of our domestic policy actions including fiscal policy and action in support of the financial sector. We will not retreat into financial protectionism, particularly measures that constrain worldwide capital flows, especially to developing countries;

• we will notify promptly the WTO of any such measures and we call on the WTO, together with other international bodies, within their respective mandates, to monitor and report publicly on our adherence to these undertakings on a quarterly basis;

• we will take, at the same time, whatever steps we can to promote and facilitate trade and investment; and

• we will ensure availability of at least $250 billion over the next two years to support trade finance through our export credit and investment agencies and through the MDBs. We also ask our regulators to make use of available flexibility in capital requirements for trade finance.

23. We remain committed to reaching an ambitious and balanced conclusion to the Doha Development Round, which is urgently needed.

This could boost the global economy by at least $150 billion per annum. To achieve this we are committed to building on the progress already made, including with regard to modalities.

24. We will give renewed focus and political attention to this critical issue in the coming period and will use our continuing work and all international meetings that are relevant to drive progress ensuring a fair and sustainable recovery for all.

25. We are determined not only to restore growth but to lay the foundation for a fair and sustainable world economy. We recognize that the current crisis has a disproportionate impact on the vulnerable in the poorest countries and recognize our collective responsibility to mitigate the social impact of the crisis to minimize long-lasting damage to global potential. To this end:

· we reaffirm our historic commitment to meeting the Millennium Development Goals and to achieving our respective ODA pledges, including commitments on Aid for Trade, debt relief, and the Gleneagles commitments, especially to sub-Saharan Africa;

· the actions and decisions we have taken today will provide $50 billion to support social protection, boost trade and safeguard development in low income countries, as part of the significant increase in crisis support for these and other developing countries and emerging markets;

• we are making available
resources for social protection for
the poorest countries, including
through investing in long-term
food security and through
voluntary bilateral contributions
to the World Bank's Vulnerability
Framework, including the
Infrastructure Crisis Facility, and
the Rapid Social Response Fund;

• we have committed, consistent
with the new income model, that
additional resources from agreed
sales of IMF gold will be used,
together with surplus income, to
provide $6 billion additional
concessional and flexible finance
for the poorest countries over the
next 2 to 3 years. We call on the
IMF to come forward with
concrete proposals at the Spring
Meetings;

• we have agreed to review the flexibility of the Debt Sustainability Framework and call on the IMF and World Bank to report to the IMFC and Development Committee at the Annual Meetings; and

• we call on the UN, working with other global institutions, to establish an effective mechanism to monitor the impact of the crisis on the poorest and most vulnerable.

25. We recognize the human dimension to the crisis. We commit to support those affected by the crisis by creating employment opportunities and through income support measures. We will build a fair and family-friendly labor market for both women and men. We therefore welcome the reports of the London Jobs Conference and the Rome Social Summit and the key principles they proposed.

26. We will support employment by stimulating growth, investing in education and training, and through active labor market policies, focusing on the most vulnerable. We call upon the ILO, working with other relevant organizations, to assess the actions taken and those required for the future.

27. We agreed to make the best possible use of investment funded by fiscal stimulus programmes towards the goal of building a resilient, sustainable, and green recovery. We will make the transition towards clean, innovative, resource efficient, low carbon technologies and infrastructure.

We encourage the MDBs to contribute fully to the achievement of this objective. We will identify and work together on further measures to build sustainable economies.

28. We reaffirm our commitment to address the threat of irreversible climate change, based on the principle of common but differentiated responsibilities, and to reach agreement at the UN Climate Change conference in Copenhagen in December 2009.

Delivering our commitments

29. We have committed ourselves to work together with urgency and determination to translate these words into action. We agreed to meet again before the end of this year to review progress on our commitments.

Source: Number 10 Downing Street

Global Plan Annex: Declaration on Strengthening the Financial System Statement Issued by the G20 Leaders, April 2, 2009, London

We, the Leaders of the G20, have taken, and will continue to take, action to strengthen regulation and supervision in line with the commitments we made in Washington to reform the regulation of the financial sector. Our principles are strengthening transparency and accountability, enhancing sound regulation, promoting integrity in financial markets and reinforcing international cooperation. The material in this declaration expands and provides further detail on the commitments in our statement. We published today a full progress report against each of the 47 actions set out in the Washington Action Plan. In particular, we have agreed the following major reforms.

Financial Stability Board

We have agreed that the Financial Stability Forum should be expanded, given a broadened mandate to promote financial stability, and re-established with a stronger institutional basis and enhanced capacity as the Financial Stability Board (FSB). The FSB will:

- assess vulnerabilities affecting the financial system, identify and oversee action needed to address them;
- promote co-ordination and information exchange among authorities responsible for financial stability;
- monitor and advise on market developments and their implications for regulatory policy;
- advise on and monitor best practice in meeting regulatory standards;

- undertake joint strategic reviews of the policy development work of the international Standard Setting Bodies to ensure their work is timely, coordinated, focused on priorities, and addressing gaps;
- set guidelines for, and support the establishment, functioning of, and participation in, supervisory colleges, including through ongoing identification of the most systemically important cross-border firms;
- support contingency planning for cross-border crisis management, particularly with respect to systemically important firms; and

- collaborate with the IMF to conduct Early Warning Exercises to identify and report to the IMFC and the G20 Finance Ministers and Central Bank Governors on the buildup of macroeconomic and financial risks and the actions needed to address them.

Members of the FSB commit to pursue the maintenance of financial stability, enhance the openness and transparency of the financial sector, and implement international financial standards (including the 12 key International Standards and Codes), and agree to undergo periodic peer reviews, using among other evidence IMF / World Bank public Financial Sector Assessment Program reports. The FSB will elaborate and report on these commitments and the evaluation process.

We welcome the FSB's and IMF's commitment to intensify their collaboration, each complementing the other's role and mandate.

International cooperation

To strengthen international cooperation we have agreed:

- to establish the remaining supervisory colleges for significant cross-border firms by June 2009, building on the 28 already in place;
- to implement the FSF principles for cross-border crisis management immediately, and that home authorities of each major international financial institution should ensure that the group of authorities with a common interest in that financial institution meet at least annually;

- to support continued efforts by the IMF, FSB, World Bank, and BCBS to develop an international framework for cross-border bank resolution arrangements;
- the importance of further work and international cooperation on the subject of exit strategies;
- that the IMF and FSB should together launch an Early Warning Exercise at the 2009 Spring Meetings.

Prudential regulation

We have agreed to strengthen international frameworks for prudential regulation:

- until recovery is assured the international standard for the minimum level of capital should remained unchanged;

- where appropriate, capital buffers above the required minima should be allowed to decline to facilitate lending in deteriorating economic conditions;
- once recovery is assured, prudential regulatory standards should be strengthened. Buffers above regulatory minima should be increased and the quality of capital should be enhanced. Guidelines for harmonization of the definition of capital should be produced by end 2009. The BCBS should review minimum levels of capital and develop recommendations in 2010;

- the FSB, BCBS, and CGFS, working with accounting standard setters, should take forward, with a deadline of end 2009, implementation of the recommendations published today to mitigate procyclicality, including a requirement for banks to build buffers of resources in good times that they can draw down when conditions deteriorate;

- risk-based capital requirements should be supplemented with a simple, transparent, non-risk based measure which is internationally comparable, properly takes into account off-balance sheet exposures, and can help contain the build-up of leverage in the banking system;

- the BCBS and authorities should take forward work on improving incentives for risk management of securitization, including considering due diligence and quantitative retention requirements, by 2010;
- all G20 countries should progressively adopt the Basel II capital framework; and
- the BCBS and national authorities should develop and agree by 2010 a global framework for promotıng stronger liquidity buffers at financial institutions, including cross-border institutions.

The scope of regulation

We have agreed that all systemically important financial institutions, markets, and instruments should be subject to an appropriate degree of regulation and oversight. In particular:

- we will amend our regulatory systems to ensure authorities are able to identify and take account of macro-prudential risks across the financial system including in the case of regulated banks, shadow banks, and private pools of capital to limit the buildup of systemic risk. We call on the FSB to work with the BIS and international standard setters to develop macro-prudential tools and provide a report by autumn 2009;

- large and complex financial institutions require particularly careful oversight given their systemic importance;
- we will ensure that our national regulators possess the powers for gathering relevant information on all material financial institutions, markets, and instruments in order to assess the potential for their failure or severe stress to contribute to systemic risk. This will be done in close coordination at international level in order to achieve as much consistency as possible across jurisdictions;

431

- in order to prevent regulatory arbitrage, the IMF and the FSB will produce guidelines for national authorities to assess whether a financial institution, market, or an instrument is systemically important by the next meeting of our Finance Ministers and Central Bank Governors. These guidelines should focus on what institutions do rather than their legal form;
- hedge funds or their managers will be registered and will be required to disclose appropriate information on an ongoing basis to supervisors or regulators, including on their leverage, necessary for assessment of the systemic risks that they pose individually or collectively.

- Where appropriate, registration should be subject to a minimum size. They will be subject to oversight to ensure that they have adequate risk management. We ask the FSB to develop mechanisms for cooperation and information sharing between relevant authorities in order to ensure that effective oversight is maintained where a fund is located in a different jurisdiction from the manager. We will, cooperating through the FSB, develop measures that implement these principles by the end of 2009. We call on the FSB to report to the next meeting of our Finance Ministers and Central Bank Governors;

- supervisors should require that institutions which have hedge funds as their counterparties have effective risk management. This should include mechanisms to monitor the funds' leverage and set limits for single counterparty exposures;
- we will promote the standardization and resilience of credit derivatives markets, in particular through the establishment of central clearing counterparties subject to effective regulation and supervision. We call on the industry to develop an action plan on standardization by autumn 2009; and

- we will each review and adapt the boundaries of the regulatory framework regularly to keep pace with developments in the financial system and promote good practices and consistent approaches at the international level.

Compensation

We have endorsed the principles on pay and compensation in significant financial institutions developed by the FSF to ensure compensation structures are consistent with firms' long-term goals and prudent risk taking.

We have agreed that our national supervisors should ensure significant progress in the implementation of these principles by the 2009 remuneration round. The BCBS should integrate these principles into their risk management guidance by autumn 2009.

The principles, which have today been published, require:

- firms' boards of directors to play an active role in the design, operation, and evaluation of compensation schemes;
- compensation arrangements, including bonuses, to properly reflect risk and the timing and composition of payments to be sensitive to the time horizon of risks. Payments should not be finalized over short periods where risks are realized over long periods; and

- firms to publicly disclose clear, comprehensive, and timely information about compensation.
  Stakeholders, including shareholders, should be adequately informed on a timely basis on compensation policies to exercise effective monitoring.

Supervisors will assess firms' compensation policies as part of their overall assessment of their soundness. Where necessary they will intervene with responses that can include increased capital requirements.

Tax havens and non-cooperative jurisdictions

It is essential to protect public finances and international standards against the risks posed by non-cooperative jurisdictions. We call on all jurisdictions to adhere to the international standards in the prudential, tax, and AML/CFT areas. To this end, we call on the appropriate bodies to conduct and strengthen objective peer reviews, based on existing processes, including through the FSAP process.

We call on countries to adopt the international standard for information exchange endorsed by the G20 in 2004 and reflected in the UN Model Tax Convention. We note that the OECD has today published a list of countries assessed by the Global Forum against the international standard for exchange of information.

We welcome the new commitments made by a number of jurisdictions and encourage them to proceed swiftly with implementation.

We stand ready to take agreed action against those jurisdictions which do not meet international standards in relation to tax transparency. To this end we have agreed to develop a toolbox of effective counter measures for countries to consider, such as:

- increased disclosure requirements on the part of taxpayers and financial institutions to report transactions involving non-cooperative jurisdictions;
- withholding taxes in respect of a wide variety of payments;
- denying deductions in respect of expense payments to payees resident in a non-cooperative jurisdiction;

- reviewing tax treaty policy;
- asking international institutions and regional development banks to review their investment policies; and,
- giving extra weight to the principles of tax transparency and information exchange when designing bilateral aid programs.

We also agreed that consideration should be given to further options relating to financial relations with these jurisdictions

We are committed to developing proposals, by end 2009, to make it easier for developing countries to secure the benefits of a new cooperative tax environment.

We are also committed to strengthened adherence to international prudential regulatory and supervisory standards.

The IMF and the FSB in cooperation with international standard-setters will provide an assessment of implementation by relevant jurisdictions, building on existing FSAPs where they exist. We call on the FSB to develop a toolbox of measures to promote adherence to prudential standards and cooperation with jurisdictions.

We agreed that the FATF should revise and reinvigorate the review process for assessing compliance by jurisdictions with AML/CFT standards, using agreed evaluation reports where available.

We call upon the FSB and the FATF to report to the next G20 Finance Ministers and Central Bank Governors' meeting on adoption and implementation by countries.

Accounting standards

We have agreed that the accounting standard setters should improve standards for the valuation of financial instruments based on their liquidity and investors' holding horizons, while reaffirming the framework of fair value accounting.

We also welcome the FSF recommendations on procyclicality that address accounting issues. We have agreed that accounting standard setters should take action by the end of 2009 to:

- reduce the complexity of accounting standards for financial instruments;
- strengthen accounting recognition of loan-loss provisions by incorporating a broader range of credit information;

- improve accounting standards for provisioning, off-balance sheet exposures and valuation uncertainty;
- achieve clarity and consistency in the application of valuation standards internationally, working with supervisors;
- make significant progress towards a single set of high quality global accounting standards; and,
- within the framework of the independent accounting standard setting process, improve involvement of stakeholders, including prudential regulators and emerging markets, through the IASB's constitutional review.

Credit Rating Agencies

We have agreed on more effective oversight of the activities of Credit Rating Agencies, as they are essential market participants. In particular, we have agreed that:

- all Credit Rating Agencies whose ratings are used for regulatory purposes should be subject to a regulatory oversight regime that includes registration. The regulatory oversight regime should be established by end 2009 and should be consistent with the IOSCO Code of Conduct Fundamentals. IOSCO should coordinate full compliance;

- national authorities will enforce compliance and require changes to a rating agency's practices and procedures for managing conflicts of interest and assuring the transparency and quality of the rating process. In particular, Credit Rating Agencies should differentiate ratings for structured products and provide full disclosure of their ratings track record and the information and assumptions that underpin the ratings process. The oversight framework should be consistent across jurisdictions with appropriate sharing of information between national authorities, including through IOSCO; and,

- the Basel Committee should take forward its review on the role of external ratings in prudential regulation and determine whether there are any adverse incentives that need to be addressed.

Next Steps

We instruct our Finance Ministers to complete the implementation of these decisions and the attached action plan. We have asked the FSB and the IMF to monitor progress, working with the FATF and the Global Forum, and to provide a report to the next meeting of our Finance Ministers and Central Bank Governors.

Source: Number 10 Downing Street

446

CHAPTER 45

POLICY RECOMMENDATIONS
TO PREVENT ANY FUTURE CRISIS

In terms of additional factors which may be deemed as worthwhile policy objectives, these two deserve special attention:

1. Enhanced risk management systems to control systemic risk to financial markets. This is a short, mid and long-term strategy as continual monitoring of risk profiles at banks, insurance companies and other financial intermediaries is crucial on an ongoing basis.

2. The Green America initiative is part of a global approach to controlling the level of emissions in the environment and slowing down the global warming process. President Obama has taken this initiative one step further by recommending exploration of alternative energy sources like solar and wind power, with recommendations to improve the fuel efficiency of American cars in the next few years. But the green initiative is ultimately concerned about having a zero emissions policy in the next few years.

a. President Obama has also shown the initiative to suggest reduction of dependence on foreign oil as one more motivating reason to achieve two goals: firstly balance the national budget by reducing oil costs and secondly improving national security by reducing dependence on the whims and fancies of foreign oil interests. But in the final judge of whether we are moving in the right direction is a concerted action by governments to design cities where people can breathe---- setting up bicycle lanes and bicycle parks and walking areas, where people can move easily. Development of public transportation infrastructure is another way to stop the unbelievably wasteful use of cars in richer countries in North America, where everyone uses his or her own car to go to work and contributes massively to the global emission level, which fuels the greenhouse gas effect, which adds to global warming.

3. A specific policy plan, with a well thought out PR, advertising and marketing plan is required to increase public confidence in their elected officials, in the economy and in their ability to live a better life for themselves and their families. I will discuss this a little later at the end of this chapter.

Now, I would like to talk a little more about enhanced risk management controls.

The financial crisis in America developed as a direct result of two major errors in risk management:

1. The faulty mathematical models at banks and other financial institutions and rating agencies, which resulted in no consideration being provided for free falling real estate values and wholesale defaults on sub-prime   mortgages. Had the calculations been done well, numerous synthetic financial products, which bundled mortgages of different risk levels, would never have been rated AAA by the major US rating agencies. This would mean that there would be much less participation in investments in these products by domestic and international investors---- this would have softened the blow and created some stability early on in the financial market. It seems hard to understand how and why banks and other financial institutions with access to the brightest and best business minds failed to design proper mathematical models to assess the true risk of their investments. It finally boils down to greed, where banks in spite of probably knowing the risk levels of their activities continued to multiply their risks exponentially in shadow banking off-balance sheet investment items and in the massive subprime securitization process. The profits from these activities were very high and in fact the banks made billions of dollars in profits before the financial crash--- in one word there was an overemphasis of profit and greed over financial

prudence, which brought the deck of cards down in a hurry.

2. Alan Greenspan's infamous policy of keeping interest rates very low for a prolonged period of time contributed to a climate of financial irresponsibility and excessive risk taking by speculators and banks alike. This again was a major risk management blunder, since the Federal Reserve controlled financial markets through setting of the national interest rates and their inability to see the future impact of their actions caused devastation in the market place.

3. The financial authorities like the SEC, the Federal Reserve, the FDIC and other trusted organizations were basically sleeping at the wheel. In situations like the Madoff scandal, there were specific complaints against him more than a year prior to the Ponzi scheme scandal becoming public knowledge. However, all the SEC did was to rap him on his fingers and give him a fine. There were numerous other instances where the authorities were aware of alleged financial wrongdoings but no one nowhere took the time or trouble to investigate, prosecute and control these problems. There was a "laissez-faire" attitude in these institutions, something which has changed now post- financial crisis. Now all of a sudden everyone has woken up. But it is a little too late. The damage is done and it will take time for

complete restoration to normalcy in the market. The lack of regulation was a major governmental blunder in controlling poor risk management systems enacted in the private sector.

THE ROLE OF PSYCHOLOGY IN THE CURRENT CRISIS

It is really a shame that economics, in general, does not take into consideration the importance of human psychology in resource employment decisions. When studying the stock market, we are quite familiar with the theory of herd mentality. In boom times in the stock market, everyone is buying because they feel they will get rich fast and because everyone else is buying. This euphoria and irrational exuberance then gets replaced with a feeling of fear and depression when the stock market starts tanking. Now due to fear, no one is buying. The current financial crisis is a reflection of extreme fear and risk aversion by the ordinary investor. In the United States, this feeling of fear and depression is particularly felt as people stopped buying anything other than what is required to survive--- shopping malls are empty and hungry as people stop paying their mortgages and credit card bills. For some individuals who resorted to such actions, these moves were necessary because they had lost their jobs and had no income to pay their obligations. However, generally the risk aversion level was very high and this was accompanied by a lack of trust in all financial organizations whether these were banks, stockbrokers, insurance companies or any other financial intermediary.

The press lambasted the financial community for irresponsible decisions and rightfully so, but the after effect of the "doom and gloom" was a little too much for the average American to withstand. So people responded by cutting down on consumption, "en masse".

This resulted in lower Gross Domestic product, an economic contraction and the worst recession since the Great Depression. People had lost hope.

As a policy initiative, it is the government's obligation, to manage the level of expectation. But this expectation management must be done honestly and efficiently and not in a deceptive manner. People must be told that America is still one of the best places to live in the world, and that the American people have the resilience, strength, courage and character to overcome this problem. It is critical at this juncture to provide hope to the average person and to negate all the bad publicity and fear mongering which is present in the media today. President Obama has already started this process by maintaining a special website, which tells people how the government is spending its money. This demonstration of accountability and transparency is the first thing which is required to win back the trust of the people. But much more than this is required. A dedicated policy platform with a Consumer Affairs department, manned with thousands of PR, advertising and marketing people, who constantly extol the virtues of America is required. Confidence or lack of it is the predominant contributive factor to the anxiety, depression and malaise in the public mind.

And unless this malaise is overcome positively and ethically, people will not spend as they did before. And unless the consumption process is started the economy will stutter around, Do not forget that more than 65 per cent of the national US economy is fueled by personal consumption.

It is most imperative as a policy recommendation to keep in touch with people. Keep in touch often and assure them that things will become better.

The new self-confidence will start the consumption process. As people consume more, additional jobs will be created and the economy will improve. Everything and everyone is interconnected and one person's consumption will help another person's economic position---- a process which will in time improve everyone's wellbeing. Hiding your money under a mattress or buying bars of gold will not solve anyone's financial problems forever and this should also be part of the Government advertising and marketing theme. Good management of the public disposition will go a long way in restoring America to its original economic glory.

CHAPTER 44

ITS NOT ALL ABOUT MONEY

This Chapter is a distance away from the main theme of this book, which focuses on the financial crisis and its causes and consequences. However, there is an intimate connection between the contents of this chapter and everything else.

Let us talk a little bit about spirituality and peace of mind. You may say, what role do these play in understanding the financial crisis? And what relevance does this have in my Life? To understand the relevance to the crisis, we must start a journey inside ourselves. It has been said and truly so, that all Life starts from the inside and projects itself on the outside. If we are happy and enthralled, we create circumstances and conditions on the external front to reflect our basic optimism and Love of Life. The financial crisis, which is unfolding, is a reaction of our loss of confidence in others, particularly people like banks and insurance companies we trusted and who let us down. However, this is not the end of Life. There are numerous personal lessons to be learned from this crisis. Here are some pointers, which I hope you will find valuable.

MOVING AWAY FROM MATERIALISM

In the developed world of North America, Europe and Australia we take materialism for granted. In a recent conversation with a North American girl who wanted to teach in India, I was told that she was so concerned that she would not have 24 hours electricity and 24 hour running water and in my mind, this was one of her predominant fears and a motivating factor to go or not to go to a foreign country. We are really wired into materialism. We want a bigger car, a larger home, a better sex life and more money. Although none of these objectives are necessarily bad, what is important to understand and accept is that this concept of materialism in and by itself does not guarantee happiness. A survey done fifty years ago and one done recently indicated that Americans did not feel any happier today than they did fifty years back as a result of access to more materialism. If you don't give a priority to happiness, peace and balance in your Life I respect your decision and in that case I would suggest you skip this chapter. There is nothing you can learn from this Chapter. However, if you are like the majority of people I have met in all my wide and far travels through the world, happiness and good relationships is the reason why they are alive and this is their primary objective, whether consciously stated or unconsciously known.

So, what is your definition of happiness? If you have not articulated it, then maybe this is a good time to bring it out to the fore. What is it that your really want?

And why do you want so badly what you think you want? Do you need these objects of desire and pleasure? Or do you merely want these materialistic things? And where does this stop? Where do this end? Is your Life going to be expended in the endless pursuit of pleasure? And what about Pain? Do you see pleasure and pain as the opposite sides of a coin?

Does non-acquisition of pleasure in any pursuit automatically result in pain? And what pain management systems are you using?

Although, no one has the right or privilege to define individual happiness, this is a Life journey you are in. And you need to give some thought to maximize this Life trip. Make it as happy as you can. The financial crisis has got everyone so worried, insecure and anxious. However, like all other crises this will go away. Why not be happy and make the best of a very bad situation? Why not stay positive and enjoy the quiet, beautiful things in Life? A move away from extreme materialism may just open up your Life doors to beauty and peace and is this not what Life is all about??????

COMMUNITY AND SOCIAL RESPONSIBILITIES

For those of you who have got economically dispossessed as a result of this financial crisis, why not consider involvement in community and social organizations? Is it not better to go out and help others worse off than you and give something back to the world instead of sitting at home and quarrelling with your wife all day and drinking beer round the clock?

Why not enjoy your temporary unemployment period? Be in touch with others, get involved to make someone else's life better. Some consideration for allocation of time and energy to others through community work will go a long way in bringing some peace and order in your Life in these tumultuous times.

LOVE AND CARE INSIDE THE FAMILY UNIT

Love and care symbolize the meaning and purpose of Life. Nowhere more is the opportunity of giving and receiving love than inside your very own family unit. Your family represents the sum of your hopes and desires. If you are in a good family relationship, then utilize this excellence in communication and relationship to share some of your burdens with your spouse or significant other. If that person really loves you, she will stoop to serve you in a happy and non–servile way. If your relationship is not that hot, then this is a good time to spend more time with your spouse and get to know her better. Spend more time with your kids. Tell them you love them. Tell them you care for them; tell them you will always be around them; that you are committed to do the utmost to love and protect them. The financial crisis may be a way of bringing you closer to your family unit.

LOVE BEYOND THE FAMILY UNIT

Love is universal and in the heart and spirit of the Good Lord, love is everywhere. In the Bible, great care is taken to explain to the common man the understanding of the doctrine to " love thy neighbor".

Ethical and religious theories in the world propound the fact that you must love and do to your neighbor what you would do to yourself. So, in a moment of grief and misery, why not share happiness with others?

It is very easy to be and stay negative in this world. The financial crisis is a perfect instigator of disharmony. You have less money to spend and more bills. You do not have a job. Is this the end of the world? I guess it is if you think it is so. And it is not if you choose to thing, feel and act positive, happy and self-fulfilled. If you realize and act from a center, which says You are OK irrespective of what happens on your outside then you draw the power of the universe into your small but meaningful life. Act and feel good about yourself and others. If you are an empty nester or have no significant other this is not the end of the world. Try to help others. Try to be kind. Try to smile at Life and thank God---- maybe, there are hidden lessons in the all enveloping misery of this financial crisis.

A GLANCE AT GOOD HEALTH

In times of personal and financial crisis, it is imperative to keep your health up. There is intimate linkage between the mind and the body.

If the mind is depressed and angry, then this energy effects the normal functioning of your body. Numerous psychosomatic illnesses can be avoided by controlling the energy levels in your mind. And therefore you need to practice both good mental and good physical health. If you are unemployed, or underemployed as a result of this financial crisis, now is the perfect time to spend a few hours in a gym to refresh and replenish yourself. Get into a structured exercise program and also do fun things like swimming, sailing, biking and boating. Read positive thinking books and practice the ideas and techniques therein. Good mental and physical health will provide the opportunity for you to both withstand the shocks of this crisis and take you one step beyond.

PRAYER AND RELIGION

In a time of crisis, one needs to muster all of one's energy, intelligence and emotion to face the problem squarely in its face. You do have a choice. One should have an understanding and awareness of the well known "fight or flee" theory. You either flee away from the problem, through alcoholism, fighting with your loved ones and depression or you face the situation boldly, positively and lovingly.

If you belong to any particular religion, this is a perfect time to invest more time and energy in exploring in depth, the religion of your choice. Spend time at church, a temple, or mosque or whatever makes you happy. Pray that your condition will change soon.

Expect the miraculous change.... And act as if the change has already happened. Prayer and religion are strong motivators of positive change. And I truly hope you fight for your happiness, sanity and peace of mind.

MEDITATION

Many of you probably have a strong idea or opinion about meditation. However, meditation can play a great role in keeping your balance and peace. Meditation starts with a process of acceptance of yourself wherever you are. In meditation, and I would urge you to try it to see if it has relevance in your Life . Why not start the experimentation process by spending a few minutes with yourself every day in unattached, unbiased awareness. A simple exercise, which could work wonders in your life is to spend ten to fifteen minutes first things and last thing in the night in quiet, unbiased energy attention. In the morning, look at your life for that day by paying conscious attention to any particular challenges and trials you may have to face in the day and at night before you relax and sleep try to review everything you have done that day and ask yourself if you could do anything better or could you change anything or improve in any way.

Most important, leave at least ten minutes in the morning or night to suspend thinking. Just watch all your thoughts impersonally without any reaction. If thoughts come and go inside your mental system, just watch them: do not react to them.

Believe me, you will be more powerful, centered, and awakened and there will be a flood of positive energy and hope in your life. Make Life what you want ----do not be dictated by negative circumstances of the financial crisis. Meditation can be a great tool for advancement of personal happiness and Love.

PUTTING EVERYTHING TOGETHER TO SMELL THE FRAGRANCE OF WELLBEING

Now that we come to the end of this chapter, I want to share with you what I believe is the ultimate significance of Life. Life is nothing but relationships--- the better they are, the more wholesome and loving your Life is. Relationships exist, whether you are aware or not, with not only people but with things, ideas, opinions and with Nature. Optimizing your relationships will create a more health, purposeful and peaceful life. And is that not what we all want desperately--- more Love, more togetherness, more Peace and in the end more inner wisdom?

Take care of your inner needs. Understand yourself more intensely and passionately. Understand the fact that everything you do or express on the outside has a start in the inner realm. Relax and enjoy yourself. Money is a great servant but a poor master. Enjoy money and enjoy your Life. But most important discover yourself and be happy. This crisis will pass but you will be still around. Do not allow this crisis from ruining your life, not even for a second.

CHAPTER 47

CONCLUSION

Thank you for taking the time and care to go through this incredible financial journey with me. As you must have realized, this crisis is one-of-a-kind in a century and is difficult to understand easily.

The crisis started at the epicenter of the financial world, the United States of America and the cancer spread worldwide. Starting with some major policy blunders at the Federal Reserve through a policy of reduced interest rates to the point we are at on April 2009, the crisis has become worse. Over relaxation of interest rate policies started a period of intense speculation. Numerous individuals and institutions joined this party including what were the honorable banks and insurance companies.

With a negative real rate of borrowing, it was a period too good to be true. And all these accomplices amassed a fortune worth billions of dollars. But this house of cards came stumbling down. The subprime crisis started the real problems in America. One after the other, the big and mighty financial institutions came down. First it was Bear Stearns and then it was Lehman Brothers. But the bankruptcy of Lehman brothers and the refusal of US authorities to bail it out started the real intensification of this downfall.

From far and wide, international investors saw that the US government was not really committed to all its financial institutions and this started the downward spiral of lack of investor confidence.

Shortly after, Merrill Lynch was sold off in a fire sale to Bank of America. And then we saw the conservatorship of Freddie Mac and Fannie Mae, two venerable government charted mortgage institutions. The problem now mysteriously transformed into a deeper liquidity and credit crisis. No one anywhere would lend anyone any money.

Even well known investment banks like Morgan Stanley and Goldman Sachs were not spared. In addition to Countryside being sold to Bank of America, Wachovia Bank went down and was eventually sold to Bank of America. The problem at Wachovia and Countryside was reckless and uncontrolled investments in subprime mortgages. In a little while, all of America's banking and insurance system was exposed to this crisis. In fact, there was no place for an investor to hide.

The great financial and credit crisis did not spare Europe, Asia or Australia. The seismic shock effects were felt everywhere as there was a total loss of market liquidity and huge banking losses in Europe, which were tied to bank investments in securitized products and subprime loans.

Finally, some relief was available at the financial horizon. America had a new leader. President Obama responded to this crisis by pulling all stops out.

His initiative is very fresh and marks a new beginning to solving the American financial crisis and by default the world credit crisis. Through numerous initiatives and stimulus packages he is attempting to make a change.

The Obama initiative has been followed by the G20 initiative. In a meeting in London on April 2,2009 the top 20 economic countries in the world pledged to work jointly to solve the problems emanating from the financial crisis.

There is definitely great hope in change and stability in the financial crisis. It appears that the worst is behind us. Already there are signs of improvement in the US. And there will soon follow stabilization in the marketplace. The US stock markets show signs of health and this will be followed by economic stabilization, which will probably take till end of 2010 to show positive results.

The most important lessons to be learnt from this financial crisis is the need for international and national regulation of all financial institutions in addition to institution of new accounting rules to determine fairly the real value of corporations, securities and hedge funds alike. Only in an atmosphere of complete transparency, fairness and openness can we guarantee that another crisis of this kind never reoccurs. And this to be is the most important lesson of all. We should never ever make this kind of mistake again, whether it be policy errors by the Government or greedy unconscionable moves by callous bankers. I hope and pray that the worst of this crisis has taught us to live in better ways in the future.

Best wishes in your continued exploration of this crisis which has affected each and every one of us. May each of us become a better human being who learns to co-operate with another for our mutual satisfaction and inner fulfillment. Only in complete trust in each other and an acceptance that we are all linked together, wherever we live can we start building a positive happy world around us.

CONSULTATIVE APPENDIX

"QUANTUM CRISIS I"
-"ORIGIN OF GLOBAL FINANCIAL CRISES "

TABLE OF CONTENTS

PART ONE: THE BACKGROUND HISTORY OF PAST FINANCIAL CRISES

CHAPTER 6
THE DUTCH TULIP BUBBLE OF 1636

CHAPTER 7
THE SOUTH SEA BUBBLE OF 1720

CHAPTER 8
THE FLORIDA REAL ESTATE BUBBLE OF 1926

CHAPTER 9
THE GREAT DEPRESSION

CHAPTER 10
THE REAL ESTATE AND STOCK MARKET BUBBLE
IN JAPAN 1985-1989

CHAPTER 11
THE REAL ESTATE & STOCK MARKET BUBBLE IN
SCANDINAVIA 1985-1989

CHAPTER 12
THE ASIAN FINANCIAL CRISIS OF 1997

CHAPTER 13
THE NASDAQ BUBBLE IN THE UNITED STATES 1995-2000

CHAPTER 14
THE SAVINGS AND LOANS CRISIS IN THE UNITED STATES

CHAPTER 15
CONCLUSION

QUANTUM CRISIS III

-WINNING INVESTMENT STRATEGIES TO PROSPER THROUGH THE 2007-09 GLOBAL FINANCIAL AND CREDIT CRISIS

TABLE OF CONTENTS

SECTION 1
FUNDAMENTAL FINANCIAL PLANNING CONCEPTS

CHAPTER 5
THE FIRST PILLAR OF YOUR FINANCIAL FOUNDATION:
SAVINGS
LEARN TO SAVE FIRST
THE PIGGY BANK EPISODE
THE CANADIAN BANK BOOK EPISODE
THE AMERICAN SAVINGS QUANDARY

CHAPTER 6
THE SECOND PILLAR OF YOUR FINANCIAL FOUNDATION:
INVESTMENTS
LEARN TO INVEST--- SIMPLE LESSONS IN INVESTING
MASLOW'S MODEL OF HUMAN NEEDS
RAJPAL INVESTMENT SUITABILITY PYRAMID

CHAPTER 7
THE THIRD PILLAR OF YOUR FINANCIAL FOUNDATION:
RISK MANAGEMENT
LEARN TO PROTECT:
YOUR LOVED ONES
YOUR BUSINESS
YOUR RETIREMENT INCOME NEEDS
YOUR CHILDREN'S EDUCATION NEEDS
YOUR WEALTH IN EVENT OF DISABILITY

CHAPTER 8

THE FOURTH PILLAR OF YOUR FINANCIAL FOUNDATION:
EFFECTIVE TAX MANAGEMENT OF YOUR RESOURCES
DIRECT VISIBLE TAXES
INDIRECT & SOMETIMES HIDDEN TAXES
OTHER TAXES
SIMPLIFIED ASSET PROTECTION CONCEPTS

CHAPTER 9

THE FIFTH PILLAR OF YOUR FINANCIAL FOUNDATION:
ESTATE PLANNING
THE NEED FOR EFFECTIVE INTER-GENERATIONAL WEALTH
TRANSFER
ONSHORE STRUCTURES-LIFE INSURANCE AS CHEAP
CREATOR OF WEALTH FOR ESTATE PLANNING PURPOSES
OFFSHORE STRUCTURES

CHAPTER 10

THE SIXTH PILLAR OF YOUR FINANCIAL FOUNDATION:
ACTIVE COST-CUTTING STRATEGIES
LEARN TO CUT COSTS OF ALL KINDS OF
INSURANCE STRUCTURES
LEARN TO LIVE SIMPLE LIFE
THE THREE WAYS OF GETTING RICH

SECTION 2
ADVANCED INVESTMENT TECHNIQUES

CHAPTER 14
OVERALL RISK MANAGEMENT STRATEGY FOR THE ORDINARY INVESTOR
WHAT IS RISK MANAGEMENT
UNDERSTANDING OF LIFE, DISABILITY,
GROUP AND HEALTH INSURANCE

CHAPTER 15
INVESTMENT/ASSET ALLOCATION STRATEGIES
FOR THE SMART INVESTOR

CHAPTER 16
SUPERCHARGING YOUR RETIREMENT STRATEGY
CHAPTER 17
COLLEGE FUNDING STRATEGIES

CHAPTER 18
HOUSE MORTGAGE, HOUSE REFINANCING &
HOME INVESTMENT STRATEGIES

CHAPTER 19
CREDIT CARD DEBT REDUCTION STRATEGIES

CHAPTER 20
COMPREHENSIVE INSURANCE STRATEGIES
WITH PRIORITIZATION OBJECTIVES

CHAPTER 21
SAVINGS STRATEGIES FOR WEALTH GENERATION

CHAPTER 22
SMALL BUSINESS WEALTH CREATION STRATEGIES

SECTION 3

PERSONAL GROWTH STRATEGIES FOR WEALTH ACCELERATION

"QUANTUM CRISIS 1
- THE ORIGIN OF GLOBAL FINANCIAL CRISES"
($29 USD-Free shipping)

The first of a three-book series on the current Global Financial and Credit Crisis. This book provides a historical perspective on the major financial crises in the last four hundred years. In this journey, it weaves through difficult financial conditions in Asia, Europe and North America. It concludes with looking at the predominant causative strand running though such crises ---- the universal factors of greed and fear. It then provides some prescriptions in terms of how individuals can protect themselves in such dire conditions. A great starting book for anyone interested in understanding the current 2007–2009 global financial and credit crisis.

"QUANTUM CRISIS III
Winning Investment Strategies to Prosper through the
Global Financial and Credit Crisis"
(39 USD-Free shipping)

This publication marks the final installment of the 3 book series entitled Quantum Crisis. This book deals with specific investment strategies to assist an investor save, grow and protect his hard earned wealth. It starts with a section on Basic Financial Planning concepts and then graduates to discussion of advanced investment strategies. It concludes with an understanding of health and other wellbeing strategies, suggesting that a total balance of physical, emotional, mental and spiritual factors assist in building not only a financially successful Life but also a happy one. A great read for any individual wanting to learn to employ better investment and insurance techniques to grow his wealth in Challenging financial times.

"OFFSHORE INVESTMENTS
–The Millionaire Vision."
$99 USD(Free Shipping)

This book deals with the challenges of investing in offshore locations. It explains brilliantly the basic investment principles involved in saving, growing and protecting your capital. Then it deals with the advantages and drawbacks of world offshore centers. It continues with an understanding of trusts, foundations and other asset protection mechanisms. A must read for anyone planning to diversify his investment portfolio offshore!!!!!

"OFFSHORE HAVENS
-"The four best kept secrets of millionaires."
$99 USD(Free Shipping)

This book presents the top four offshore havens in the world in terms of the most important factors of superiority: privacy, safety, wealth management services and availability of professional expertise. The book then proceeds to explain the advantages/drawbacks of each of these top four centers. In the process it deals with current tax and investment legislation for international investments. This is a great book for international investors who seek advanced tax, investment and asset protection knowledge.

"YOU HAVE IT ALL-
Your Life is yours to truly discover and enjoy."
$29 USD(Free Shipping)

The author takes you through a marvelous journey, which ultimately questions the value of money in its relationship to Personal Happiness. Through his real Life experiences with his clients, the author discovered that Successful Living challenges one to achieve an optimal balance between Material pursuits and Happiness. He suggests means, methods and processes to live a more balanced and integrated Life leading to Wealth and Happiness simultaneously. A valuable book for anyone aspiring to Wealth and Happiness!!!!!

"QUANTUM SELLING"
$ 29 USD(Free Shipping)

This book deals with modern, practical and time-tested methods of achieving success in any Sales Endeavor. Through his business and sales experience of more than twenty years, culminating in achievement of all the top business awards in North America, the writer expounds a simple, time -proven technology of finding, growing and retaining clients in any field of business. This book is a must read for anyone desirous of building a successful Sales Practice/New business.

"QUANTUM SALES MANAGEMENT"
$ 29 USD(Free Shipping)

This publication focuses on proven success methods essential to the optimal management of a sales force. It discusses brilliant ideas addressing the four major challenges in professional sales management----- recruiting, training, developing and motivating salespeople. The research in this book is based on live studies and experiences of the author, who captured every major management award in North America, both at the corporate and professional body level in his field of financial service management. This book is extremely valuable to both new and experienced sales managers, who want to increase their sales numbers and achieve an even higher level of professional success.

"QUANTUM MARKETING"
How to create & grow profitable business opportunities
$ 29 USD(Free shipping)

This publication deals with the time-honored principles of marketing management. This book is truly unique in the sense that it approaches marketing from a 360 degree view. It does this by focusing on all aspects of marketing management, starting from the traditional 4 P's (Product, Price, Promotion and Place) to more elaborate concepts of the psychological, societal and philosophical implications of the marketing process. A must read for both marketing practitioners and enlightened marketing students, who want a deeper and significant understanding of the marketing process and their role in it.

"QUANTUM ETHICS"
$29 USD(Free shipping)

This book deals with some of the ethical concerns besetting the world today. It specifically discusses how major world corporations have ripped customers, investors and government authorities in their blind pursuit of money and fame. It throws a fresh light on some of the major world scandals and proposes ways and means of organizing, controlling and delivering a higher quality of ethical care to consumers. Through the process, it provides an understanding of the twin challenges of World Sustainability and Global Warming------these constitute two of the most important ethical considerations of our age. A great book for anyone interested in exploring how Ethics and Business clash and how to protect oneself from dishonesty, misrepresentation and poor business practice.

"QUANTUM PUBLIC SPEAKING"
How to Influence People through Superlative Communication(29 USD-Free Shipping)

Here, for once, is a fresh and entertaining book on Effective Public Speaking. The author has shared his twenty plus years of experience as a major public speaker, debater and trainer of sales people. This brilliant and enjoyable book discusses how anyone can master Public Speaking through one-on-one communication and in group public speaking. A must read for anyone who wants to increase his communication power with a view to positively influencing people!!!!!

BOOKS CAN BE ORDERED DIRECTLY AT:
www.pioneer-communication.com or at
rdrajpal@yahoo.com

10% DISCOUNT FOR 2-3 BOOKS
15% DISCOUNT FOR 4-5 BOOKS
20% DISCOUNT FOR 6-7 BOOKS
25% DISCOUNT FOR MORE THAN 7 BOOKS

**** NOTE ALL BOOKS MUST BE ORDERED AT
THE SAME TIME FOR DISCOUNT TO APPLY
FREE SHIPPING AND DISCOUNTS ONLY PROVIDED WHEN
ORDERS PLACED DIRECTLY AT ABOVE WEBSITE
FREE SHIPPING APPLIES ONLY TO CONTINENTAL UNITED
STATES DELIVERY